England in the Age of Caxton

Geoffrey Hindley

❧❧❧❧❧

England in the Age of Caxton

St Martin's Press
New York

© 1979 Geoffrey Hindley

All rights reserved. For information, write:
St Martin's Press, Inc. 175 Fifth Avenue, New York, NY 10010
Printed in Great Britain
First published in the United States of America in 1979

ISBN 0–312–25274–9

Library of Congress Cataloging in Publication Data
Hindley, Geoffrey.
England in the Age of Caxton.
  Bibliography: p.
  Includes index.
  1. England–Civilization–Medieval period, 1066–1485.   2. Caxton,
William, ca. 1422–1491–Contemporary England.   I. Title.
DA245.H53   1979   942.04   79–4329
ISBN 0–312–25274–9

Contents

To Dr Tom Parker

1

Who Were the English?

The first thing to be established about the English fifteenth century is that it was not the Age of the Wars of the Roses. Victorian legend and school-book history still conspire to anchor the idea firmly in the popular calendar of the past. This book is called 'England in the Age of Caxton' because William Caxton's life (1422–91) sums up so many of the themes that were important in his century. He was a distinguished man of business, he was well read and a competent translator and stylist, he had close ties with the nobility; and he had intimate knowledge of a major branch of England's trade. William Caxton was also responsible for one of the truly significant events in the English social history of the fifteenth century. The publication of the first printed book in England in 1477 held implications for the future beside which the tragic tussle on Bosworth Field in 1485 appears a somewhat old-fashioned episode. Nobody at the time considered it decisive and few people today consider it significant.

This was the century in which England moved from the ranks of the underdeveloped primary producers to the position of an industrial exporter. It was the century in which popular dissent began to become literate, the century in which English merchants made their first large-scale bid for overseas penetration, with women taking a newly active role in trade. It saw the beginning of a reshaping of English landscape by enclosure. It was a time of ambition, much harsh injustice but also much social mobility, and a time of excitement. The nobility were struggling with a constitutional crisis precipitated by the collapse of government under Henry VI for which there was no adequate precedent and which, despite their heavy-handed methods, they solved surprisingly well. It was, after all, from their ranks that Edward IV came and it was he who laid the firm foundations of a restored monarchical government.

The fifteenth century was the age, too, in which the English found themselves. Only the nineteenth-century coinages such as 'nationalism' and 'jingoism' will do to describe the upsurge in self-awareness and aggressive pride that followed the decades after Agincourt. The anachronistic overtones of such words are outweighed by the clear evidence of their general aptness in Caxton's England. This book begins with an attempt to assess who the English saw themselves to be. We will then examine their view of the cosmos, their outlook on the world, their own history, their own language – a new and potent force – their standing in the community of Christendom and their less lovely view of foreigners. Our picture is drawn from their own comments, notebooks and account books and from the books which an increasing number of them could read and many more hear read. The books that William Caxton published show what his educated compatriots rated as important, a wide spectrum of other documentary evidence allows us to probe the attitudes of the unlettered majority of English men and women.

The ability to read did not represent quite such a wide and divisive social distinction as we might expect. The vast majority of literates were, in any case, men already distinguished from society at large by their membership of ecclesiastical orders. For them reading was more a professional qualification than an everyday necessity while for the populace at large it was quite unnecessary. Exact percentage estimates of literacy in fifteenth-century England are very difficult (see below, p. 237) but most people could not read and as a result illiteracy did not carry the social stigma it does today. More importantly, while modern living must be virtually impossible for someone who cannot confidently handle the notices, notifications, forms and hundred other documents it breeds, the great majority of Caxton's contemporaries could conduct happy and successful lives without ever learning their alphabet. Margery Kempe, citizenness of Lynn and pilgrim extraordinary, with the help of a secretary, even produced the first autobiography in English.[1]

Homes without books or newspapers, shops and streets without advertisements: the almost total absence of all reading matter is probably the biggest yet least emphasised difference between modern and medieval society. But there were many others, perhaps more easy to grasp, which can give us some flavour of this remote society.

The average English man and woman of the fifteenth century confessed the Christian religion, acknowledged the spiritual supremacy of Rome and expected, if they proclaimed views contrary to the Church's accepted doctrine, to be interrogated, possibly under torture, and in the last resort to be burnt alive. Executions of all kinds were commonplace, of course, and provided men and women of all social ranks with a popular spectacle in an age where the entertainment industry was unknown. There was no organised sport; beer, introduced from Holland in the 1420s, was regarded as a new-fangled foreign invention and, as in most parts of Europe, foreigners were regarded with robust contempt. In England the category firmly included the Irish, Scots and Welsh. The Cornish, their own Celtic language still very much alive, were of course subjects of the king but were hardly ranked among his compatriots by the Londoner or Yorkshireman. Even among the English themselves regional variations in the language were so great that, as Caxton tells us, a Northerner could be mistaken for a Frenchman by a Kentish woman.[2] Not the least of Caxton's contributions to the future was his pioneering work in making the

Midlands dialect which Chaucer had used, the basis of a stan-
dardised English.

Yet whatever their strange foreign ways, the Irish, Italians,
French, were, at least in theory, reckoned as all members of
Christendom, that great family of peoples who held a privi-
leged place in the plans of the Creator.

To the ordinary simple Christian, God's purposes might
be mysterious, but his universe was built on a satisfying and
simple plan. The face of the great clock in Wells Cathedral
still reminds us of its salient features. The hour hand is in the
form of a sun which circles in an outer star-spangled firma-
ment once every twenty-four hours. Nearer the centre is a
disc showing the moon in its changing phases, which revolves
every thirty days. At the centre is the Earth, composed of
the four elements of Earth, Air, Fire and Water. The whole
is summed up by the inscription: 'This circular dial shows
the actual universe in miniature.' Few people then, as now,
had much interest in the nature of the universe, but anyone
who did want to know soon discovered that, gratifyingly
enough, academic theory squared with his everyday experience and observation of the phenomena. The structure of the
universe held few problems but the diversity of the earth
and its people almost defied belief. Even within the shores
of Britain where, it was believed, there had anciently been
eight kingdoms, there was a multitude of different customs.
The thousands of people who followed the pilgrim roads to
Spain, to Italy or to Palestine, learnt something of the still
more fabulous world overseas. Many others read about it.

Mandeville's Travels, one of the century's most popular
books, bequeathed in wills, alluded to by preachers and plagiarised without stint, was devoted to this exciting foreign
world. Written in French about the year 1375 and probably
at Liège, it purported to be the journal of an English knight
called Sir John Mandeville who had set out on his travels in
the year 1322. It soon had translations in all the major European languages and nowhere was it more popular than in

England, home of the supposed author. In fact its French or Flemish writer almost certainly never left Europe and probably never even crossed the Alps. But while Marco Polo's true accounts of his own astonishing voyages earned him the nickname of *Il Milione* – 'the man who talks in thousands' – Mandevile's book was accepted as gospel by generations of readers. Today, the book, based in part on the records of true travellers, in part on fables encrusted with credibility from endless regurgitation in encyclopaedias and story collections, seems an odd mixture of fancy and fact. Its success shows the eagerness with which people looked for information about the world outside, a strange and largely unknown place where anything seemed possible. Who would believe in a camel unless he had seen one, or a sea in which things would not sink? And if these, why not men with their heads in their chests – a legend first reported in the venerable pages of Herodotus.

People were not convinced any more or less easily than they are today. They found Mandeville trustworthy because he claimed to report only what he had himself seen and because he gave circumstantial evidence about things that mattered. A pilgrim, setting out on the tedious and expensive journey east, could save himself a good deal of money if he knew that the cross in the Abbey on the Hill of the Holy Cross, in Cyprus, was in fact the one on which Dismas the Good Thief was hanged. Not everyone did know this and 'that is evil done for, for the profit of the offering they say that it is the cross of our Lord Jesus Christ'. Mandeville also expounded the mystery of the Cross itself. It was made of four woods. Because the Jews 'trowed our Lord should have hanged on the cross as long as the cross might last...made they the foot of cedar, which may not in earth nor in water rot...For that they trowed that the body of Christ should have stunk they made that piece that went up from the earth upward of cypress for it is sweet smelling.' The cross piece from which Christ hung was of palm because, according to the Old Testament, this was the wood with which to crown the defeated, and the Jews 'trowed they had the victory of Jesus Christ'. The board which carried Pilate's superscription was of olive to symbolise the peace that would follow the death of this trouble-maker.

While he gives due attention to the geography and sanctuaries of the Holy Land the author of *Mandeville's Travels* did not intend to write merely a pilgrims' guide. There were plenty of those (see below, p. 17). His theme is the marvels of the whole world and among the chief of these were the granaries of Joseph, which he had built in Egypt to garner food for the seven lean years. Mandeville discounts the theory that they were royal tombs on two grounds. In the first place Joseph's part in their building is confirmed by the traditions of the local Arabs. (It is highly probable that this particular myth started with the Arabs, for whom, as for Christians and Jews, Joseph was one of the patriarchs.) In the second place – 'ye may well know that tombs and sepulchres be not made of such greatness nor of such highness, whereof it is not to believe that they be tombs or sepulchres'. Time and again Mandeville reinforces the evidence with such an appeal to the experience and common sense of his readers.

And so the geography of the world, and particularly the mysterious east, builds up. In the desert there are men who wrap their heads and their necks in a great quantity of white cloth and at the back of the desert, beyond Armenia the great, lies Mount Ararat, with Noah's Ark visible on the top on a clear day. Unfortunately the Ark cannot be reached because the mountain is snow-covered throughout the year; only one man has ever made the climb and he was an intrepid monk who brought down one of the planks of the ship. This can still be seen in the church at the foot of the mountain. Still further east lies India full of yet more wonders, of which the most incredible is the festival of a god at which 'young women fall down under the wheels of the car of the god and let it go over them and so that they be dead anon'. At this point, just half way through his book, Mandeville presents evidence that the 'earth and the sea be of round form and shape', a view familiar in intellectual circles.

From the way he approaches the idea it would seem that it did not strike him as particularly remarkable but because he clearly anticipated some incredulity he buttresses the contention with more evidence than usual. First he quotes the accounts of shipmen that in the remote parts of the world the night sky is quite different from the one seen over Europe. Then follows a list of the changing declination of stars as the observer moves south – observations which Mandeville claims to have verified with his own astrolabe. Next he describes what are claimed as well-attested circumnavigations. Finally, to 'simple unlearned men' who argue that people 'may not go under the earth because they should fall toward the Heaven under', he answers that, in the first place, in a round world there is neither top nor bottom – so that we equally run the risk of falling – and in the second place, if men can fall, then 'by greater reason the earth and sea, that be so great and heavy, should also fall'.

Mandeville's Travels, lively in style and full of incident, was one of the first great books of popularisation. Though cast in the form of a travelogue, it gave a pretty comprehensive survey of the state of knowledge at the time and is our best introduction to the world as seen through the eyes of a fifteenth-century English reader. For more than a century before Columbus set sail, this consistent best-seller had given a reasoned and convincing account of the world as a globe. In 1481 the *Trinity* and *George* were chartered out of Bristol 'to serche and fynde a certain isle called the Isle of Brasil'.[3] Throughout the century Europe had been alive with speculation and exploration into uncharted waters and the English, though latecomers, were soon to follow up these Bristol pioneers once the great Genoese had justified their intuition.

Yet to most Englishmen the history of their own land was more interesting than the world beyond and here too there were books to meet the growing demand. The *History of the Kings of Britain* by the twelfth-century writer Geoffrey of Monmouth was widely read. Still more popular were the books of the contemporary John Lydgate. His history of the kings of England, *Troy Book*, from the Conquest to Henry VI, was favourite reading with the patriotic and we can assume that his biography of the Anglo-Saxon king, St Edmund, had equally wide popularity.

Lydgate was a monk at Bury and a life of its patron saint was a natural enough work of piety for him; moreover the great abbey was one of the most important of medieval English shrines. But from many parts of the country we find signs of an awakening interest in all things Anglo-Saxon — as though the English of the fifteenth century were eagerly embracing the pre-conquest tradition as part of their Englishness. At Worcester the memory of the last Anglo-Saxon bishop was lovingly revered in the cult of St Wulfstan; at Hereford the martyred king, St Ethelbert of the East Angles, was the centre of a considerable cult; Juliana of Norwich, the great mystic of the early part of the century, paid special reverence to St John of Beverley; and in the city of London St Dunstan was honoured as the patron saint of the goldsmiths. It was not only a matter of religion, for William Worcestre names Alfred's son, Edward the Elder, as the first king of England of that name while the widely read *Libelle of Englyshe Polycye* (1436) found in the pre-conquest period one of the greatest moment's in the nation's history. Tradition has it that King Edgar (d. 975) was rowed on the River Dee by eight tributary kings; for the author of the *Libelle* this ranks him with Cyrus the Persian or Charlemagne the Frank.

Search for past glories indicates a burgeoning nationalism which in one form or another is a recurrent theme in the fifteenth century. By the 1430s it was also a symptom of bewilderment. Agincourt is so wreathed in Shakespearian allusions that we may forget the wild jubilation which greeted Henry the Conqueror on his return to England that year. Fifteen years later his young son was crowned King of France in Paris itself. Yet, despite these triumphs, the English cause in France was waning. Just as many contemporary Britons in the 1940s and 1950s were angered and confused by their country's undeviating decline from the victory year of 1945, so Caxton's contemporaries looked for explanations of what seemed to some a national collapse.

In his exultant *Troy Book*, which he had dedicated to Henry V, John Lydgate told a noble story. To us it seems a web of fantasy and myth; to his contemporaries it was a proud history they were heirs to. Britain took its name from Brutus, son of Priam, king of Troy. From him descended the royal house of England and Lydgate bitterly rejected the mendacious and slanderous account of Troy's fall as given in the pages of Homer the Greek. For him the Trojans were victims of Fate, defeated by a combination of treachery at home and the hostility of Mars. The disaster drove Brutus into exile and with twelve companions he made landfall on the coast of Devon. So it was that the kings of England could boast a more ancient and more noble lineage than any other.

The English church had equally venerable antecedents. Indeed, a tactless Englishman might feel tempted to claim priority in conversion to Rome itself. For the Apostle of Britain was, supposedly, Joseph of Arimathea, who had laid Christ in the tomb. After the Crucifixion he had taken ship and found sanctuary in the south-west of Britain. There the local king had granted him and his companions twelve hides of land and there they had laid the foundations of Glastonbury. In this historic plot Arthur, King of Britain, had been laid to rest. The founder of Chivalry and a greater Paladin of the Faith than Charlemagne himself, he was but one of the heroes of Christendom which the English claimed as their own. St Helena, Discoverer of the True Cross and mother of Constantine, the first Christian emperor, had been the daughter of King Cole of Colchester. The emperor himself had been born at York. In more recent times the royal line

The presentation of a book to Margaret of Burgundy, patron of Caxton's *History of Troy*.

St Bride's Printing Library

of England had been graced by St Edward the Confessor, renowned throughout Europe.

The voice of Englishness, often so strident in the fifteenth century, had been given its first intellectual formulation in the very year of Agincourt in a diplomatic coup that matched the military triumph. The Council of Constance, convened by the Emperor Sigismund to restore the unity of the papacy after forty years of schism, brought ecclesiastical delegations from all over Europe. The emperor's policy, supported by the English, was to reform the abuses in the Church before electing a new pope. The delegations from Italy and France favoured the opposite course and, because of their greater numbers, were bound to out-vote the Anglo-German bloc if voting was to be by simple head count. Hence the English proposed, and successfully pushed through, a system of voting by nation.

Since at least the thirteenth century the University of Paris had been organised by birthplace or *natio* categories. The term had nothing to do with political boundaries. The Italian *natio*, for example, comprised a group of Europe's most powerful city states; the English were included for administrative convenience within the German nation; the Spanish 'nation' embraced the independent kingdoms of Castile and Aragon. The fact that the Spanish were absent at the beginning of the council meant that the 'traditional' four nations – Italian, French, German and Spanish – were not complete and gave the English the chance, as they saw it, to claim the vacant place. The French drew up a long and persuasive case against the English claim to be a separate nation. In their reply *Anglorum contra Gallos. Vindiciae pro jure nationis*, the English made ingenious play with the fact that the papal constitution on which the French founded their case had been issued by a French pope. Among numerous detailed arguments, the French also objected that the Welsh, supposedly subjects of the English king, did not obey him while the Scots, with a king of their own, were not members of the English nation.

The English, ignoring the awkward fact of Owen Glendower's rebellion a decade earlier, denied the first charge and pointed to the number of Welsh prelates in their delegation. As to the second, they pointed out that the Scots and English shared the same language and that it was in any case 'astonishing for intelligent men' to advance political obedience or lack of it as proof or disproof of nationhood. What about Spain? Indeed, what about France itself? The Duke of Burgundy, to name only the most notorious instance, ignored the French king's authority, yet Burgundians undoubtedly belonged to the French nation.

Some salient facts in England's long and noble history follow. Aided by the uncertainties of contemporary geography, their own ignorance of the outlying parts of their own country, and the fair assumption that the foreign delegations knew even less, they even claimed that Britain was bigger than France. In addition, they asserted it had more subject kingdoms, more dukedoms and other temporal lords, more cathedrals, more monasteries, more collegiate churches and more ecclesiastical provinces.

This long and highly interesting document extends the medieval concept of the *natio*, but shows that it had little in common with the modern nation state, since it comprised neither political nor territorial unity nor homogeneity in race or language. In fact, even the idea of national sovereignty was awaiting clear definition and general acceptance. Henry V's own grandiose claims in France infringed the whole notion and the German emperor still claimed, as heir to the empire of Charlemagne, the theoretical overlordship of the Christian west.

A century before Constance, French writers had been claiming for the French king the right to supreme authority in his own dominions. They argued that he too was 'emperor' within his frontiers. The word was then the only one available to express the unreligious, even unfeudal, concept of untrammelled lay authority. Other kings, even the powerful merchant princes of northern Italy, were still under the cloud of imperial pretensions. In 1416 even England felt it necessary to make a demonstration against them.

In that year, Sigismund paid a state visit. As his state launch approached the shore it was met by an armed and mounted figure brandishing a sword. It was, perhaps, Humphrey of Gloucester. In the name of his brother, Henry V of England, he called on Sigismund to renounce his claim to England's liege homage. Since the emperor came as a friend and was to leave as an ally, everyone enjoyed the pageant, but no one discounted its importance. In 1194, captured by imperial agents as he returned through Austria from the Holy Land, Richard I had formally reaffirmed the feudal subjection of England to the empire as part of the price of his freedom. The oath had never been anulled. The colourful ceremony on Dover sands also reminded those whom it might concern that King Henry had not renounced by any such forms his claims on the crown of France.

In their catalogue of titles to 'nationhood' the delegates at Constance had listed the, to us remarkable, claim that the number of different languages within the English *natio* should be taken into account. These were five in all – English, Welsh, Irish, Vasconish (possibly Gaelic?) and Cornish. The absence of French from the list is hardly surprising in the circumstances. Even so, it is significant that even in so disingenuous a piece of special pleading the omission could seem plausible.

Until the middle decades of the fourteenth century, French had remained the true vernacular of a large section of the upper classes. However, by 1400 it had been taught as a foreign language in the business schools at Oxford for a generation.[4] Further down the educational ladder, English was even being used as a medium of instruction by 1385 when the Oxford magister, John Trevisa, thundered that the children from the grammar schools knew 'no more French than their left heel'. Soon this appalling state of affairs was seeping up the social scale. Even the court listened to Chaucer reading his *Canterbury Tales* in English and in the 1390s the renowned condottiere, Sir John Hawkwood, was writing home from Italy in English. Eight years later George Dunbar, the Scottish Earl of March, used it in a letter to Henry IV, though he felt obliged to explain his lapse. 'Noble prince, marvel you not that I write my letters in English, for that is more clear to mine understanding than Latin or French.'[5]

By the 1420s the great English nobles, among them royal dukes, were commonly writing in the language of the country. Perhaps this had something to do with the fever against France, but whatever the reason the habit was catching. In 1422 the London Brewer's Guild decided to keep its records henceforth in English because the king used 'our mother tongue for his letters missive'. A few years later the water bailiff at Southampton went over to English for his harbour accounts. Even educated diplomats were pleased to use their new-found mother tongue as a negotiating weapon. On one occasion, angered by an attempt to force the use of French instead of Latin as the medium of debate, they blandly claimed that they no more knew French than Hebrew.[6]

French was almost completely displaced in routine administrative business by 1460. In the last year of Henry V's reign we find a royal safe conduct being issued in English and from then on, as the Brewers had noted, the Privy Seal used English more and more frequently. From 1437, the more conservative Office of the Great Seal began to follow the trend. In the country at large the pattern was much the same though surprisingly inconsistent. From at least 1380 some people had been writing their wills in their native tongue and the last one in French was drawn in 1431. At Oxford the Ascension Day and Corpus Christi sermons to joint town and gown congregations, at St Frideswide's open-air cross, began to be given in English rather than Latin. There was also a spate of translations of the standard Latin sermon books. Yet ecclesiastical institutions, such as the Oxford colleges, continued to use Latin not only in their accounts but also in instructions to their bailiffs and masons, while the estate officers of the nobility used French in their instructions for a surprisingly long time. As a result, masons, carpenters, clock makers and other master craftsmen needed a working knowledge of the dog Latin and French relevant to their trade. Often enough the languages got a little confused. In 1474 the bursar of Magdalen College in Oxford recorded payments to two men from Headington for digging out sixty yards of earth at the college's quarry 'usque ad lapidos vocatos *le freebedde*'. And a little later on, in the same accounts, we find him listing the purchase of 'uno instrumento vocato *a crowe*'.[7]

It was natural that men whose professional life had begun when the use of English was still in its infancy should continue to prefer the familiar Latin or French terminology. The notebooks of William Worcestre, for many years the secretary and agent of Sir John Fastolf, reveal how unfamiliar an idiom written English could be to a trained administrator. For him Latin was a far more precise and expressive tool. In his retirement the old man began a series of journeys, recorded in his *Itineraries*, which reveal the England of the 1470s as a prosperous place, with stately mansions and parks and thriving industries.

It was equally rich in tradition and romance. After a busy professional life William was no expert in history – he thought the Brutus who founded Britain was the Roman consul – but he made notes when possible. In a London library he found the 'Chronicles of Gildas'; at Bristol he made jottings on the history of the Order of the Temple from an information sheet posted in the Temple church there. He carefully records the lists of local worthies found in parish records and was specially interested in anything about the Great Plague, more than a century in the past but still a dread memory. At Bodmin he noted from the church register that the pestilence had begun among the Saracens, and this because they were pagans. Such divine interventions were

a commonplace and the spirit world was immanent everywhere. Even the homely English River Wye ran 'through
a valley called Dimin Dale where spirits suffer torments,
where there is the marvellous entrance into the earth of Peak
where souls are tortured'.[8] While in the Aran Isles off Ireland,
men cannot die but when they decide, in extreme old age,
that the time has come to depart this world, they have themselves carried out of the island.

Worcestre's objective was the discovery of his native
country and today he is acknowledged as the first topo-
grapher of England. But sometimes his fellow travellers gave
him information worth noting down. Bartholomew Ros-
synel, a young Dublin merchant he met on the pilgrimage
to Walsingham, furnished him with a list of the towns and
harbours of the Isle of Man, and a hermit from 'Elsing' in
Denmark gave him a good deal of accurate information on
the Scandinavian countries.

Such occasional encounters, or the chance glimpse of a
hurrying merchant or solemn ambassadorial cavalcade, gave
many English people, if only momentarily, an authentic experience of the foreign. But a far deeper impression was made
by the departure of neighbour or friend on pilgrimage. There
were radical thinkers like William Emayne the Lollard who
denied the spiritual benefits of the pilgrimage, but for most
it was a foundation idea of their experience. In the idea of
Palestine, medieval Europeans shared a concept which even
in Christendom's most introspective periods had kept a window open to the world beyond. And the fifteenth century
was by no means introspective. Familiar from Bible reading
and sermon, the Holy Land was probably the only foreign
place that the average person could conceptualise. Mount
Olivet, Calvary, Bethlehem, the Holy Sepulchre, all evoked
quite precise responses while beside them places such as
Rouen or Paris were misty.

When someone set out to see these places the whole town
assembled to see them off. Friends and well-wishers asked to

be remembered in the prayers at the sacred places because a pilgrim was thought to enjoy special merit; the Bishop of Lincoln was not ashamed to ask Margery Kempe to pray for him when she set out for the Holy Land.[9] The day of departure was a time for high, devotional commitment and communal ceremony, but behind it lay months of preparation. A papal licence had to be obtained, for a fee, from the bishop. One's will had to be made and creditors warned, probably by a pulpit announcement, to present their claims. Then there was the packing. Clothes obviously, but also books – perhaps John Poloner's *Description of the Holy Land* or the anonymous guide *Information for Pilgrims* – and the practical fitted themselves out with a set of cooking utensils. William Wey, a Devon man, recommended 'a little cauldron and frying pan, dishes, bowls and glasses'. In a book of *Itineraries* based on a pilgrimage he made in 1458, he had a lot more of such practical advice for pilgrims. In fact his book was the basis for the *Information*. Among other matters, Wey gave advice on shopping, on how to negotiate the most favourable terms with the Venetian galley master, and above all on the exchange rates which governed Europe's multiplicity of currencies. On no account, he urged, should one hold on to local coins longer than necessary, for those 'of the one lordship will not go in the next lordship'.[10]

The routes taken varied according to the starting point of the travellers and the state of relations with the French. Pilgrims from the Midlands and East Anglia generally crossed from Yarmouth to Zeeland. From there the route ran up the Rhine valley to Constance, then on to the Inn valley and from there through the pass at Resia into the headwaters of the River Adige and thence to Venice. The more common Dover–Calais route crossed the Alps by the Great St Bernard or the St Gotthard and approached Venice down the Po. Despite good hostels, with stabling and laundry facilities, the journey over the mountains was dangerous and frightening. Bandits lurked to cut off stragglers and for some the plunging gorges and jagged heights of the mountain scenery were terrifying in themselves. The Welshman Adam of Usk had himself blindfolded and carried rather than face the horrors of the St Gotthard.

It was only common sense to travel in a party and every guide book stressed the importance of keeping on good terms with one's travelling companions. Parties formed themselves on the Channel crossing. Sometimes one member was appointed as treasurer and since well-to-do pilgrims might be carrying as much as twenty pounds it could be a responsible job. In addition to their money, many pilgrims, even the poorer, carried jewellery and precious stones which were to be impregnated with the spirit and virtue of the Holy Land by being pressed against the relics. People often contributed to the expenses of a poor friend willing to do this service. On the pilgrim's return the stone was incorporated into a rosary or some other object of devotion.

A well-organised traveller would arrange an itinerary to get him to Venice just before a galley sailing, since there could be delays of up to three months in this beautiful but expensive city. One of the wonders of Europe, the city drew a considerable income from the tourist trade and was organised accordingly with a department of the senate specifically charged with the welfare of pilgrims. The board employed twelve full-time guides to help with sight-seeing, lodgings, shopping and money, and these were instructed not to take tips of any kind, either from the pilgrims or from the shopkeepers of Venice. There was a good deal of shopping to be done, quite apart from souvenirs and relics. There was food, hens and hencoops to be bought and bedding to be hired. This consisted of a mattress, feather bed, pillow, two pairs of sheets and a quilt with an all-in price of three ducats, of which half was a returnable deposit when the goods were brought back in decent condition. In view of the filthy conditions on shipboard and the hazards that still lay ahead, it is doubtful whether many of these deposits were returned.

A rich man could travel comparatively well. John Tiptoft, Earl of Worcester, one of the noblemen in the 1458 party joined by William Wey, hired the galley captain outright as his own personal guide and courier. In addition he was permitted to set up a bed under an awning on the poop and walk the decks more or less at will. Conditions below decks however were, according to Wey, 'right evil, smouldering hot and stinking'. Bedding, laid out according to rectangles chalked out by the ship's crew, covered the whole of the decking so that the travellers slept head to toe, shoulder to shoulder, as best they could. In the stampede at meal times, the clumsy, weak or drunk could be bowled overboard.

The basic charge of 50 ducats for the round trip, included the fees at the Holy Places, but from the moment they disembarked at Jaffa, the pilgrims were systematically fleeced by Muslims and Eastern Christians alike. The Franciscan community of Mount Syon made some attempt to introduce the newcomers to the customs and hazards of the land in a sermon preached by one of their number at Ramleh, the last stage on the road before Jerusalem. He gave special warning against being involved in brawls which street urchins and traders tried to provoke, so as to extort money in 'compensation'. At the end of his harangue the friar pleaded with each congregation in turn not to carve their names or coats of arms on shrines or buildings and, above all, not to help themselves to souvenirs. He was generally wasting his breath. William Wey, for one, brought back stones from Calvary, the Holy Sepulchre, Mount Tabor, the place where the cross was discovered and the cave at Bethlehem.

Once they reached Jerusalem, most pilgrims supposed there would be ample time for quiet and private devotions at each of the holy sites. Instead, they found pandemonium. The din was worst in the church of the Holy Sepulchre where shouts of admiration burst out above the hubbub of polyglot conversation and the cries of hawkers selling candles or relics rang out stridently against the monotonous hymn singing of a party moving from one to another of the score or so shrines. Periodically the air was rent by the screams and groans of ecstasy from some overwrought devotee.

Besides Jerusalem there was so much to be seen that to cover everything needed careful planning. Wey's guide book divides the sights into convenient day trips. For the English the main attraction was the excursion to Lydda, to see the site of St George's martyrdom and also, according to some authorities, the place where he slew the dragon – though others said this had happened outside Beirut. To complete all the itineraries required a minimum of nine days, but most pilgrims stayed for three weeks. For these three weeks, an English pilgrim had been on the journey for up to six months. A month to six weeks from England to Venice; perhaps three months' wait for a passage and then five to six weeks at sea. It is not surprising that people boasted of their travels and the hardships they had seen, though the church strictly disapproved of such vanity. Many kept journals, though these contain little on the people and native customs, being devoted instead to the objectives of the pilgrimage. Occasionally a rich man would take an artist with him, as a friend urged Tiptoft to do.

Poor pilgrims sometimes ran out of funds and got stranded en route. When she was looking for a guide and companion in Constance Margery Kempe, herself well-to-do, was able to engage the services of William Weaver, an old Devon man. In similar straits on her return to Venice she found a beggar called Richard the Irishman.

But most people's idea of things foreign was based on hearsay or the occasional visits of businessmen, Italian church officials or foreign embassies on their way up to London. In the winter of 1400–1401, the towns and villages along the Dover road were treated to the exotic spectacle of the embassy of the Byzantine emperor, Manuel II. The oriental cavalcade was glamorous, but it came with a begging bowl, for Constantinople was surrounded by the Turks and the emperor was touring Europe to implore help. Sixteen years later Kent cheered a still more magnificent pageant as the royal dukes and their following waited to greet the progress of the German emperor, Sigismund. Two emperors in a generation would not have been quickly forgotten and as a boy Caxton must have heard old men reminiscing over these brilliant events. Kent, on the high road between London and the Continent, was used to foreign faces, but in other parts of England, too, the foreign experience was a regular part of life.

The alabaster quarries at Chellaston in Derbyshire had a European clientele and in 1414, Alexander Berneville, master mason to the Abbey of Fécamp, came to supervise the cutting of a large consignment of stone and arrange its shipment through Hull. Italian faces and fashions were a familiar sight on the narrow lanes and rolling hill roads of the Cotswolds. Peasants working in their fields or the shepherds on the hills watched as the agents of the Alberti or some other great Florentine house cantered by on their way to the next wool town. In 1480 George Cely, one of the many English merchants who bitterly resented the concessions granted by the king to these foreigners, wrote in disgust: 'There is but little Cotswold wool here at Calais, and I understand Lombards have bought it up in England.' In the busy streets of Chipping Campden, or Burford or Northleach, the soft Oxfordshire and Gloucestershire accents mingled with those of Lombardy while in Oxford magister Stefano Surigone held classes in the new humanist studies for a few enthusiasts, outside the official curriculum.

In remoter parts of the country and along the coasts, the contact with the foreigners was less urbane. Raiding was endemic along the Scottish border and the streets of the south coast towns were often bloodied by French or Breton swords. In 1416, just a twelvemonth after Agincourt, a French fleet blockaded Spithead and ravaged the Isle of Wight and Sandwich was sacked as late of 1457. Bodiam

Castle is now, thanks to land reclamation, so far inland that it seems it must have been designed as an old soldier's dream. But in fact it was an important fort behind a deeply indented shore. During the forties London itself had many sleepless nights while Dutch and French pirates ranged at will in Thames mouth. After an especially rough episode in 1441 the government was bitterly informed that men of Dieppe and Boulogne had taken the king's subjects, 'in your water of Thames and then robbed and ransomed to great summs, beaten and slain, and their wives horribly despoiled to their uttermost shame and confusion'.

Not that the English were only victims. Piracy was a cosmopolitan profession and one of the busiest centres for it was the Cornish port of Fowey. French, Flemings, Dutchmen and Danzigers swaggered the waterfront while other unlucky seamen, mostly Mediterraneans, trudged the narrow streets as prisoners and hostages. In 1434 the town's chapmen and taverners no doubt beamed to see a great Genoese galley being warped into the harbour under orders from the famous Cornish pirate, John Mixtow. The flotilla which seized her had been manned by 200 seamen, all now with their pockets well lined. A few years later Fowey offered a placid welcome to the Dutch sea rover, Hankin Selander, who had plundered many an English ship in his time. This would be little disqualification in a Cornish port but even in what might be considered England proper no one bothered unduly about a pirate's mother tongue if he had goods to sell. A Breton–Dieppoise crew found no difficulty in fencing an English cargo in Yorkshire.

In places like Bristol or Sandwich or Southampton the contacts with other Europeans were generally on a more sophisticated level. For most of our period the galley fleets of Venice and Genoa and then Florence took in Southampton and/or Sandwich, on their round trip from the Mediterranean to the Netherlands. There was a considerable Italian resident community in Southampton, generally on excellent

terms with its neighbours. Mayors and aldermen coopera-
tively eased the anti-alien laws promulgated from time to
time by the government. They also bought up prime residential properties and sites to let them at inflated rents to the
wealthy southerners. There were occasional affrays. Richard
Hortensell, for instance, was fined half a mark for brawling
in East Street with a black drummer from one of the Venetian
galleys.[11] Equally there was cooperation. If a galley needed
new timbers, the ship's carpenter would go down with local
foresters to fell them in the woods of Beaulieu. On another
occasion the ships' masters raised a work party from their
crews to help with repairs to the town's forts.

Along the coast and in many inland centres, too, English
men and women had good opportunity to see and assess
something of foreign ways. Richard Bradley, an Oxford taverner, did his own importing from Southampton. On his
visits there he must from time to time have seen into the
cabins of one of the rich southern sailing masters he did business with. Lined with Arras tapestries, the tables laden with
gold and silver plate with, in a corner, a coffer containing
illuminated books, the state apartments were often so magnificent that captains of Venetian ships entertained royal
ambassadors and even royalty itself, on board.

The Italians tended to stay in the ports or in the capital
though some lived for a time further inland and occasionally
married English women. Belisaro de Bardi found himself an
heiress in Northampton and Lorenzo de Plataea a rich widow
from Essex. Some even settled in England, having been duly
naturalised by royal letters of denizenation, and rose to
elected municipal office.[12]

The Venetian, Gabriel Corbet, had been given denizenation papers by Henry V for services rendered in 1415 – presumably in connection with the Venetian ships the king had
commandeered to transport the army across to France. During a long life he became one of Southampton's leading
citizens, holding office as town steward and water bailiff

during the early 1440s and even being elected sheriff in 1453. The London merchant community was too hostile to foreign traders to allow them such privileges but craftsmen might attain civic rights. After twenty years' registration as 'a stranger', the German-born goldsmith Bartholomew Naylond achieved the freedom of the city on payment of a £4 fee and was formally admitted to the guild as a 'brother of St Dunstan'. At the same time he was registered as a denizen by royal letters patent.[13]

Even so the goldsmiths did exercise tight control of foreign artificers. The London guild was painfully aware that the latter were generally more skilled than the English and the wardens made regular inspections of the foreign communities. The largest was in the parish of St Martin's le Grand and though protected by royal charters did not evade the guild's control. The right to work could hardly be withheld, but they were forbidden to sell their goods retail within the city boundaries. Race relations in the city were generally in a state of tension. The alien community played a vital role in England's commercial and financial life but the city merchants were convinced, usually quite wrongly, that the foreigners' royal concessions were damaging to local interests while craftsmen and apprentices feared to lose their jobs to the immigrants.

Suspicion and hostility flared up into ugly riots in the 1420s, 1430s, and 1450s and parliament was frequently petitioned to limit alien privileges and freedom of action. In 1425 their wholesale expulsion was demanded on the grounds that they were spying for the king's enemies.[14] Thirty years later the charge is made again with the additional, and for the king none too flattering, rider that the 'Italians who ride about for to buy wool and tin in every part of the realm', gained 'knowledge of the privities of the same and of the poverty of your people as of their penury'. But the underlying grievance was always the same – the foreigners were, by fair means or foul, too successful. They

were accused of using their knowledge of English conditions
to advise newcomers from abroad on how to beat down the
price of native merchandise, and in 1449 parliament voted
a poll tax to be paid only by alien merchants. These were
listed as Venetians, Italians, Genoese, Florentines, Milanese,
Lucchese, Catalans, Albertyns, Lombards, Hansards and
Prussians. Especially interesting is the inclusion of the 'Albertyns', since the Florentine family of the Alberti had virtually
ceased trading since the collapse of the firm in the 1430s.

Up to that year they had been a power in England for more
than a century and the memory died hard. That collapse had
given many English merchants a genuine cause for grievance.
William Willey, a woolman of Chipping Campden, had
accepted a bill for £666 13s 4d that very year and had little
hope of recovering a penny of it until he was granted royal
letters of marque to distrain any of the firm's assets he could
lay hands on. He was not the only sufferer, and others, without waiting for authorisation, tried to recover their losses at
the expense of any Florentine trading in England, whether
Alberti or not. The danger to the whole community eventually became so great that in 1450 the home city formally
accepted responsibility for all the debts of the Alberti. The
débâcle seemed to many English businessmen the vindication
of their attitude to foreigners in general. The trouble was that
not only were they everywhere but there was no effective
check on their activities. For a time, during the late 1430s
and 1440s, parliament had been persuaded to pass 'hosting'
laws by which a foreign merchant was obliged to live with
an English host. It was his duty to scrutinise all the transactions of his 'guest' to ensure that the profits derived from
trade in England were spent in England and that he did not
stock-pile to force a rise in prices.[15]

The merchant community dressed its xenophobia with
specious economic arguments. For the mob virtually any
pretext would serve. The continuance of English power in
France, a source of considerable pride, depended in the last

resort on the alliance with Burgundy. At the Treaty of Arras in 1435 the duke dramatically overturned the alliance in favour of France, and the Flemish community in London received the news with apprehension. The following year the duke even laid siege to Calais and the London mob went on the rampage, killing and looting in the Flemish quarter. When the siege failed, hatred turned to derision and 'many rimes were made amongst Englishmen after the Flemings were thus shamefully fled from Caleis'. Where the Burgundians had wounded national pride the Genoese, a few years later, were thought to have offended English religious sensibilities. In 1442 news came through that Genoa had attacked the Knights of St John of Rhodes, a Christian outpost against the Turk. Immediately parliament petitioned that the Genoese in England should be treated as the enemies of all Christian people. It was too good an opportunity for harrying the foreigner to be missed and the fact that there were a number of English knights in the Rhodes garrison may have had something to do with the outcry.

When the Earl of Worcester visited the island on pilgrimage some years later, the prestige of the English was at its height as one of its members was castellan of the whole garrison.[16] He gave a dinner party in his private garden in honour of the earl and his Italian travelling companions. Thanks to the diary of the Milanese pilgrim, Roberto Sanseverino, we have a living picture of this English party under a Mediterranean sky. As the guests rode through the olive groves to the host's estate, sweet herbs crushed by the horses' hooves scented the air. In the spreading acres of the garden grew 'beautiful trees, especially cedars and chestnuts; here were thickets of bay, there orange groves, graced with ornamental fountains'. Low tables were set in the dappling shade and finely woven tapestries and carpets were hung over the bushes to give dignity and opulence to the *al fresco* setting. Garlands of flowers hung everywhere, yielding their fragrance to the perfumed air. The Italian was delighted and

impressed and as the shadows lengthened the two Englishmen talked.

Although the most distant. the knights on Rhodes were
not the only English community overseas. Caxton was head
of the English merchants in Bruges while others were settled
in the lands of the empire. Like the Germans in London they
sometimes found themselves being held to ransom for the

Peter Schoeffer is considered by many historians of printing to have been
a finer master than Gutenberg. He was succeeded by his son Johann.
This early sixteenth-century woodcut shows a printing works much as
it must have looked at the time of Gutenberg and the elder Schoeffer
and as it was to remain in essentials, for the next 300 years.

St Bride's Printing Library

policies of the home government. In 1440, a treaty had been signed with the Prince Archbishop of Cologne which guaranteed him an annual pension in return for an alliance. The advantages to England were exiguous and the expense soon beyond the capacity of the several times empty exchequer. By 1454, the archbishop reckoned he was owed the sum of 40,000 florins and dispatched two of the resident English merchants back to London with the message that, unless he was paid, the English community would be fined. Inevitably the merchants found themselves making the archbishop a voluntary advance.

Like most other nations the English maintained representation at Rome. In addition to the royal proctorial delegation there was a small company of monks who maintained the Hospital of St Thomas as a hostel for English pilgrims to the Holy City. Thomas Polton, Bishop of Chichester, who led the royal delegation, became the centre of an angry exchange between London and the Holy See in 1422. By that time he, and his officials, had been living in Rome for more than a decade and reckoned their long residence had given them the highest seniority in the 'diplomatic corps' at the papal court. Accordingly when the recently arrived Archbishop of Santiago was given precedence as the fully accredited ambassador of the King of Castile, angry scenes followed. The climax was an unseemly struggle between the two prelates as they celebrated mass. When news reached London Henry V dashed off a furious letter in his own hand protesting at the insult to his own dignity implied by the treatment of Polton.

The niceties of diplomatic protocol were beginning to be formulated at Rome and as the century progressed the upsurge in diplomatic activity all over Europe brought with it categorisation in procedure that laid the foundations for modern practice. The embassies that went out yearly from London gave some Englishmen a chance for first-hand contact with the world – Polton himself had not only held the Rome job but had also been the English representative on the secretariat of the Council of Constance. Some years later London sent a still more impressive delegation to the Council of Basel while throughout the century royal embassies were penetrating to the remotest parts of Europe. In the winter of 1435 Stephen Wilton and Sir Robert Clifton were riding the harsh snow-bound roads of Germany seeking alliances to compensate England for the loss of Burgundy's friendship. Their achievement was the dubious treaty with Cologne. On a less contentious mission Dr John Norton was dispatched to distant Lithuania as the government's representative at the marriage of King Jagiello. The activity of royal foreign agents came to be matched as the century advanced by the trading community. For a time Englishmen dominated the trade with Iceland and in the second half of the century they made forays into Mediterranean markets. In 1478 John Neve, despairing of recovering by correspondence the money owed him by Antonio Martelli, travelled to Florence to plead in the courts there, while a few years later we find a Hugh Clopton and Thomas Hawes running a warehousing business in Pisa.

Though they had little love for foreigners, the English saw a good deal of them both at home and abroad. Their own reputation was mixed. But few foreigners tried to deny them their reputation as soldiers. Philippe de Commines, chronicler and councillor of Louis XI of France, says simply that they are the best archers in the world. As to the rest of their army he comments: 'When the English first come over no one is more stupid or clumsy but in a very short space of time they become very good, clever and brave soldiers.' To the French, who had been fighting them for centuries, there was nothing very surprising about the Henrician invasion, but a thoughtful Spaniard looked for deeper explanations. 'They have no wish to live in peace,' he wrote, 'for peace does not suit them, seeing that they are so numerous that they cannot keep within their country and in time of peace many cannot find subsistence there... They have no liking for any other nation.'[17] Generally they were considered the odd men out of Europe. The legend that the English had tails was centuries old. When, in the spring of 1436, they were finally expelled from Paris, the French collaborators who had supported the regime were driven from the city to cries of, 'After the Foxes! Have their tails!'

The English soldier's favourite oath of 'Goddam' earned him in France the nickname of *godon* and his superstition had become a proverb. To it was attributed the English belief that Joan of Arc had won victories through witchcraft, and there may have been some basis for this reputation for superstition since in one of his concordats Pope Martin V observed that the English seemed to be more prone to the plague of pardoners than other people. Commines put the same point in another way when he spoke of the English love of prophecies, 'of which they are never short'. When peace was signed between Louis XI and Edward IV at Amiens in 1475, some of the English averred that the Holy Spirit was responsible since a white pigeon had perched on the English king's tent where the discussions were taking place. 'But others', continues Commines drily, 'were of the opinion that the pigeon had perched itself on this tent, which was the highest, to dry itself after a light shower.' In the early years of our period the English themselves worried less about their reputation for superstition than about their looming reputation as heretics. The Council of Constance had arraigned Jan Hus on the charge, among others, that he was spreading the doctrines of the English heresiarch, John Wyclif. Oxford University was desperately anxious to repudiate its association with him and the English delegation at the conference pressed for a fresh condemnation of Wyclif.

But most Englishmen of Caxton's day cared nothing for their ill reputation abroad. The fact that M de Commines regarded them as polite would have been as uninteresting as the fact that he also considered them superstitious. Writing his treatise on the *Governance of England* as an exile driven from home by civil war, Sir John Fortescue found even in his own plight cause for pride in his countrymen. For was it not 'only the lack of heart, and cowardice that kepen the French men from rising'? Conclusive proof of their pusillanimity was to be derived from a comparison of the crime statistics of the two countries. For more were hung for robbery and manslaughter in England in one year than were hung in France in seven years and the reason is 'that they have no hearts to do so terrible an act'.

'Nationalism' is a nineteenth-century coinage, and the battle over the English claim at Constance to be considered a 'nation' reveals all too clearly how differently the Middle Ages used the word. While the French were prepared to concede England the status of a *natio particularis,* being a small state governed directly by only one ruler, they denied the application of the term *natio principalis* which should properly be reserved for large bodies politic with several political obediences within their frontiers. We have seen the English arguing with fervour and ingenuity against this. But though the debate was conducted in terms strange to us, it belongs unmistakably to that cluster of concepts we call 'nationalism'. Such sentiments were equally strong elsewhere in Europe. Commenting on the 'Salic' law which, according to French tradition, prevented the crown of France from passing to the daughter of a king, Commines decided that it originated in divine favour. It prevented the rule by a foreign prince which the French people would not have been able to tolerate. Nor, he goes on, would other nations. 'In the long run there are no lordships, in particular no powerful ones, where in the end the country does not remain in the possession of its people.' The reasons he adduces to explain why even the wisest foreign prince would find it difficult to hold a land for long against the will of its people are custom, temperament and love of country.

In this chapter we have seen something of the English, at home and abroad, becoming aware of themselves and displaying in the process an unlovely contempt of foreigners. In the words of Commines this self-awareness consisted, at least in part, in pride in their customs and love of country. Chief Justice Fortescue proudly outlined the superiority of the English constitution and rooted it firmly in the past. It was a past which stretched back to Troy and up to Agincourt, a past in which England had been great even before the coming of the Normans. One of the best loved stories of the time was the romance of Sir Beves of Hamtoun (i.e. Hampton), an English hero who defeated the pagans and then returned to clear the streets of London of foreigners. The character is entirely mythical, but the story is set in the reign of the Anglo-Saxon King Edgar. In Caxton's lifetime, in part thanks to his work, the English found a common language. They had already begun the building of a common folk mythology and it was in this century that they acquired a fully mature patron saint. The Feast of St George became a major festival in the year of Agincourt.

2

The French Connection

During the first half of the fifteenth century English involvement in Europe was more continuous and at times more decisive than at any other time until the nineteenth century. The great victory of Agincourt in 1415 established an English occupation in northern France which endured close on forty years and gave some Englishmen of all classes a continental interest and experience which fed back into domestic affairs and which is possibly underestimated by historians. The military adventure, indeed, was not finally closed until a bloodless but profitable campaign by Edward IV in 1475. But there were important non-military episodes throughout the century. Diplomatic ties with the Emperor Sigismund not only produced the Treaty of Canterbury in 1416 but also gave England a leading role in the Council of Constance called by the emperor to end the papal Schism. For some twenty-five years agents and officials of the English king and council governed large tracts of France. For much of that time the alliance between England and the Duchy of Burgundy was one of the determining facts of European politics. There were strong trading links with Bordeaux, Flanders and the towns of the German Hanse which led in turn to further diplomatic entanglements. During the civil conflict in England both Lancastrians and Yorkists and even Henry VII were decisively helped by foreign patrons. William Caxton, being an English merchant who made his career in Bruges, is a telling and not untypical instance of the way Englishmen of the period felt themselves a part of Europe in a sense unusual for centuries to come. And there were Europeans who for practical purposes acknowledged themselves subjects of the English king. At the Congress of Arras, convened in 1435 under the auspices of Pope Eugenius IV and the Council of Basel to settle the disputes between England, France and Burgundy, the English delegation was composed of the king's 'ambassadors born in his realm of England and...his other ambassadors born in his realm of France'.

When Charles IV of France died in 1328 his nearest blood relative was his sister Isabella, the mother of Edward III of England. In 1340 Edward formally adopted the title of King of France and quartered the fleur de lys with the leopards of England. Six years later, after his triumph at Crécy, he laid siege to Calais which was to remain in English hands for the next 200 years. The English kings had been hereditary dukes of Normandy since 1066 and of Guienne since 1153; the town of Bordeaux and its hinterland was English and remained so to the 1450s. This was the position when Henry V crushed the French army at Agincourt. In 1420 he entered Paris and a marriage was arranged between him and the French king's daughter Katherine. At the Treaty of Troyes in that year Henry was proclaimed the 'true son' and heir of Charles VI of France and the Dauphin was declared a bastard, with the explicit endorsement of his own mother. There were members of the University of Paris who argued the legality of Henry's claim and many ordinary French men and women were prepared to give allegiance to an undoubted if remote member of the royal house rather than to a prince whom even his mother had disowned.

Henry V died in 1422 but under his brother John, Duke of Bedford, Normandy enjoyed a government more just and more efficient than it had known for generations. For a time, in Normandy at least, there were practical reasons for accepting the alien rule. Joan of Arc changed all this. In 1429, against all expectation, she inspired the French to raise the English siege of Orleans. She then persuaded Charles VII, the Dauphin disowned at Troyes, to go to his coronation at Rheims, cathedral of the kings of France. The English remained in France another twenty years but now no Frenchman could doubt who was the true king. The crowning of the nine-year-old Henry VI at Paris had been a meaningless ceremony – in the wrong church, by the wrong bishop, with the wrong regalia. Years later, Edward IV, toying with the idea of a French coronation, extracted a guarantee from his ally Charles of Burgundy that he should have for the ceremony the ampulla of the sacred unction of St Rémi held at the cathedral of Rheims.

By the mid-1430s English rule in France had degenerated into tyranny. The Bishop of Lisieux looked out on a countryside 'deserted, uncultivated, abandoned, empty of inhabitants, covered with scrub and dead branches', where even the cattle lumbered for shelter when the tocsin sounded the approach of brigands, both French and English.[1] William Worcestre, who frequently visited Normandy, could only admit the oppressiveness and brutality of the regime. Sir John Fastolf, his employer whose fortune was founded on his French revenues, had no time for pity. A hardliner, he urged that the 'traitors and rebels must needs have another manner of war...more sharp and more cruel'.

After his conquest of Calais, Edward III had expelled almost the entire French population and resettled the place with English. The colony continued to flourish because Calais was a major link in the English wool trade to the continent. Henry V's settlement in Normandy, without the same economic raison d'être, never took root. He had hoped to make Harfleur a second Calais and planned for 10,000 settlers. The target was never even approached and by the late 1440s there were only 400 English citizens. Despite tax and other inducements few English had risked the French adventure; government employees in the French branch of the service had no alternative. William Wymington, who worked in the Rouen *chambre des comtes*, bought a house with a garden in the city; soldiers of the Normandy garrison bought houses in Caen and elsewhere, some even married French wives. Assimilation at this level squared with royal policy, but it was rare and many settlers sold their properties to French buyers and returned home. This compounded their desertion and Henry V, foreseeing how the English presence could be weakened by this kind of thing, had legislated against the selling of lands acquired by royal grant to any but the 'king's English subjects'.

Yet those who did stay often found themselves out of pocket. When the home government surrendered the county of Maine in 1448 there were bitter protests from those who found their lands confiscated by the incoming French authorities without compensation from London. It must have seemed that only the unscrupulous could flourish in the king's 'realm of France'. And some undoubtedly did.

Thomas Overton began his career as a poor clerk. He carved himself a comfortable niche in the outworks of the bureaucracy and was soon able to employ seven footloose soldiers to help him in a profitable protection racket. When Sir John Fastolf engaged him as receiver-general of his lands in France Overton widened his scope. The wise traveller in the disturbed conditions provided himself with a safe conduct through the lands of the chief magnates. Overton derived a handsome supplementary income from bogus safe conducts in Sir John's name about which his master knew nothing. When he was at last examined on corruption charges it was found that he had a well-appointed house in Falaise, French properties worth £300 a year, lands in England, a mistress, a string of bastards and cash assets reckoned at 2000 salus.[2]

But the really large fortunes went to the powerful men. The crown had many French offices of profit in its gift: the captaincies of Calais and Brest, the lieutenancy of Normandy, governorship of Anjou or keepership of Cherbourg. Fastolf, Constable of Bordeaux even before the re-conquest of Normandy, was for eighteen years the king's councillor in France with the large salary of £110. He held twenty other appointments and the revenues from a string of French lord-ships. Later he joined the stream of returning Englishmen and began to sell his lands in advance of what he foresaw was the inevitable collapse. Yet even as late as 1445 his French properties were bringing in £400, rather more than a third of his English revenues. His French income went to increas-ing his English holdings and to the £6000 worth of building and improvements at his great castle of Caister in Norfolk.

Fastolf is the classic example of the *nouveaux riches* bred by the wars. But the old established aristocracy made their profits too. The Regent, the Duke of Bedford, controlled the revenues of Alençon, Anjou, Maine, Mortain, Harcourt and Dreux and many smaller lordships. Two years before the English were driven from the duchy the Duke of Buck-ingham reckoned his French revenues at close on £450. There are many other cases and none of these figures includes the traffic in ransoms which came out, on balance, in favour of the English.

For aristocrats and adventurers France meant big money; for most Englishmen it came to seem a costly extravagance. For the French it was, in general, disaster. To the extortions of English landlords and the brutality of freebooting soldiers and brigands were added rapacious tax demands for the maintenance of the garrisons. Between 1419 and 1435 the Norman estates voted £350,000, of which two-thirds was actually collected; from other sources another £330,000 was raised in the duchy. Had this been merely for the defence of the duchy the Normans might have been less restive; but it was also used to finance further campaigns of conquest. The fateful siege of Orleans had been begun as part of this policy. The triumph of Joan of Arc before the city, although little mentioned in English sources, obviously seeped through from the army to affect public opinion. The natural reaction was that she had won her victories by sorcery. But this, while it satisfactorily diminished the repute of the French military, was hardly reassuring. Writing four years after the event, Bedford revealed something of her impact on the soldiery. She 'not only lessened in great part the number of our people there but as well withdrew the courage of the remnant in marvellous wise; and couraged the adverse party and enemies'.[3]

Joan's advent was the more disturbing as maintaining English opinion in support of the French venture already required news management. Naturally enough, when Sir John Talbot presented a copy of Christine de Pisan's *Fayttes and Armes of Chyvalrye* to Henry VI and his bride in 1447 he had the copyist omit a passage deploring the actions of the English army of invasion. But the government's propaganda reached out to the population in general. Verses commissioned from a French writer, Laurence Callot, justified the claims of Henry to both thrones. The Duchy of Normandy's new gold coinage (the *salus* in which Overton amassed his fortune) represented England in the shape of an angel announcing to the French the coming of a new saviour, the infant Henry VI. These Callot verses were displayed, together with a pictorial representation of the royal genealogy, on the doors of Notre-Dame in Paris and at the banquet for Henry's coronation in Paris the decorative tableaux, or 'sotelties' between courses, depicted such inspiring themes as St Edward the Confessor and St Louis IX of France leading young Henry 'armed in cote armours'. The accompanying verses proclaimed:

Lo here two kings right perfect and right good
Holy St Edward and St Louis;
And see the branch born of their blessed blood
Live, among Christians most sovereign of price,
Inheritor of the fleur de lys![4]

The coronation was naturally celebrated with pageants in London too. In remote Shropshire, where the artificiality of the propaganda was perhaps less obvious, John Audelay, a priest, wrote a glowing and notably inaccurate picture of the young monarch's splendid future.

Thoughtful people, however, were not impressed. As early as the 1410s Thomas Hoccleve, poet and civil servant, had been urging Henry V to honour his talk of a crusade once he had united the two realms by marriage with Katherine of France. About the same time the monk Thomas Elmham suggested that the king should reform the government at home before fighting abroad and saw the export of an unruly soldiery as the only advantage of a French campaign.[5] These ideas were as premature as they were generally unpopular. But peace policies did come to seem more attractive; few shared in the fortunes won by the captains in France. In 1431 a parliamentary resolution on negotiation with France baldly asserted that it was 'not convenable nor suiting, nor like to be to the pleasure of God, nor of the world; for a Christian prince to refuse peace offered with means reasonable'. A little further on it bemoaned 'the burden of the war, and how grievous and heavy it is to this land and how behoveful therefore the peace were to it'; two years later a Commons motion observed that Englishmen were leaving the French settlements because they saw 'peril' ahead. Others seriously argued that success in France would subject England to French laws and customs. A Burgundian observer noted among the English growing disillusionment with the war.

But the English government held on to its precarious position in northern France to the bitter end. As they saw it, and as all regimes involved in a hopeless and costly war have always seen it, there was no alternative. Duke John of Bedford, who had shaped English diplomatic strategy for the Congress of Arras and who had struggled manfully to make the Henrician system in Normandy work, summed up the position. He was willing to concede much. But on the question of the English king's claim to be also king of France, almost the only question that mattered, he would yield nothing. If Henry VI were to abandon his claim the world would think he was too weak to maintain it and, moreover, that 'all the wars and conquests hath been but usurpations and tyranny'. It was precisely because they now believed that England's wars and conquests in France had become a tyranny that the advisers of the Duke of Burgundy urged him to abandon the English alliance. It had been cemented in 1419 when the duke's father had been assassinated by the faction of the Dauphin. Now, sixteen years later, argued the courtiers, Burgundy had honoured the vendetta for long enough and as Frenchmen by nation if not by allegiance they could no longer honourably maintain their alliance with England. Bedford died during the Congress, before the reconciliation between France and Burgundy which spelled the end of English power in Normandy.

The end, when it came, occurred a decade later, and was humiliating and bitter. In 1415 London had greeted its hero king with pageants and jubilant strains of the Agincourt Carol.

> Our king went forth to Normandy
> With grace and might of chivalry,
> There God wrought for him marvellously,
> Wherefore England may call and cry,
>   Deo Gratias!

> He set a siege, the sooth for to say,
> To Harfleur town with royal array;
> That town he won and made affray,
> That France shall rue till Doomsday.
>   Deo Gratias!

Thirty years later Londoners watched the straggling streams

of returning refugees '...men and women and children in right poor array, piteous to see, driven out of Normandy'.[6]

The collapse of the English position in Normandy was inevitable and was probably recognised to be so by most people. It was more than 200 years since there had been an English presence there and the occupation played no structural part in England's economic or social or political life. In Bordeaux and Calais the position was quite different. The Bordelais had been English for three centuries and its economy had become structurally integrated into the English system. Wine had become the exclusive industry and the region's economy seemed totally dependent on the wine trade with England. Even so, expulsion from Normandy was quickly followed by expulsion from Guienne. The home government had lost the will and the ability to withstand the surging momentum of French military recovery. Nevertheless the reconquest was not straightforward and the final months of the English in Gascony show that the age-long tie was no longer merely dynastic.

The armies of Charles VII recovered Bordeaux in June 1451. Contemporary manuscript illuminations show the victory procession through the gates being led by a riderless horse bearing a book upon its back, as if to symbolise the return of French law after its long exile. The king struck a victory medal. This, however, proved a premature gesture. In October 1452 an English force, commanded by the seventy-year-old John Talbot, Earl of Shrewsbury, recovered the city. They held it for a twelvemonth. What had gone wrong? With characteristic caution Charles had not moved until he had bought the leading Gascon families with handsome pensions. Even then he had granted six months' grace for clearing up their affairs to those who preferred to leave rather than take the oath to France. And yet, ten months after this had expired, the town opened its gates and welcomed back the English.

When news of the French capture of Bordeaux reached

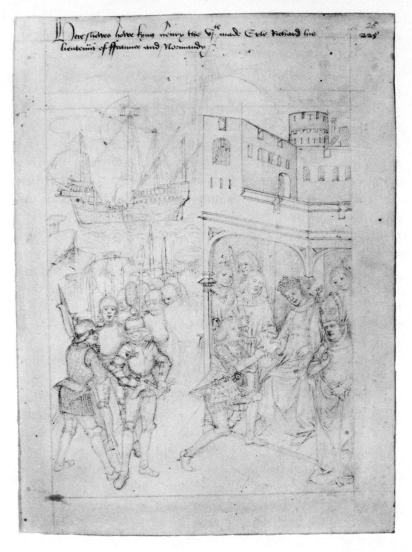

Richard Beauchamp, Earl of Warwick (1401–39), whose estates passed by the marriage of his daughter to Warwick 'the Kingmaker', was a powerful figure early in the reign of Henry VI. The boy king's tutor from 1427, he displaced Richard, Duke of York as English commander in France when Henry came of age at sixteen, in 1437. Here he is seen receiving his commission.   *The British Library*

London in June 1451 among those most affected were members of the Gascon delegation to parliament which had been in the English capital for some eighteen months. Of them Pey du Tasta and Grimond de Bordeaux decided to take up permanent English domicile and had their goods shipped out to them. Others accepted grants of land in French-held Gascony, anticipating return. Their hopes seemed well founded. A group of Bordeaux citizens, led by Pierre Merlanes, was secretly prepared to assist the English expedition under Shrewsbury. When he landed in October 1452 the Beyssac gate of the city was opened by a body of 300 men from the parish of St Michel. Yet even with evidence of goodwill, Shrewsbury's troops proved difficult to control. They pillaged merchant houses and churches and inevitably earned unpopularity. Their home government was little better. Willing to exploit pro-English feeling in the city, they did not take the expedition seriously enough. The troops' pay was soon in arrears and the commanders had to make it good from their own resources. There were strong personal ties between England and her ancient French dukedom; the Bordelais citizen Pierre Montferrand had both an English grandmother and an English wife and there were others in a similar situation.[7] But with the home government proving so half-hearted and ineffectual the complete demise of English influence in south-west France was only a matter of time. It came in October 1453.

It was the end of a remarkable chapter in English history. For the Fastolfs and the Overtons it had been a glittering and profitable chapter; for many others it had been a weary and disheartening time. In one campaign the Earl of Shrewsbury had taken sixteen tenants from his manor of Painswick to France to the war and only five had returned. It was a community disaster repeated many times in England during those years and we know about it only because the widows of Painswick 'cried out against the lord of the manor'. Their protest was not merely an emotional outburst. With the

death of their menfolk the women had also lost their right
to the family holdings and so their means of livelihood.
Shrewsbury showed himself a considerate lord. Following
an enquiry he allowed the widows not only to retain their
husbands' lands but also to choose second husbands for themselves if they wished.

The French adventure was followed by the usual horrid
consequences of war. It also had another, rather remarkable
outcome. The court of the Regent Bedford at Rouen was
also a centre of English culture in France. Hardly, one might
suppose, a fact of great moment. Poggio Bracciolini, the
humanist, once observed that when dining with an English
nobleman he found it necessary to rise after four hours at the
table and bathe his eyes in cold water so as not to fall asleep
from sheer tedium. But in one art the English were, by
general consent, pre-eminent. This was the art of music.

The Duke of Milan sent to England to recruit singers for
his chapel. English brass players astonished continental lis-
teners with their skill on the newly invented trombone or
sackbut. But it was the composers serving in the ducal chapels
of the conquerors who proved the most startling revelation
to their European contemporaries. This was the only
occasion in the history of music when the English school
headed the avant garde and decisively shaped the development of the art. The theorist Martin le Franc enthused over
the 'sprightly consonance' of their music and others excitedly
welcomed it as a new art.

The figureheads of this musical revolution were Leonel
Power and John Dunstable, in service in the chapel of the
Duke of Bedford. Their contribution was in two fundamental areas. The sprightly consonance derived from the
English tradition, probably rooted in folk song, of descant
singing in intervals of the third and sixth. This produced a
sweet concordant effect which Dunstable and Power worked
to breathe into all their music. This continuous euphony was
bound to astonish European composers used to the stark

intervals of the fourth and fifth and elaborate mathematical patterns to be fulfilled whatever the consequences. The differences between the late-fourteenth-century compositions of Machault and the fifteenth-century master, Guillaume Dufay, proclaim an evolution of style which would have been unthinkable without the intervention of the English tradition. The introduction of the interval of the third meant the introduction of the chord of the triad which was to be the basic building block of western harmony until the time of Liszt.

The second innovation of the English, equally momentous, was in the area of musical form. Unlike their European contemporaries English medieval composers were more interested in church than secular music and especially in the music of the mass. A full setting of the text resulted in a lengthy composition of up to half an hour or more and the fundamental problem was how to give a piece of music of this length a satisfying and recognisable unified form. The solution to this problem, first found in the works by English composers, was to base separate sections of the mass – e.g. the Kyrie, Gloria, Credo, Benedictus and Agnus Dei – on the same theme. This could be a familiar fragment of plainsong or even a popular song; when French composers took up the form the song 'L'Homme armé' ('the Armed Man') was, fittingly enough in view of their country's recent history, one of their most favoured themes. The unifying theme or 'cantus firmus' (Latin, 'fixed song') gave the key to the first extended musical form in the western history of the art.

This, and their vital contribution in the field of harmony, more than justified the esteem which English composers enjoyed up to the 1450s. They had arrived in the wake of a conquering army; they remained as the admired masters of a new art. The works of Dunstable survive largely in Italian manuscripts, his song 'O rosa bella' was probably the most widely copied single composition of the century. English composers after him held important posts at the court

of Burgundy. The magnificent if chauvinistic music of the
Agincourt Carol and the gentle strains of 'O rosa bella'
together sum up one of those rare moments in history when,
for a time, war and the self-seeking of national policies served
as midwives to a great cultural innovation.

A tailpiece of the wars that brought the English into
Europe with such unexpected consequences came in 1475.
On 4 September that year, after a campaign that had taken
them deep into French territory to St Quentin, the army of
Edward IV began a laborious but cheerful re-embarkation
at Calais. In a six-week promenade through the lands of the
old enemy they had fought not a single battle. Casualties
there had been, but only of soldiers pursuing conquests of
their own; a contemporary reported that 'many a man was
lost that fell to the lust of women who were burnt by them;
and their members rotted away and they died'.

On the outward and on the homeward march the army
had passed the historic field of Agincourt. Beside that heroic
victory the present king's 'great enterprise' had been an in-
glorious business, ending with the English being bought off
at the Treaty of Picquigny. The French nobility viewed the
affair with unconcealed contempt; their soldiery chanted a
cheerful little ditty of derision:

> I saw the King of England
> Come with his mighty host,
> To take the Frenchman's land
> In short and utter conquest.
>
> Our king, their style well knowing,
> Gave them such fine wine sack,
> That soon they could do nothing
> And happily went back.[8]

In fact, during a drinking bout at Amiens, paid for by Louis
XI, the English troops became so unruly that Edward had

to clear them from the town after four days and set guards on the place to stop them coming back to loot. But Louis had disbursed a good deal more than free wine to the army. He paid the English king 75,000 gold crowns to quit France in peace and had guaranteed him an annual pension of 50,000 crowns which was in fact paid in two instalments, at Easter and Michaelmas, in London for the rest of Edward's reign.

It has been said of Edward that he was that rare thing, 'a talented commander in the field with little natural taste for warfare'.[9] He won every important battle he fought and his first victory, Towton, was achieved at the age of nineteen. Yet unlike Henry V he did not seek glory, preferring solvency. Not to have led an army to France, the hereditary enemy of his country and the shifty opponent of his own house, would have been beneath his 'worship' as a Yorkist king of England. He prepared the campaign with professional care. At his back was a magnificent army and awaiting him was a promised alliance with Charles, Duke of Burgundy. When it became clear that Charles was not, in fact, planning close cooperation with the English and that France was eager to buy him off, Edward took the money and went home. There were those at the time who believed the whole expedition had been raised merely to force protection money from the French. Whatever Edward's intentions, the outcome was to give the king an income of some £10,000 a year independent of parliament.

For Louis it was a price well worth paying. The Milanese ambassador at the French court reckoned Edward's army 'the finest, largest and best equipped force that has ever left England'. Such a force, even without the support of its Burgundian allies, might well defeat the French army in the field and would certainly return northern France to the wasteful turmoil of the 1430s and 1440s when the English had been so laboriously expelled. Nor did Louis want any distractions as he conducted his tortuous diplomatic campaign against his overmighty subject, the Duke of Burgundy.

The feelings of the English themselves were mixed. The king's advisers and staff officers mostly approved the arrangements; some received pensions, that of the influential Lord Hastings alone amounting to 2000 crowns. Others received lavish gifts: Lord John Howard was said to have received 24,000 crowns over two years. Many of the soldiers were happy enough to get home unhurt, others were ashamed and others angry at their lost chance of plunder. These enlisted with the Burgundian army. Public opinion at home, however, seems to have been generally hostile. Parliament had gone to great lengths to ensure that its considerable grants were used exclusively for the campaign. On two previous occasions Edward had raised money on the pretext of wars he had then abandoned. Foreign observers expected serious trouble for Edward on his return. And there were 'numbers of people complaining of the unfair management of the resources of the kingdom, in consequence of such quantities of treasure being abstracted from the coffers of everyone'. Disturbances followed the army's demobilisation and the king made a judicial progress through Hampshire and Wiltshire at the end of 1475 to put down risings there. Yet on his return to London in September he had been escorted triumphantly through the city by the mayor and aldermen and 500 members of the guilds, and the tribute money from France cut back his future demands on his subjects. The peace and prosperity of the remaining years helped assuage the pangs of hurt national pride and, with the king's quarrel with France no longer part of practical politics, the English people returned to their own affairs.

Yet, in a reduced area, the French connection continued important in English political affairs well into the next century, at Calais. Throughout our period the town had been a major factor. Its garrison was the largest body of troops permanently in the pay of the crown. The peacetime establishment cost a massive £10,000–12,000 a year which rose to £19,000 in time of war; of this only £3500 was met from the annual revenue of the town. Inevitably the pay was often in arrears; in 1407, 1423, 1433 and 1442 the garrison seized the wool in the Staple as a pledge of payment. In 1454 the Duke of York, then Protector of the Realm, persuaded the Staple merchants to fund the garrison in return for privileges. Yet that same year the soldiers once more seized the wool and also the victuals held in the port. Eventually, disgusted by the long delay in their payment, they sold both.

But if the troops were discontented and even mutinous, for most Englishmen the town was one of the jewels in the crown. 'O only God, in whom is all/Save Calais the town royal/That ever it most well cleave/Unto the crown of England' ran one political doggerel. *The Libelle of Englyshe Polycye*, recalling that the Emperor Sigismund in 1416 had praised the strong strategical advantage that England had in holding both Dover and Calais across the Straits, pleaded with the government to 'Cherish Calais better than it is'. For a glorious period in the late 1450s, when the town was under the captaincy of the Earl of Warwick, the English saw it being used as it should be to keep the narrow seas. The flotilla Warwick commanded was his own personal possession but the humiliations he inflicted on French and Spanish shipping were reckoned national triumphs and his reputation rose accordingly.

In 1436, the year after he had patched up his quarrel with France at Arras, the Duke of Burgundy had tried to take the town. The raising of the siege and the discomfiture of the perfidious Flemings was the subject of ribald verses sung delightedly by the Londoners, and the men of Calais became national heroes. To many their resistance embodied a spirit of unity all too sadly lacking at home. 'The mayor and burgesses were ready for to defend their possession'; the common people had made preparations by filling the town with 'goods and vitaille'; even the women played a full part: 'both young and old, with stones stuffed every scaffold; they spared

not sweat nor swynk [labour]'. And the water bailiff's dog,
Goby, became a legend of folk history.

> Full swiftly would he run
> At every skirmish to travail
> Man and horse he would assail
> Full well he could them ken[10]
> [i.e. 'he read them like a book']

Yet for the government Calais could be a trouble spot. Like
Ireland it provided an easy refuge for exiles and a springboard
for rebellion. In November 1459, after his party had been
declared traitors at the Parliament of Devils, York fled to his
estates in Ireland while his son, Edward, Earl of March, Warwick and the Earl of Salisbury made Calais their base. They
had led a force to join the duke at Ludlow, from Calais
through Kent and the Midlands that September. And, despite
the débâcle that caused the Yorkists to flee, they were able
in June 1460 to bring a further 15,000 men from the French
garrison to Sandwich and with them to launch the political
and military sequence which ten months later put a York on
the throne of England.

3

♣♣♣

The Governance of England

On 26 June 1460 a flotilla put out from Calais. It carried 2000 men at arms under the command of the principal Yorkist lords: the Earl of Warwick, the Earl of Salisbury, his father, Lord Fauconberg of Kent, his uncle, and Edward, Earl of March, son of Richard, Duke of York and the cousin of Warwick. Landing at Sandwich the earls marched steadily towards London through the disaffected county of Kent. Their force swelled as Kentish men, weary of the mismanagement of the Lancastrian regime, anxious to join the popular Warwick and Fauconberg or simply hoping for a chance of loot if London was put to the sack, flocked to the banners. Henry VI was at Coventry and the Yorkists secured the capital before he could reach it. It was the essential first round in any English revolution.

For a decade the realm had been unsettled by the Duke of York and his followers trying to force their way to their rightful place in the council of the realm. Soon they were to aim at the crown itself. Yet people were reluctant to commit themselves. There was the uneasy knowledge that despite his incompetence and simple-mindedness Henry VI had been anointed with the sacred unction which, it was believed, St Thomas à Becket had received generations before from the Blessed Virgin Mary. The magic of the coronation ceremony surrounded the king with an aura which dimmed very slowly. Moreover there were those of

Henry's subjects who believed him worthy of sainthood. Frankly the English were bemused by their simple-minded king who preferred the conversation of his confessor to the affairs of state. They wanted to love him not because they were incurable romantics but because if the head of state was indeed responsible for the appalling decay of authority in the 1450s the position was more or less hopeless.

Even so, since the 1440s there had been realists in all classes of society coming to recognise their king for the simpleton he was. When Henry was in his late twenties foreigners remarked on his childish appearance and a London tradesman unwisely echoed the opinion. The king, he said, 'was not in his person as his noble progenitors have been, for his visage was not favoured for he had unto a child's face and is not steadfast of wit as other kings have been'. Unsophisticated rustics could see things as clearly as the townsman. A yeoman of Farningham in Kent bluntly observed that the king was a lunatic. Both merchant and farmer were, of course, arraigned before the justices. Thomas Carver, a gentleman of Reading, was lucky to escape with his life. On Palm Sunday, 1444, he was in the congregation of Abingdon Abbey when John Curtis, a Dominican friar, preached before the king and court on the text from Ecclesiastes: 'Woe to thee, O land, when thy king is a child.' Curtis was being outspoken even for a member of the clergy. Carver not only quoted the sermon with approval the following day, he added that, were the English king as much a man as the French Dauphin, his French lands would be at peace. This impugned not only the king's intelligence but also his honour, since the English held that Henry himself was king of France and since he had no son there was no 'Dauphin'. Carver was duly condemned to a traitor's death. He was reprieved by Henry in a character-istic if unkingly act of mercy.[1]

Despite the turbulent events of the 1450s no one in England, as late as October 1460, contemplated deposing the anointed Henry. On the tenth of that month Richard, Duke of York found this out for himself in the most pathetic anti-climax of English history. He had marched into London with 500 men at his back and a naked sword, the prerogative of monarchy, borne before him. York proceeded to West-minster Hall, marched through the ranks of the lords in the parliament chamber and, glaring round at the astonished assembly, laid his hand on the cushion of the empty throne. He awaited shouts of acclamation; he was met by silence. At length the Archbishop of Canterbury enquired whether the duke wished to see the king. 'I know of none', came the fuming reply, 'who would not more fitly come to see me than I to him.' He then stormed into the royal apartments and 'lodged there for no little time more like a king than a duke'. Five years before, at the first battle of St Albans, Henry had been struck by an arrow. John Whethamstede, the abbot, watching from the church tower, was horrified – Henry was nonplussed by what he considered an act of sacri-lege and cried out 'They do foully to smite an anointed king so.' After his death Henry was indeed venerated as a saint. As late as 1480 the London Company of Mercers, seeking to win the favour of Edward IV, resolved to discontinue their annual pilgrimage to the tomb of Henry VI. But England did not need or want a saint; the country wanted a king.

Sir John Fortescue, Henry VI's chief justice and author of the important constitutional treatise *The Governance of Eng-land*, could evidently imagine the advantages, in an ideal world, of states without kings. The ancient Israelites, discon-tented with the rule of the Judges, 'desired a king as then had all the gentiles we call paynims'. God warned them that a king 'would take from them their lands and give them to his servants and set their children in [the shafts of] their carts'. Untrammelled, kingship could be a danger, but Fortescue starts from the premise that it is the proper regime for a Christian people in the modern world. He distinguished two types: *dominium regale*, by which he meant arbitrary lord-ship, and *dominium politicum et regale*, which we would call 'constitutional'. In the first the king 'may rule his people by such laws as he maketh himself...and...may set upon them tailes and other impositions...without their assent'. The second type of king 'may set upon them no impositions without their assent'. The difference between the two derived from their origins; it was England's good fortune that her monarchy had been founded by the 'fellowship that came into this land with Brutus, willing to be united and make a body politic called a reawme...and chose the same Brutus to be their head and king'. In short the just prince 'began by the desire and institution of the people of the same prince'. Fortescue did not belittle the considerable powers of the king but clearly he felt that in a modern *dominium politicum et regale* parliament had a vital role.

And what did the average subject expect of a king? Not a great deal as it would seem to us. Today Henry VI is best remembered as the founder of Eton College and King's College, Cambridge, and it was the kind of pious patronage expected of a king at the time. But education as such was no part of a government's responsibilities. Nor was housing, social security or employment, nor was the government even required to maintain standing defence forces. Henry V's magnificent navy had been his personal possession and as such had been sold, under the terms of his will, to help pay his debts. They had been raised for the conquests in France, considered the personal concern of the monarch. A thoughtful contemporary recommended that they be abandoned and the released resources be used so that the English

> Might win Ireland to a final conquest
> In one sole year, to set us all at rest.

Another recommended the conquest of Scotland. Both foresaw economic and political advantages from their proposals but these were not based on considerations of *Realpolitik* but rather on the view that 'that parcel was of your eldest heritage'.[2] The pretext for a just war was based on inherited rights, part of the dignity and attributes of monarchy which people expected a king to vindicate.

But the chief function of the king's government was to keep the peace within the realm; to 'keep the seas' about it free of piracy as far as possible and against foreign invasion and raids; and to maintain open and honest justice. For these limited though important objectives, for the paying of his servants and rewarding of his supporters, and for the maintenance of the ostentatious magnificence which, in the words of Fortescue 'besuiteth the royal majesty', the king had large personal landed estates, occasional revenues and special taxes in time of war. The king was expected to live of his own and to spare his subjects the profligacy of corrupt ministers and unwarranted extortions by his officers.

In every important respect Henry VI failed in these obligations. He also failed the noble class which expected the king to maintain the peace and give them scope and leadership which would enable them to further their own affairs. 'It is worth remembering,' wrote K. B. McFarlane, 'that [England's] nobility was masterless for thirty years, with the certain prospect of twenty more like them, before self-restraint finally crumbled.' The state of anarchy that threatened in the final years of Henry VI's misrule upturned the conventions of the power game and so threatened all the players. 'The abuse of lordship and the prevalence of corruption were merely signs that England lacked a ruler.'[3]

The more ruffianly elements of the aristocracy were rapidly getting out of control. The Earl of Devon had terrorised his lands in the south-west; in Gloucestershire the dynastic wrangle between the Talbot and Berkeley families burst into open war. In the 1440s the Talbots won a favourable decision in the royal courts through well-placed friends. James, Lord of Berkeley, refused to yield the disputed manors and, when summoned to appear before the royal judges, forced the herald to eat the summons – wax seal, parchment and all. In East Anglia the Dukes of Norfolk and Suffolk ruled their lands like petty tyrants and obliged the lesser gentry to look to their defences with the eyes of professional soldiers.

In 1448 the stalwart Margaret Paston wrote to her husband in London for 'some crossbows and windlasses to bind them with, and quarrels'. The English longbow was no use for the domestic siege she was preparing for, 'for your houses here be so low that there may be no man shoot out with no long-bow, though we had never so much need...And also I would that you should get ii or iii short poleaxes to keep within doors and as many jacks [quilted leather jackets] as you may.' The need was urgent in view of their neighbours' prepara-tions which she outlined in detail.

> Partryche and his fellowship...have made great ordi-nance in their house, as is told me. They have made bars to bar the doors crosswise and wickets on every quarter of the house to shoot out at; both with bows and with hand guns; and the holes that be made for the hand guns they be scarse knee high from the plawnchere [floor]; and of such holes be made five. There can no man shoot out at them with no hand bows.

As the country approached the verge of civil war the govern-ment became virtually powerless in the provinces. The 1460 mayoral elections at Southampton were terrorised by a mob controlled by Thomas Payne. For the next three years he ran the city, acquiring control of valuable central properties by extorting the deeds from their owners. A government direc-tive for new mayoral elections was ignored; opposition to the Payne gang needed courage. When her husband signed away their house Christina Nymithalf and her two children locked themselves in a bedroom. The mobsters moved in at once and 'violently nailed up the door upon her and kept her in the said chamber' for more than three months of a bitter winter. They survived on food which Christina's sister smuggled to the house at night and kept themselves warm by burning the bed boards and bed straw. Eventually a crowd of townsmen summoned up courage for a rescue. They were easily driven back when one of Payne's lieutenants 'caused a gunner to shoot guns out of the said tenement at the king's liege people'.[4]

Sometimes, however, the medieval mafia got a hammering. John Aston of Somerton in north Oxfordshire ran his affairs with considerable success and total disregard for his neighbours' rights. Towards the end of his career he took out a formal pardon from chancery of 'all intrusions and entries into the inheritance of any heirs, tenants in chief without licence and of all trespasses offences misprisions etc and of...all actions, suits, quarrels against him'. A few years earlier one of the most acrimonious of these quarrels had been with the men of neighbouring Deddington. Led by John Somerton, gentleman, who, from his name, we can guess to have been an unwilling exile from Aston's territory, a company of them 'arrayed in manner of war, broke the close and houses of the said John Aston of Somerton, assaulted him and took away goods to the value of £20 and beat and wounded his servants and so threatened them that they dared not go about his business for fear of death or mayhem'.[5]

This lawlessness on land was matched during the 1440s and 1450s by an upsurge in piracy. English cargoes were freely taken in the Thames estuary and sold at Harwich; a shipment of Bordeaux wine was captured in the Channel and sold in Devon; another shipment, pirated by a Breton crew, even found its way to the London wine market. In an age when any successful law enforcement was largely a matter of chance, the elusive mobility of shipping made it virtually immune to arrest. When the pirates were sponsored by powerful men the immunity became complete.

In the West Country piracy was big business. In November 1449 the *St Anthony and St Francis*, a galley of the king's Catalan allies, was taken while at anchor in

Plymouth Sound. The ships involved were the *Mackerell* of Fowey and the *Edward* of Polruan. Cargo to the incredible value of £12,000 was taken and, of this, £7000 was distributed in protection fees. The recipients were: Sir Hugh Courtenay, MP; Sir John Coleshill; John Arundel, Esquire; Michael Power, Esquire; James Durneford, Esquire; the Prior of Kearnek; and John Trelawny, Esquire. It was also noted that the *Mackerell* was owned by Henry, Duke of Exeter, admiral of England. No one was astonished that the prosecution of the case flagged. In fact, possibly the only one to be surprised about the operation was Richard Penpons who found that he had been cut out of it. His ship *The Katharine* plundered profitably out of St Ives and only two years after the Plymouth episode he was made a JP. Thereafter he sat on regular commissions of enquiry into piracy with his friends Sir John Trevelyan, Gentleman of the Royal Household and owner of the *Edward*, and Sir John Arundel, sheriff of the county. The crown endeavoured to rescue something from the wreck, so to speak, by confiscating the *Edward*. But it was bought by Arundel and, when the dust had settled, sold back to Trevelyan at a friendly price.

All along England's coasts the gentry saw profit out at sea. The pirate fraternity of Winchelsea at one time numbered the local MP William Marfoot; the town's mayor was proud to join forces with another ship of His Grace the Duke of Exeter in the plunder of the *St George* of Bruges, off Portsmouth. Henry Bruyn, another partner in this particular venture, was a Gentleman of the King's Household, steward of the Isle of Wight and, in the same year (1450), MP for Portsmouth. In 1453 a caravel owned by Lord Say took two ships off Dordrecht and sold their cargoes at Colchester – the proceeds being shared with the victualler of the ship, the master, the purser and the seamen.[6]

Public exasperation with the government's incompetence and corruption broke surface explosively in 1450. It began to erupt on the south coast late in 1449. Adam Moleyns,

Bishop of Chichester and Keeper of the Privy Seal, had been sent down to Portsmouth to pay arrears owing to crews of near mutinous seamen. When they discovered they were not all to be paid they lynched him. With his dying words he denounced the king's chief minister, the Duke of Suffolk. Parliament introduced bills of impeachment and attainder; on 28 January 1450 Suffolk was committed to the Tower. 'Now is the fox driven to his hole; Hoo to him, Hoo! Hoo!' crowed one balladeer. Hoping to save his servant, Henry VI ordered the duke into exile before the charges could be heard against him. Suffolk evaded a London lynch mob, reached the coast and found a fishing boat willing to take him across the Channel. But the fugitives were intercepted by the Bristol ship *The Nicholas of the Tower*. After a mock trial by the crew Suffolk was 'executed' and his headless body left on Dover sands. All England 'did joyfully sing' at the news.

Throughout the country old scores came up for reckoning. For years the shire house, the only permanent administrative centre in each county, had been controlled by corrupt sheriffs who sold 'right and law...like beef cattle at market'.[7] In East Anglia the sheriffs appointed in Suffolk's interest had for seven years turned a blind eye to a protection racket directed by Sir Thomas Tuddenham of Oxborough Hall, near Norwich, and backed by the JPs John Henydon and John Ulveston. The new sheriff 'swore by great oaths that he would neither spare for gold, nor love, nor fear'. At the end of the hearing Tuddenham faced more than three hundred fines totalling £1396.[8] In Kent another Suffolk nominee, Sheriff Crowmer, vowed he would turn the whole county into a deer park to avenge the duke's death. The county did not wait; led by John Cade they marched on London in good order and on 1 June 1450 they encamped on Blackheath with such military professionalism 'that no power of horsemen should come and override them'.

Cade was an ex-soldier from France and his following included a former squire of Henry V who had fought at

Agincourt, members of the gentry, a mayor, five clerics and even armed levies summoned in due form by local authorities. They presented a bill of reasoned criticisms of government policy – the 'Complaint of the Commons of Kent'. The king was urged to dismiss all the 'false progeny and affinity of the Duke of Suffolk' from who he 'hath had false counsel, for his lords are lost, his merchandise is lost, his commons destroyed, the sea is lost, France is lost, himself so poor that he may not for his meat and drink; he oweth more than ever did king in England...' They claimed that parliamentary elections were not free; that lords of the blood royal were excluded from the king's council in favour of parvenus; that household officials embezzled royal moneys and the people were oppressed to recover the losses; that when the royal household moved about the country the purveyors commandeered food and other supplies without making payment.

King and council temporised then sent troops against Cade. He fell back into Kent and ambushed and overwhelmed the royal forces near Sevenoaks. Recruits flooded to Cade from Surrey and Sussex. The king withdrew to regroup his force at Kenilworth and on 3 July London opened its gates to the rebels.

The regime's fate was on a knife edge. Lord Say and Sheriff Crowmer, imprisoned in the capital as a temporary concession to Cade's movement, were executed; Bishop Ayscough, another royal adviser, had already been murdered by the parishioners of Edington in his own diocese of Salisbury. In Oxfordshire the sheriff, William Wykeham, 'entretened daily about him great numbers of people, defensibly arrayed...to subdue the heady rigours of the people...such as would have entended to inordinate insurrection'.[9] John Hampden, sheriff of Bedfordshire, was ordered to send reinforcements into the neighbouring county of Northamptonshire and there were demonstrations in favour of Cade as far afield as Yorkshire. At one point Cade had adopted the name of John Mortimer, the family name of the Duke of York; he had also called for the reappointment of York on the royal councils. It seemed for the moment that he had provided the Yorkist party with a powerful base from which to expel their enemies with popular support. But Cade's rising defeated itself. The riff-raff were rioting and looting in the capital within two days and the city fathers ordered out the watch to round them up. Seizing the opportunity the royalist garrison in the Tower won control of London Bridge. The rebel forces faded fast and Cade himself was killed while directing an abortive siege of Queenborough Castle on the Thames.

Public opinion seems to have rated the rising a success despite the death of its leader. After all, the six-week turmoil had stirred up the government and ended with the death of three of the king's most hated ministers. But little in fact changed. By the time Edward IV achieved the throne in 1461 the king's writ had been a dead letter in wide areas of England for a generation – in the far north men had almost entirely deserted the normal courts for powerful local patrons. Men looked for a new order under the new regime of York.

After their triumphant return from Calais in June 1460 the Yorkists defeated the royalist army at Northampton and took the king himself prisoner. It was a humble and loyal arrest. Finding Henry alone in his tent after the battle, March, Warwick and Fauconberg went down on their knees before him. They assured him that they desired only 'for to please your most noble person, desiring most tenderly the high welfare and prosperity thereof, and of all your realm, and for to be your true liegemen, while our lives shall endure'. They then proceeded to London where the king was housed honourably in the palace of the bishop.

Although they had fought openly against the king's army the lords were quite sincere in their pledge of loyalty. Richard, Duke of York, boasted a descent from Edward III which, many would have agreed, gave him a marginally better claim to the crown than Henry VI, and recently he had adopted the surname of 'Plantagenet' to emphasise his royal blood. Once before, at St Albans in 1455, he had led his men in battle against the king's army. Then too the Yorkists had won. Then too York himself had reaffirmed his allegiance to the person of the king but demanded that he be given his own rightful place in the councils of the realm. A hectoring and resentful man, he nevertheless had a point. Undoubtedly of the blood royal, he was also the greatest landowner in England and as such entitled to a senior place in the king's council. Yet he had been rigidly excluded by the advisers and favourites of the weak-willed and ineffectual Henry. He had competently filled the appointments as Lieutenant of Ireland and King's Lieutenant in France only to find himself supplanted by less able men. During the king's two brief attacks of madness in the 1450s he had forced the council to accept him as Protector of the Realm, only to be excluded once again when the king's sanity returned sufficiently for his advisers to claim to be able to act in his name. Then at the 'Parliament of Devils' in November 1459, York and all his supporters had been condemned as traitors. Successful armed rebellion was their only chance of recovering their position and their lands. York had fled to his estates in Ireland and the other members of his faction to Calais, in Yorkist hands since the duke's second protectorship.

None of them had aimed to put York on the throne. When, therefore, the duke marched into London in October 1460 and made a bid for the crown his friends were astonished and angry. Warwick even requested the Archbishop of Canterbury to remind York of his oath of allegiance. However, the Lancastrian monarchy was in such disarray following Northampton that York was able to press his case. The House of Lancaster was descended through the male line from Edward III's fourth son John of Gaunt, Duke of Lancaster; the House of York, in the male line, descended from Edward's fifth son Edmund of Langley but also, in the female line, from the old king's third son Lionel, Duke of Clarence.

Since his line descended through the senior line, York claimed the superior right to the crown. The claim could hardly be disallowed on the ground that it involved descent through a woman, since it was precisely on such grounds that Henry V had based his claims to the crown of France.

These genealogical games were not considered frivolous by the assembled lords and gentry. There was hardly a landed family in the realm which had not at some time had to decide the fate of a prosperous inheritance on just such considerations. Moreover there was, at this time, no hard and fast rule for the descent of the English crown so that these legalistic niceties were not merely matters of family and estate law, but also of real constitutional importance. No wonder that even the House of Lords demurred. Claiming that they lacked the necessary legal expertise to rule on such 'high matters' they passed the question on to the judges; and they asked the advice of the serjeants at law. At last a compromise was reached. Henry would remain king but York and the heirs of his body were declared heirs to the throne. It was a startling setback for the court party.

But there were many great families with a vested interest in the continuance of the Lancastrian regime. Henry's war-like queen, Margaret of Anjou, was raising support in Scotland and in Yorkshire the Dukes of Somerset and Exeter and the Earl of Northumberland were massing a large army. In mid-December York slogged his way north, along roads virtually impassable after a year of almost uninterrupted rain, to his family castle at Sandal near Wakefield. He was killed 'like a fish in a net or a deer in a buckstall', leading an unnecessary sortie into an easily foreseeable ambush. His head was spiked above the gates of York wearing a straw and paper crown; the Earl of Salisbury was killed after the battle, probably by retainers of the Earl of Northumberland, head of the Percy family, the traditional enemies of the Nevilles.

York's son, Edward, Earl of March, was dealing with trouble in the Welsh Marches. In February Warwick was defeated at the Second Battle of St Albans by Margaret and her northerners; they also recovered the pitiable person of Henry VI. A few months after their triumph the Yorkists were scattered and in disarray. Their only chance was to overthrow the Lancastrian regime, now in full cry, and put their own candidate on the throne. The Earl of March was proclaimed king as Edward IV. On 29 March 1461 he crushed the Lancastrian army at Towton in Yorkshire.

The attitude of the general population to the recurring faction fights of the century was generally indifferent. The power of the magnates and old traditions of loyalty to the great local family usually determined allegiance in the countryside and in the little market towns it surrounded. The larger cities sometimes showed somewhat greater independence. The city records of York contain a warm tribute to the dead Richard III, written in the first days of the reign of his successor; a detachment of Bristol men fought under the town's own banner at Towton, but this was exceptional. In the interests of a quiet life most towns, while prepared to provide taxes, loans and even contingents of 'waged men' for whichever faction controlled their district for the time being, carefully avoided any true commitment.

When Norwich received a Lancastrian order of mobilisation in January 1461, the city fathers temporised. No doubt they had had news of the Yorkist defeat at Wakefield, but the Duke of Norfolk was still loyal to the cause of York. However, following a second summons, they mustered 120 men to serve at sixpence a day from 28 January for six weeks. Finding a man of worship prepared to leave his affairs and risk his life as captain proved more difficult. Eventually, after 'great labour and constant application' and on the assurance that all his expenses would be met, William Rokewood, Esquire, agreed to serve.

When the six weeks had almost elapsed, the company was at last called up for active service – but not in the cause of King Henry. Early in March they were led out to join the forces of the Duke of Norfolk.[10] As they footslogged their way northwards through bitter and blustering March days, Rokewood and his band had little to cheer their spirits. Before they left Norwich news had reached the city of a second great Lancastrian victory at St Albans in mid-February. The wild northern army led by Queen Margaret was reported to have pillaged Stamford and Peterborough. The Norwich council decided 'for the safekeeping of the city that five gates only shall be kept open and guarded...and that the rest of the gates be kept closed and locked', the night watch was also increased. The Yorkist cause seemed in decline and, if they were not killed in the battle, the Norwich men could expect to be killed as traitors if defeated.

After St Albans London had shut its gates to Margaret. She decided to regroup her forces on York, leaving behind her a trail of devastation and sullen anger against the royalist army. On 27 February the Earl of Warwick entered the capital with the handsome young heir to the Yorkist title, the Earl of March. Edward, at least, led an army with a victory over the Lancastrians behind them; at Mortimer's Cross, in Herefordshire, a fortnight before. His triumph had been marked by a dramatic 'prophecy'. Just before the battle began a trick of atmospherics produced the illusion of three suns in the sky. The effect unnerved the superstitious troops, but the sunburst was a Yorkist badge and Edward, quick thinking as always, hailed the phenomenon as a sign that the Holy Trinity was on his side.

Within forty-eight hours of his arrival in London, Edward had been acclaimed king by an assembly of Londoners summoned to St John's Fields, Clerkenwell, by Warwick's agents. The following day, Sunday 1 March, Henry VI was publicly declared no longer worthy to be king; on Wednesday Edward was proclaimed at St Paul's Cross. From there he and a group of noble supporters went in procession to Westminster Hall where he took his place in the marble chair his father had laid his hands upon only months before. The next

day the Duke of Norfolk went to raise troops in his territories. On Palm Sunday, 29 March, Rokewood and his Norwich contingent marched under Norfolk's banner into a
battle raging on the meadows south of the Yorkshire village
of Towton. It was mid-afternoon; a blizzard swept the fields.

That morning the Yorkist commanders Warwick,
Edward and the fiery old Lord Fauconberg looked up the
bleak meadows at the largest army yet assembled on an
English field. They were outnumbered by about 10,000 men
and the Lancastrians had the advantage of the terrain,
occupying a light rise in the ground with the village of Towton about 1000 yards at their back and the vulnerable right
flank protected by the little River Cock. They were commanded by the Duke of Somerset. The king and queen were
at York; she impatient at being excluded from the battle by
her sex, he refusing to compromise his immortal soul by
fighting on one of the high feast days of the Church.

After a bitter, cold night a gusting wind from the south
whipped the cloud-heavy sky under a grey dawn. The armies
waited, Somerset secure in his positional advantage, Edward
waiting for Norfolk's forces to come up. About mid-morn-
ing snow began to fall and soon the blizzard was driving into
the Lancastrian line. Edward ordered the attack and Fauconberg, commanding the archers, seized the weather advantage
with full professional expertise. Ordering his men to use their
heavy sheaf arrows, he led them within close bowshot; then,
the volley still in the air, they retreated several yards. The
enemy, blinded by the snow, hampered by the wind and
deceived by Fauconberg's ruse, completely misjudged the
range. As their arrows fell harmlessly short they were collected as reserve ammunition by Fauconberg's men. Repeat-
ing the manœuvre drew all the Lancastrian's heavy, armour-
piercing arrows and finally drove the infuriated enemy to
attack. They lost their positional advantage but as the morning wore into afternoon their superior numbers began to tell.
Warwick in command of the centre and Edward directing

the reserve, fought prodigiously and held the line steady; but they were being slowly forced back. The dead and wounded lay so thick that foemen could only come to blows after climbing the mounds of bodies; from time to time there were lulls in the fight while both sides cleared a way to their enemy.

As the afternoon began to darken Norfolk's men loomed out of the snow on the road from Ferrybridge to the south. Without breaking their march they drove against the Lancastrian left flank. Slowly the battle shifted back, then the Lancastrians broke. As they fled desperately for safety across the River Cock many were dragged down by their armour in its freezing water and trampled underfoot by panic-stricken friends. Hundreds more were slaughtered on the plain of York. Bishop Neville of Exeter later reported to his brother Warwick that the corpses counted after the battle covered eighteen square miles. Both earl and king had ordered their troops to spare the commons; in the blood lust of battle the order was forgotten. The order to 'seek out the lords' was better obeyed. The Earl of Northumberland, Sir Andrew Trollope and a dozen more barons and knights were killed in the fighting. The Earls of Devon and Wiltshire were executed afterwards. But Margaret and Henry, Somerset and Exeter escaped to Scotland. On both sides the common soldiery mourned the loss of comrades in arms. Thomas Neve and John Ive, when they got home, founded a chantry 'to pray for their friends' souls which were slain at York field'.

Towton, the largest battle fought on English soil, involved about 50,000 combatants; among them three-quarters of the peerage. Perhaps it was the one battle of the 'Wars of the Roses' which everyone considered important. For the first time since the twelfth century the crown of England was to be decided on a battlefield. Its principal outcome was to shatter the strength of great northern lords like Percy, Clifford and Dacre who hitherto had been loyal to Lancaster and who between them dominated the north of England.

On the Monday afternoon following the battle, King Edward entered the city of York. There he remained to celebrate Easter and he held his court there for two weeks. Then he began a slow progress through Lancashire, Cheshire and the Midlands to accustom his subjects to their new-made king. He arrived in London to be crowned on Sunday 28 June. Warwick remained in the north with an army recruited to a large extent from his own retainers.

The bulk of the Yorkist army disbanded after Towton; many of the troops had still to be paid. Rokewood's contingent included a small group waged at the expense of Alderman Richard Borne who paid them for the sixty days of their contract and asked his friend John Williams to cover any additional expenses. Williams, in fact, paid the costs of the journey back to Norwich, only to find on his return that Borne had died and his executors were refusing to pay. But if Williams was out of pocket the soldiers got their money. Not so the company raised by Alderman John Smyth of Bury St Edmunds and led by William Alleyn. When they went to court to recover £30 in back pay and expenses they found the alderman was more than a match for a bunch of battle-scarred war veterans.

The driving force behind the new dynasty was thirty-one-year-old Richard Neville, Earl of Warwick. He was now the greatest man in the realm, second only to the king, and most people assumed that he would be able to rule the young monarch whose proclamation as king he had engineered. For the first three years of the new reign it was he who held in check Lancastrian machinations in the north. But Edward came to resent this overmighty subject and the influence of the whole Neville clan. As the decade advanced the struggle between the two most powerful men in England rose in intensity. Where Warwick advocated alliance with France Edward favoured Burgundy; where Warwick arranged a suitable royal marriage Edward married secretly a beautiful but penniless widow of a former Lancastrian knight; when

The Wheel of Fortune, humbling the great and exalting the fallen in its revolutions, was one of the most hackneyed images of the later Middle Ages. Nevertheless, it must have seemed fresh and vivid to the contemporaries of Edward IV. An English illuminated MS of the early 1460s shows the king in person enthroned upon a Wheel of Fortune. In this picture the figures are generalised types. *The British Library*

Edward forbade the marriage of his own brother, the Duke of Clarence, to Warwick's daughter Isabel, no doubt fearing a still closer tie between the great earl and the royal family, Warwick publicly celebrated that marriage at Calais on Tuesday 11 July 1469.

The break was complete and a new round in the 'Wars of the Roses' about to begin. After the marriage Warwick and Clarence published a manifesto against the king's evil advisers; took ship for Kent, and marched unopposed through London to join friends coming down from the north. Edward's support melted away and by the end of July he was a prisoner in Warwick Castle. But now the great earl was troubled by insurgent forces on the borders and to his dismay found he could not raise the troops to meet them. In a sullen but effective demonstration of opinion the English commoners refused to fight except in the name of King Edward. The king had to be released and by May 1470 had successfully outmanœuvred his rivals. Warwick, who since 1461 had seen himself as the arbiter of England, had hoped to make a new king out of the pliable George, Duke of Clarence; instead he found himself and his candidate forced to flee the kingdom. On 5 May 1470 they landed in France at Honfleur.

The situation was made to order for the wily Louis XI of France. His sole interest in English affairs was to keep the old enemy distracted by civil war for as long as possible. The Lancastrian Queen Margaret was already in exile in his country. During the next few months he presided over a sensational *entente* between Warwick and Margaret. They made common cause, not on behalf of the senile Henry VI still held in the Tower of London, but of Edward, Prince of Wales, his son and heir by Margaret. He was betrothed to Warwick's daughter, the Lady Anne Neville, and following the restoration was to become regent for his father under Warwick's tutelage. On 13 September, with men, money and ships provided by Louis, the new Lancastrian landed in Devon.

Edward IV was caught unawares and had to flee to the Low Countries.

What Warwick called the 'Readeption' of Henry VI lasted barely eight troubled months. In March 1471 Edward, the only English king to lose and win back his crown, landed at Ravenspur in Yorkshire. His reception was cold. Yet, thanks to his enemies' mistakes and his own cool and brilliant strategy he brought Warwick to battle on Easter Sunday 14 April at Barnet and there defeated him. The great earl and his brother Baron Montague were killed and their bodies exposed for two days in St Paul's to scotch any 'feigned seditious tales' that they still lived. On the day of Barnet, another Lancastrian army landed at Weymouth. Led by Margaret it made a brilliant march up the west of England, twice outmanœuvring Edward until, on the morning of 4 May, it was forced to turn and fight in the meadows where the River Avon joins the Severn below Tewkesbury. It might have gone better for them had they let their remarkable queen command their battle. As it was, after a hard fight and confusion in their high command, they were routed and then massacred in the bloodiest battle of the civil wars. Prince Edward was among those killed and his death finally broke the 'determination' of his mother. She placed herself 'at the commandment' of King Edward and ended her life in France as a pauper. Her husband was murdered in the Tower on Edward's orders.

England remained at peace for fourteen more years. When Edward died in 1473 he was succeeded in mysterious circumstances by his brother Richard, Duke of Gloucester. In his brief two-year reign Richard III demonstrated the considerable abilities which he had loyally devoted to his brother's service. In August 1485 King Richard died on the field of Bosworth. The outcome was decided by treachery but the king died heroically spurring his horse into the enemy line in defiance when he could easily have withdrawn and regrouped to fight another day.

Once again the English faced the prospect of civil war. There were a dozen Yorkist nobles with better claims to the crown than the young Henry Tudor, whose only tenuous link with the blood royal was through the bastard line of the Beauforts which had been forever barred from succession by parliamentary statute. The outlook was bleak for England. When the troubles started, some thirty years before, the cause had been a palpable failure of the monarchy; their pretext a strong, well-argued claim of hereditary legitimacy. Now the crown had been tumbled in the mud of battle by an adventurer supported by French money, an army barely 5000 strong and by treachery, at a time when the monarchy was effective and England was well and peacefully ruled. Bosworth was a frightening precedent for a new and still more unprincipled round in the wars which now seemed endemic.

Few at home, and no foreign power, believed in Henry's survival. Before William Caxton died he saw three rebellions against the usurper. As late as 1495 Henry VII, who had cynically dated his own reign from the day before his victory and so put all the loyal supporters of King Richard at his mercy, was so insecure that parliament passed an act pardoning in advance any who assisted the reigning monarch, against possible future impeachment or attainder. It marks a vivid contrast with the stability that Edward IV had established.

He had introduced a new style in English kingship. In place of the wet-faced, shabbily dressed Henry in his drab gown and round-toed peasant-style shoes, the Londoners acclaimed a young hero. Nineteen when he came to the throne, six foot four in his stockinged feet, dazzlingly handsome and a man of ready personal charm, Edward was a confirmed glutton, a renowned lecher and, as was to become apparent, a tireless and efficient executive. It was a contradiction that perplexed his contemporaries and misled foreigners. The French courtier, diplomat and chronicler Philippe de Commines thought him fitful and idle and reckoned that his re-entry into England in 1471 was contrived by 'several noblewomen and wives of rich citizens with whom he had been closely and secretly acquainted who won over their husbands'. It is, however, improbable that the kings' mistresses were enthusiastic fifth columnists. He had a habit of handing on his consorts to favoured courtiers 'much against their will'. The practice caused resentment certainly, but also, perhaps, broke a few hearts. Edward's charms were potent. An Italian observer noted that though 'he pursued with no discrimination the married and the unmarried, the noble and the lowly, he took none by force'. Later, when indulgence had made him fat, a kiss from the king was still able to double a rich widow's donation towards the 1475 campaign from ten to twenty pounds.

But even Commines recognised Edward's ready memory. When they were introduced at Picquigny, Edward immediately 'mentioned the places where he had seen me and that previously I had put myself to much trouble serving him at Calais'. It was an important talent in a ruler which Edward's own subjects also noted and which impressed them. 'The names and estates used to recur to him of nearly all the persons throughout the shires of the kingdom, just as though he were in the habit of seeing them daily and this even if...they held the rank only of private gentleman.' Edward's remarkable memory gave social sinew to his renowned bonhomie, it also served his natural shrewdness well. The Paston family, interminably at odds with the Duke of Norfolk, had learnt to recognise the duke's corrupt adviser Sir William Brandon as the chief instigator of his oppressions. The family correspondence records with obvious gratification that the king had the same view, and quotes the king as saying: 'Brandon, though thou can beguile the Duke of Norfolk and bring him about the thumb as thou lists, I let thee wit thou shalt not do me so; for I understand thy false dealing well enough.'[11]

Edward IV made decisions at all levels; his personal style is stamped on the reign. Routine orders to representatives in the shires have autograph additions in his bold and legible hand: 'We pray you fail not to be done'; or 'John, we pray you fail not this our writing to be accomplished.' Letters, warrants and petitions are stamped with the king's personal monogram or marked by the clerk as authorised by 'the king by word of mouth'. The king's appetite for detail inspired the mobilisation of the 1475 campaign, producing a commissariat that would have been the envy of generations of later English officers.

Edward chose his officials with care but, as in any court of the period, behind the departments of state stood the monarch's body servants; men who served his food and drink, who helped him dress and undress, whose daily close attendance on the king could give them significant influence in his private discussions. In the first weeks of his reign Edward IV made Sir John Howard sheriff of Norfolk to push on the recruitment for the Towton campaign. Soon after he received also command of the castles of Norwich and Colchester and then the position of the king's carver. The job, a natural one for a man who was to remain among the king's most loyal and effective councillors, carried a salary of £40. The scope of influence open to such personal servants under a weak king was fully exploited in the previous reign. Henry VI had granted his carver the lordship and castle of Berkhamsted – even before the holder, the Duke of Exeter, was dead. The terms of the grant reveal how the king's servant had used his position to confuse the feckless monarch. 'Understanding now that our cousin John, Duke of Exeter was either dead, or inpoint to die, and not fully ascertained how it was by him, we showed our grace unto our trusty and well-beloved knight Sir Edmund Hungerford, one of our carvers...' Small wonder that John Paston, hoping to persuade the king to 'take my service and quarrel together' approached 'Sir George Brown, James Radcliffe and others of my acquaintance which wait most upon the king and lie nightly in his chamber'.

This kind of access to central government, then as now, was what any sizeable provincial operator wanted. But while Edward IV did restore the power of central, royal government, he continued to exercise it through the local strong men. Domestic offices continued to be filled by men of property, 'worship and wisdom . . . of sundry shires by whom may be known the disposition of the countries' (i.e. counties). The lesser gentry of the shires were always seeking ways of strengthening their links with the centre; parliament was one way of doing this. During the fourteenth century interest in parliament had often been so weak that sheriffs had frequently returned themselves, finding no one else willing to serve. In the fifteenth century this changed. The sheriff, often a royal appointee, found a new and less exhausting interest in arranging the election in favour of local gentry eager to serve. Bargaining for the seats began as soon as the summons for the parliament reached the shire house. Only two knights could be returned for each county but within the county there were a number of boroughs and, as John Paston ruefully discovered at Yarmouth in September 1472, these were fixed in a matter of days. The competition was fierce.

The mechanics of a fifteenth-century election were straightforward enough and not very different from the ones familiar today. The suffrage was more restricted of course – restricted in fact to a small clique of well-to-do citizens. But the election, when it occurred, was won by the man who had been nominated by the most powerful local group, and it was the nomination that mattered. Today a Tory would have little chance in Huyton just as a Socialist would have little chance in Esher. And then as now. By a statute of 1445, the member had to be elected from the burgesses actually living in the borough and also by the whole community of burgesses, 'freely and by one assent'. Once the election was made the sheriff was to be notified and the result recorded in an indenture which he then forwarded to the chancery offices in the Tower of London. Since the statute required that the member be elected by free and general assent of the burgesses, the sheriff's indenture naturally showed that they had been so elected. However, borough authorities devised various methods to ensure that this 'free consent' returned the right man.

The procedure varied. In King's Lynn the procedure was complicated but effective. It began openly enough with the mayor reading the sheriff's notification of a forthcoming election in an open assembly of those burgesses qualified to vote, in the Guildhall. He then nominated four burgesses – who nominated another four – and the eight then nominated a further four. The twelve conducted the 'election'. They handed the mayor a slip of paper bearing the names of the two members. Without surprise he read the names to the candidates. Indeed, few present would have been surprised. These gentlemanly proceedings were once rather rudely interrupted. In the 1419 election Robert Gill and Thomas Middleton demanded that the election should be conducted openly; by this they did not of course wish a public ballot of the citizenry at large but only that those present in the guildhall should give their 'free', one might almost say their 'full-hearted', consent. This modest venture into political radicalism was firmly silenced by the mayor. At Hull, by comparison, the arrangements seem positively democratic; the election there was made, in open forum, by all the town's freemen – however, the candidates were nominated by mayor and aldermen.

Such arrangements indicate how important the choice of member was to the town's prosperous ruling group. The same thing is found in the shires. Up to 1430 the knights of the shire were chosen by an open shire court. From the late fourteenth century the 'quality' were pressing for this to be changed, claiming that the elections were disturbed and interrupted by the lower orders. A statute of 1430 brought in the desired 'reform', by restricting the suffrage to free-holders with land to the value of forty shillings or more. It also provided that in the case of a contested election the successful candidate would be the one who had 'the greater number of the forty-shilling freeholders'.

This is the first statute reference to the principle of the majority; an unfamiliar and suspect one to the medieval mind. The divisive principle of the greater ruling the less in important community decisions contradicted the ideal that on such matters the will of the community was informed by God and should therefore be unanimous. Even after 1430 the poll was not general. The statute did not specify how the majority should be decided but various methods were available and the poll count, the most divisive of all because it actually quantified the division, was not always, or even generally, used. Preferred were: by show of hands, as in the modern union shop floor meeting and for the same reasons; by voice, the volume of the 'ayes' and 'noes' being judged by ear; by view, when the rival parties were divided into two groups of which the larger was assessed by eye. However, at least as early as 1450 the poll or head count was being used. It too derived, if indirectly, from the 1430 statute.

There were three candidates at the Huntingdon election in that year and, not surprisingly, there were claims that some of the voters were not in fact qualified. The sheriff began by an examination of the supporters of Henry Gymber. There were seventy of them but the sheriff was able to examine only forty-seven of them before he was forcibly prevented from going on. The other candidates, Sonteham and Styuecle, had 424 supporters, of whom 124 were claimed to be forty-shilling freeholders. The figures scattered through the report must have struck the clerk who copied them as odd and new-fangled, yet, inevitably, to find out how many electors were qualified to vote, the sheriff had to make a count. Thus, indirectly, the poll was introduced into English parliamentary elections.

Besides prescribing the manner of the election, the law also stated that members should be natives of their boroughs. In fact seats often went to outsiders, either because the electors decided that this would be to their advantage or because they had no option. In 1483 Wells returned a Bristol lawyer and throughout the century boroughs often elected lawyers from outside because they were better qualified or because the borough had no lawyer among its citizens. MPs were often charged with purely town business while they were in the capital and an efficient professional man might well have handled it better. The burgess representatives for Lynn in 1419, besides attending the king's parliament, were: to present a petition against Prussian incursions into Lynn's overseas markets and another against English rivals at Southampton; and to conduct negotiations with the Hanse headquarters in London. They wrote numerous letters home, not only for additional funds but also for advice and instructions. A couple of skilled lawyers would have served the town better.[12]

More often the borough members were outsiders – a result of external influence. In 1478 the Cornish borough returns were blatantly tampered with to return king's men, not one of which was a Cornishman. The powerful northern families regularly intervened in their own counties to arrange borough MPs friendly to their interest. Elsewhere the lesser gentry were competing for borough seats. There was little the burgesses could do about all this and often little they wanted to do. Merchants whose trade took them to the capital went there on their own account to fit their own schedules. A parliamentary session might last weeks and the expenses allowance of two shillings a day, though four times the average labourer's wage, was not likely to compensate the loss to a businessman away from his affairs for such a length of time. Moreover, while handling the town's business in London might bring prestige back home, it could also earn enemies and failure would kill a reputation. Indeed one's reputation might be in danger from quite unexpected causes. One of the MP's duties was to give a report of parliament's doings on return to the constituency. On their return from the 1420–21 parliament the King's Lynn members described among other things how the session had been graced by a sermon from the Archbishop of Canterbury on the text *Justicia et Pax osculate sunt*. In fact the sermon had been given by the Bishop of Durham on a different text. Evidently the two worthies were not in church that day and hoped that no one would expose their little deception.[13]

For the gentry parliament had greater importance. Like the modern conference it was an ideal place for making contacts. Apart from approving taxation the Commons had little part in the deliberations. Legislation was devised by the royal council; Commons' petitions, supposedly embodying petitions which formed the basis of statutes, could be reworded without redress in the Lords; the statutes themselves often received their final form at the hand of the judiciary after the session was over. Yet this was the ideal opportunity for the men from the shires, whether shire or borough members, to contact the government and highly placed officials. Contacts at court were vital to their affairs and the high court of parliament was the national arena in which to make them. By the end of the century parliament was rapidly becoming the preserve of the landed gentry.

From the latter part of Edward IV's reign parliament was called less and less frequently. Henry VII, who continued the pattern, even claimed it as evidence of royal consideration for his subjects, sparing them the expense and trouble of attendance. But if Edward dispensed with it when he could, he was careful to flatter it when he must. The speech from the throne is first recorded from his reign. His monarchy was rooted in popular acclaim. The Londoners did not forget their part in the assembly in St John's Fields, Clerkenwell, and in the West Country, where many towns had risen in support of his father's abortive rebellion; many reckoned the king had the Commons to thank for his crown. 'We brought King Edward to his prosperity in the realm of England,

and if he will not be ruled after us we will have him; as able as we were to make him king, as able we be to depose him and put him down and bring him there as we found him!'

4

Town and Country

The campaigns of the civil wars were fought over thinly populated terrain, thickly wooded in the lowland areas and much undercultivated. A Venetian visitor at the end of the century, comparing England with his own densely peopled country, was surprised that so fertile an island should support such a small population. More surprising still, to the foreigner, were the open towns of England. Here and there the walls still stood. At Canterbury the West Gate had gunports built into it during renovations in 1380. The earliest known English fortifications designed specifically for artillery, [1] this sample of modern military architecture was still a tourist attraction for army veterans in the early fifteenth century. From time to time gentlemen pilgrims, reminiscing loudly about their war service in France, were to be seen showing their sons over the fortifications and explaining the 'dangers from arbalest bowe and gun'.[2]

Caernarvon and the other Welsh garrison towns still had their walls, and south coast towns maintained defences. Southampton's were thoroughly overhauled in the 1460s and at Dartmouth the battery was fitted with improved, square gunports to permit a wider sweep of fire.

The great frontier town of Berwick, together with others along the Marches with Scotland and Wales, was fortified and walled but whereas in France or Italy or Germany even the smallest market town had its castle or tower and walls, the English had, since the time of Henry II, tended to use their town walls as convenient quarries of dressed stone. St Albans, where Henry VI raised his standard in 1455, was one of the many towns which had never been walled; it was protected only by a pallisaded ditch, designed to keep out night marauders and footpads and nothing more.

St Albans was basically a one-street town. The broad St Peter's Street, lined by the houses of the leading inhabitants, was the site of the market based at the south end. Behind this was the abbey with another cluster of houses. The gardens and orchards ran back from the houses and merged with the fields over the ditch. Today it would seem more like an overgrown village which is how it appeared to many foreign visitors, accustomed to the thriving and populous townships of northern Italy or the Low Countries. Even the rich and important wool towns of the Cotswolds were not much bigger. The modern visitor to Northleach or Chipping Campden or Broadway, impressed by the magnificent town houses of the fifteenth-century woolmen that still line the main streets, soon discovers that behind the opulent frontage the town meets the country once again, over the garden wall so to speak. These places, once the great centres of English trade, have changed little over the centuries – an hour spent in their spacious and handsome streets gives a vivid evocation of the feel and scale of medieval town life in Caxton's England.

A population as small as two or three hundred might be considered a town if the place had the right to hold a market; a large market town had rarely more than two thousand inhabitants. Outside London the greatest cities were Bristol, York, Coventry and Norwich, none with a population of more than fifteen thousand. Despite their growing wealth they could not compete with the power of the great magnates whose houses and castles lowered with menace in the surrounding countryside. A detachment of Bristol men fought, under the town's banner, at Towton, but this was exceptional. Elsewhere the citizens were uneasily aware of their vulnerability to the bully boys of the local Mister Big. John Mason proudly began the chronicle of his native Yarmouth, one of the east coast's major ports and noted for the sumptuous liturgy of its churches and the beauty of its buildings, with a brief history of the world from the time of Enoch the Just. But as he approaches the modern era local realities blot out this grand vision. From 1459 we find him dating events, not from the Creation of the World or from the birth of Christ, but from the death of Sir John Fastolf, lord of Caister Castle, just ten miles up the coast. A few years before, life at Exeter had been totally disrupted by the Earl of Devon and his retainers. In October 1455 they made a show of force which stopped the Justices of the Peace holding their session and in November they forced the cathedral treasury to surrender valuables which the earl had pledged as security for a loan from the bishop.

The earl had seized on the opportunities offered by the Duke of York's rebellion at the beginning of the decade to prosecute his own interests in the West Country while posing as the loyal ally of the duke and a champion of English rights against the central government. Hereford, another centre of the disturbances, had found itself in danger of a takeover by the men of Sir Walter Devereux, a powerful landowner of nearby Weobly and one of York's agents in the area. The town oligarchy, although loyal to the king, found itself helpless when Devereux enlisted thirty odd craftsmen and artisans to his livery and prepared a demonstration in the duke's favour in the centre of the town.

Small and weak and, in modern eyes, barely independent of the rural landscape which surrounded them, these medieval towns had, nevertheless, a strong sense of identity. The distinction between town and country was as clear-cut to medieval men and women as it is to us. In one respect it was more so, for the ruling bodies of the towns and their guilds were the only organs of authority controlled by men who were neither noble nor cleric. In the national context these carried little weight, but they were important focal points for local pride. The citizens of a place like Southampton or Bristol, seeing the daily stream of wagons which left and entered their gates for the markets of Oxford, Ludlow, Salisbury, Coventry, saw also that their town was in a different league from the surrounding manorial economies. Their merchants not only did business with these distant parts but levied tolls and exchanged privileges which had nothing to do with requirements of the manorial court. On extreme occasions they even levied war on their neighbours.

At Hereford the tailor John Weobly, later an associate of Sir Walter Devereux, mobilised a faction among the craftsmen living outside the town and others recently settled there, to force his election as MP. The oligarchy, furious at this takeover, contemptuously dubbed Weobly and his people 'Welshmen' though most had English names. Yet to the tight-knit community of the little marcher town these upstarts and newcomers were foreigners in the worst sense of the term.[3]

For the neighbouring farms and estates the town was the market: the outlet for local produce and the distribution point for luxuries and necessities, such as salt, not produced in the locality. But one distinction between town and country, to us virtually a *sine qua non*, was much less marked. Industry, growing slowly in importance as the century advanced, was not yet an exclusively urban phenomenon. Any important town had its craft guilds; some towns were major centres of industry. Coventry, thanks to the qualities of its water, was internationally known for its blue cloth – 'true as Coventry blue' was none the worse as a proverb because the woad dye had to be imported via Southampton and Bristol from France. Bristol was equally renowned for its red cloths. There were flourishing textile centres at Winchester and Romney where the Italian community in Southampton sent large quantities of Flemish cloth for finishing on its voyage back with the galley fleets to the Mediterranean. At the beginning of the century York had a sizeable colony of cloth workers and was a big centre of iron working; in the same county Sheffield had been renowned for its cutlery since the time that Chaucer's yeoman sported his 'Sheffield poignard'. Metal working and especially wiredrawing was another important trade at Coventry, while the Bristol wire-drawers and pin-makers were incorporated by royal charter in the 1460s. The luxury craft of the gold and silver smith was concentrated in London. Other cities earned local reputations for the skill of their craftsmen, but a surprising amount of what today we would call 'heavy industry' sprang up along the wooded banks of rivers far from any town or in straggling villages well placed to exploit local raw materials.

In the cloth industry a gradual shift from the towns had begun as early as the 1200s soon after water power had been harnessed to the process of fulling. Before raw wool can be worked it must be cleaned of the natural oils and grease. Throughout the Middle Ages the bleaching agent was a heavy clay known as fuller's earth which had to be dried and pulverised before it could be used and then trodden into the wool fibres and finally washed clear in running water. Water-powered trip hammers had been used on the Continent, mostly in Cistercian monasteries, for this laborious operation a century or more before the first fulling mill mentioned in England (1185). Thereafter fulling mills were set up along the tumbling streams and torrents of the Pennines, the Lake District and the Cotswolds. The movement gathered momentum in the fourteenth century, keeping step with the growth of the English cloth industry. The fine quality cloths of Beverley, Lincoln or Northampton, which had rivalled the best Italian or Flemish materials, were to be displaced by 'West of Englands', 'Cotswolds' and 'West Ridings'.

Up to about 1400, the wealth of England had rested with her wool exports and the taxes levied on them had been a main source of royal revenue. During the fifteenth century, although its fortunes fluctuated, the home industry took more and more of the finest English wools, the best in Europe. Soon it had a flourishing export trade and 'White Cotswolds', 'Suffolk medleys', 'Swindons' and many others flooded into the docks of Pisa, the port of Florence. By the 1480s the Florentine *Arte della Lana* was ordering affiliated workshops to produce a specified quota of imitation English cloths.

England, so far one of the 'underdeveloped' primary producing countries of Europe, was preparing to graduate into the ranks of the industrial exporting nations. The expansion of the industry rested on a capitalist base that had been developing since the thirteenth century. There is reason for believing that it was organised not by the weavers, the fullers or any other manufacturing craft, but by the dye merchants. The essential raw materials of wool, fuller's earth and teasles for raising the nap on the unfinished cloth, were all home products but almost all the dyes had to be imported for quantity production. From an early date the men who handled this foreign trade cut loose from the craft, leaving the actual dyeing to their hired servants. By natural progression, their dealings with foreign merchants expanded from buying to the selling of finished cloth and then to organising its manufacture – distributing the raw materials to the town workshops of weavers and fullers and the cottages of the housewife and girl spinsters. Their wealth and influence gave dyers access to the guilds merchant, the chief governing bodies of medieval towns, while weavers were specifically excluded. A Leicester man was expelled the guild for continuing to work as a weaver after being admitted to membership.[4] Thus the craft guilds were shut out, not only from the government of their town but also, because the guild merchant settled wage rates and quality controls, the direction of their own crafts. As the industry expanded the water-powered fulling mills became its new growth points. Because they were in unchartered towns and unorganised communities, they offered the excluded craft guilds a new independence.

By the middle of the fifteenth century the most prosperous of these centres were in Gloucestershire and in Wiltshire – notably along the Stroudwater valley. Next door to the Cotswolds, it had access to England's finest wool district; large deposits of fuller's earth along the valley guaranteed the second basic raw material; the river not only supplied power to the fulling mills but was also rich in salts chemically compatible with the dyes used; and finally, the nearby port of Bristol gave easy access to export markets. A nationwide reassessment of non-clerical tax liabilities of the 1520s shows this area five times as prosperous as it had been in the fourteenth century; local records fill out the picture.

In the 1450s fulling mills, subject to a fixed ground rent of 15s, were being sub-let at 66s 8d and during the same period sixteen water leases were granted at various points along the river. Some of the finishing work was done to contract for clothiers from Cirencester, the largest town in the area, but the valley's own clothiers were sending their stuff to London and abroad. In nearby Castle Combe Richard Halwey had nine men working for him and when William Haynes died in 1435 his estate paid a £20 subscription to the church tower fund. His business had obviously been large and prosperous and, after haggling with the agents of the landlord, his widow finally agreed to pay the considerable sum of £140 as a relief to enter on his properties. It was her misfortune to be a tenant of the canny and grasping Sir John Fastolf. One of the few soldiers who made a fortune from the French wars, he invested it in English properties and employed men like William Worcestre to see they were run properly.

Cloth-making began in Castle Combe in the 1370s. When Fastolf bought the manor some forty years later, it was booming. He had little interest in the old agricultural settlement of Upper Combe on the plain above the river but the thriving industry of Nether Combe provided him with liveries for his regiments in France and with revenues. Worcestre reckoned that his master spent £100 annually in the valley for the red and white uniforms of between one hundred and two hundred troops. It is doubtful, however, whether the local clothiers greatly appreciated the trade. Their neighbours of Minchinhampton and Bisley in Stroudwater were untroubled by landlords – the Duke of York and the Abbot of Syon, apparently ignorant of the fortunes being made by the newcomers to the valleys of their remote manors, were content with the traditional income based on the fossilised and decayed farming communities on the hill.

Fastolf devised new levies to meet the new industrial situation. Haynes' widow was assessed not on any theoretical agricultural value of her husband's holdings, but on their actual and immense commercial worth. Master craftsmen were obliged to guarantee 2d per head per annum for residence permits to any journeymen or labourers they brought into the manor to work for them. And the population was rising all the time. In the year Haynes died fifty new workmen had come to settle in Castle Combe; fifteen years later there were seventy newcomers. Under instructions from the lord of the manor, land or properties that reverted to the estate were to be leased to the highest bidder. But security of tenure was not granted for a twelvemonth. If within that time a better offer was made he had either to improve on it or relinquish the property to his rival.

But in exchange for these cash penalties, the masters of Castle Combe were entirely free from the interference of manorial officials in running their affairs and, still more important, they were free from the guilds merchant which ruled in the towns. According to Worcestre, the first 'inhabitants who were artificers of wool and cloths' were William Touker and his men who established a fulling business there in the 1370s. Tucker, the West Country word for fuller, crops up regularly in the records and it was men of this craft who became the great clothiers both here and in the Stroudwater manors. So long as the guilds merchant maintained their grip on the towns the new rural sites of industry were bound to attract ambitious craftsmen.

It was a new style of management and it was a new style of community. The scores of wage labourers brought in changed the whole pattern of life. The 1523 assessment showed that more than half the tax-paying population were wage earners, a class that had not appeared on the fourteenth-century roll for the district. They came from as far afield as Wales and Ireland and, at least in the eyes of their masters, were an unruly lot. Regulations governed the closing times in the public houses – eight pm in winter and nine pm in summer – and forbade all gambling there. After nine in the evening, gambling 'tables' were banned even in private houses.[5]

The fulling mill, which had made possible such dramatic if localised changes in rural England, was more than two and a half centuries old. Yet during our period the only advance in the application of power seems to have been a gigmill for raising the nap on the cloth. In the iron industry, however, the century opened and closed with important advances in technique. Both were imported from the Continent for, compared to the leading European centres like Styria, England was industrially backward. Despite expanded production during the century much steel had to be imported even for such basic jobs as ploughshares. Iron arrow heads, tipped with steel, were produced in quantity from workshops in such counties as Gloucestershire and Yorkshire, but crossbow quarrels, important in siege warfare, tended to be imported from Spain and elsewhere. The finest English steel matched the best from abroad, as the fourteenth-century helmet made for Sir Richard Pembridge of Hereford shows, yet in Caxton's day the fashionable young gentleman tended to commission his jousting equipment from the armourers of Milan or Nuremberg.

Nevertheless, the fifteenth century was an important point

of departure in the English industry. The first advance was
the gradual introduction of water-powered bellows. Even in
the simple bloom hearth process then used, temperatures of
1400° C were needed and the high-quality bellows for this
were the most expensive part of the iron-master's equipment.
At least two pairs were needed with four men to operate each.
Water power, introduced on the Continent in the early thirteenth century, had reduced this to one or two supervisors.
Cams on the revolving drive shaft of the mill forced up the
lower wing of the bellows against the upper fixed wing and
so compressed them. From figures calculated for a bloomery
at Byrkeknott in County Durham, we know that an efficient
master could increase his output by as much as tenfold with
such equipment.[6]

Even so, iron-making was heavy and technically demanding work. First the ore had to be washed, roasted to remove
the grosser impurities, pulverised and sieved. The master's
wife helped in the first operation and when her husband had
broken down the larger chunks of ore with a hammer weighing half a hundredweight or more, would help him finish
the pulverisation and with the backbreaking work at the
sieve. The prepared ore was now brought to molten white
heat in the bloom hearth where further impurities drained
away through the slag hole and the molten mass (called the
'bloom') worked and stirred so as to agglomerate it with
charcoal which hardened the iron. It was the admixture of
further carbon which yielded steel. Since most iron-masters
worked for the manorial lord, the wood for the fires and the
ore were obtained at cost from the forests and mines on the
estate; the charcoal, produced by lengthy and costly slow
burning, was thus the most expensive of his raw materials.
The cheapest charcoal came from old or dead wood but by
the fifteenth century 'green' charcoal was generally used
because of the finer results it yielded. In the 1430s the Bishop
of Durham's estate managers were planting saplings exclusively for charcoal. Another refinement, discovered in the

early 1400s, was the use of slag from ancient disused iron hearths. Rich in basic ferrous silicate, it combined chemically with the phosphorous impurities of the ore. The master at Byrkeknott got his from the nearby prehistoric site of Hoppyland. Another Durham hearth at West Crawcook on Tyneside gained permission from the bishop's officers to use slag from the old workings at Ambrosegarth.

Once prepared, the bloom, which might weigh up to 200 pounds, was transferred from the bloom hearth to the string hearth. Here it had to be forged and reduced still further. This final stage not only strengthened the metal but also extruded further impurities so that the forged bloom might lose as much as a quarter of the weight of the crude state. When it had been split for a last check on the purity of the metal the bloom was cut into blocks for sale to the smith.

Although the trip hammers of the fulling mill had long been known, the same principle was not applied to the iron forge until a 'great water hammer' was installed at Newbridge mill at the end of the century. The 'Oliver', still in use in the seventeenth century, was the sole mechanical aid the medieval iron-master in England had in shaping and pounding his recalcitrant material. A hammer let into a heavy spindle was operated by a treadle and swung back by a tension spring. The most important advance, introduced to England just a few years before the water hammer at Newbridge, was the blast furnace. It replaced the two-stage operation of the bloom and string hearths and the manual manipulation of the bloom, with a continuous flow process which both increased output and improved quality. The first hint that the process was known in England comes at Buxted in Sussex in the year 1490. A few years later it was being used by Henry Fyner, a member of the London goldsmiths' company, who had been commissioned by Henry VII's government to produce iron and steel in quantity for armaments.

By 1450 there were water-powered bloomeries in most parts of England where iron was mined. Kent and Sussex were isolated centres in the south-east. The bulk of such little mining as there was went on in the Forest of Dean in Gloucestershire, where the surface coal seams provided the fuel, and in the northern counties. Isolated as they generally were from the towns their more or less continuous working rasped on the nerves of any unfortunate enough to be their neighbours. Robert Kyrhous, 'ironbrenner' of West Crawcook near Ryton on Tyne, with his licence to keep his 'smithies going at all reasonable times when water shall serve him', no doubt interpreted the vague proviso as widely and ruthlessly as any nineteenth-century iron-master, to the misery of his assistants and the irritation of the neighbourhood at large. An outraged provincial rhymester found relief in the good old-fashioned alliterative traditions of northern verse:

> Swart smocked smiths, smattered with smoke,
> Drive me to death with din of their dints.
> Such noise at nights nay heard man never.
> What knavish cries, and clatering knockes
> The damned dolts call for 'Coal, Coal!'
> And blow on their bellows though their brain bursts.[7]

The poor man's indignation at being kept awake at night is only less than his traditional clerk's contempt for the manual worker. Yet even at this time the attitude was wearing a little thin. For centuries successful craftsmen had been amassing sizeable fortunes. None had emulated merchant families, like the de la Poles, and reached the ranks of the nobility. Yet they could rise to prominence in the secular world; Henry of Lewes, master smith to Edward I, had been able to leave houses in the City of London, Lewes and Seaford to his widow. The workers in the industry, paid piece work at a rate of $7\frac{1}{2}d$–$9\frac{1}{2}d$ per bloom, were generally better off than the agricultural labourer. Like every other group in medieval society they had considerable *esprit de corps* with their own traditions and craft legends which built them into their

society. The smith ordered to forge the nails for the crucifixion, so ran the story, refused on the pretext that his hand
was too badly injured. Commanded to show the supposed
injuries he stretched out his hand and found that it had been
miraculously wounded and that indeed he could not forge
the nails. Instead, with a typically medieval twist, his wife
did the job.[8]

The smith was ubiquitous and indispensable for the repair
and manufacture of such agricultural machinery as was in use,
shoeing horses, repair of mill machinery, the manufacture of
the clamps and other iron sections used by masons and
builders, the production of nails, arrowheads, in fact everything made of iron. Most sizeable villages and every important country estate employed its own smith – if only to avoid
the sharp practice of smiths along the road. A rider whose
horse threw a shoe was advised to watch the repair job like
a hawk. A favourite trick was to drive a long nail into the
hoof itself so that a few miles up the road the horse would
go lame. As if by a miracle, the stranded traveller would find
himself met by a kindly rustic with a hack which he was willing to trade for the crippled mount. While the gentleman
rode on his way the horse dealer ambled back to his colleague
at the smithy, the nail was extracted and after a few days' rest
a fine horse was ready to be sold to the next unfortunate gull.

The smith's forge was also the regular feature of any large
medieval quarry. The wedges, mauls, picks and chisels of the
rough masons and stone cutters did heavy duty and had to
be constantly repaired and sharpened. The forge typically
had a labour force of five: the smith himself and his servant,
a charcoal burner and his servant 'for the bellows' who kept
the fire, and finally a boy '*portehache*' to fetch and carry the
iron blocks for the smith and the tools in need of remaking
from the masons. On a job like this a smith had the occasional
chance to meet the aristocrats of the medieval craft world,
the master masons. The rough hewing of the block from the
living stone was done by labourers but a master mason who

was involved on a large commission generally went to the quarry to choose his stone and ensure that it would be cut by competent workmen. Such a visit, however, would be a pretty rare occurrence. A reforming preacher, attacking the vast revenues and luxurious life style of his ecclesiastical superiors, found an illustration in the building industry. 'The masters of the masons,' he railed, 'carrying rods and their gloves in their hands, say to others "cut it for me thus" and do no work for themselves, and yet they receive higher wages than the others.'[9]

Their wages were about ten times higher in fact. Where the labourer earned an average daily wage of 6d, a master with the reputation of a man like Richard of Winchcombe could look forward to top professional fees at a rate of 5s a day. Stephen Lote was paid 6s 8d for a survey of the bridge at Rochester in Kent, and this from a council clearly reluctant to pay for anything but the most routine maintenance. Faced with Lote's report they sent the resident bridge mason, William Champneys, to consult his retired and now bed-ridden predecessor. He was accompanied by a council repre-sentative, no doubt to ensure that the old man would give the failing structure a clean bill of health. Twelve years later Champneys set up another outside expert, only to have him overruled when the town authorities hired the king's own master mason, Thomas Mapyldon. Rochester's penny-wise merchants were not to be stampeded though in many other counties the authorities seem to have been gripped by some-thing of a bridge-building mania.

Abingdon in Berkshire built a new bridge over the Thames there in 1416. Later in the century, Wadebridge over the River Camel, Looe and Bideford – where the timber bridge was replaced by a stone one in the 1460s – were just some of the seventeen bridges listed by William Worcestre on his visit to Cornwall and Devon. The building of a bridge was reck-oned a pious act before God and a charity to travellers. The Church even granted indulgences to those who helped finance such projects, while the builders could confidently appeal for the prayers of travellers. The people of Stockbridge in Hampshire, crossing the River Test on their daily business, took little notice of the brass plate on the bridge. But the curious long-distance traveller perhaps did pause to say 'of his charity' a 'Paternoster and an Ave for the souls of John Gylmyn and Richard Gater and Margaret the wife of the aforesaid John and Richard, founders and makers of this bridge'.[10]

For the mason a bridge was a valuable commission and a job as resident architect to a major bridge was a major step in a man's career. Richard Becke, who began as a member of the staff of London Bridge, was appointed master mason to Canterbury in 1435. When, three years later, the mayor and aldermen received a shock survey on the structure of some of the arches, they at once wrote to the chapter to release Becke on secondment for he was the best qualified man in the country on such work.

Top masons were members of the elite though by Church convention they had no qualifications and in the gentry's view lacked birth and breeding. When John Wode of Colchester took a long-term commission for work at the abbey of Bury St Edmunds, the abbot agreed that he should have board in the convent's hall 'for himself as a gentleman and for his servant as a yeoman'. At York, Master Allan worked in the closest collaboration with Sir Thomas de Haxey, overseer of the works, who was directed to hurry the delivery of stone to the site so that the master could get on with the work. The sheer achievement of the masons broke down social conventions and commanded respect. The contemporaries of Caxton lived in an England humming with new building activity.

To the bridges of the West Country must be added those over the River Ouse at Huntingdon and St Ives and the one at East Farley over the Medway. New centres of industry were burgeoning into townships – William Worcestre reckoned fifty new houses had been erected at Castle Combe during the first half of the century and the Cornish fishing ports of Mevagissey and Bude graduated out of hamlet status in the same period. There were the considerable building works of the nobility and, more familiar to the average man and woman, the fine new town houses of the thriving merchant class, the churches built by the woolmen, or the chantry chapels set at some remote crossroads as haven and sanctuary for travellers. Beyond all these were the great cathedrals and city churches. The stone, in many cases but a generation old, still glowed and glistened over the low roofs of the surrounding town. Work was in progress at York Minister throughout the century; at Winchester Master William Wynford, with Sir Simon Pembury supporting him as paymaster and supervisor, had begun the new nave which was to replace the great Norman structure, demolished under the will of Bishop William of Wykeham. At Oxford the university, after long and careful planning, launched on the new Divinity Schools. At Eton and Cambridge King Henry's magnificent foundations were rising, while in proud and prosperous Bristol these superb achievements of the art and science of vaulting were matched by the great church of St Mary Redcliffe. It is not surprising that sensitive and intelligent observers paid homage to the 'inventive casting marvellous of such as can the craft of "gemetry"'.[11]

While it was the master mason, who 'carried his gloves in his hand', rather than wear them as protection against the abrasions of the rough stone, many less talented or successful members of the profession earned a handsome living. Generally, because the costs of transport were so high, units of window tracery, columns or vaulting were carved at the quarries, carefully numbered, and then assembled on the site. This adaptability to prefabrications, it may be suggested, was a principal reason for the popularity of the perpendicular style with the merchants and money-conscious noble patrons of the day. The great single shafts of Purbeck marble, in the thirteenth-century Early English style, had been carved and shaped on the site from massive blocks which might need three or more carts to transport them. It was obviously more economical when the carving could be done at the quarry by masons who set up their 'lodge' or hut for the duration. Those in charge of the actual erection of the sections on site also set up such a lodge. When work was in hand for the fourth great column in the nave of York Minster the lodge was built, by agreement with the chapter, between 'the council chamber [*consistorium*] and the door of the chapter house'.

The lodges were to provide secrecy as much as accommodation. Working plans, drawn up on parchment, were jealously guarded and usually destroyed once the work was completed. On site calculations and detailed drawings were sketched on a plaster bed in the hut and the drawing obliterated by a clean plaster skim as soon as done with. The workings behind the finished plans were the masons' mystery, handed down from father to son or master to journeyman. The arcane play acting of modern Freemasonry is the invention of a later generation but it is easy to see how the secrecy of the medieval lodge fascinated eighteenth-century minds, looking for the mystique of religion in the traditions of science.

Sometimes, however, a travelling freemason would be commissioned to advise and draw up plans for work to be done by a local master. When John Marys of Stokegursey was engaged to build a tower for the church of Demster, he was instructed to work 'according to a patron [pattern] made by the advice of Richard Pope, freemason'.[12] Pope, like Stephen Lote, was a travelling consultant. When the merchant guilds of Lynn wished to build a new chapel in honour of the Holy Trinity in the Parish Church, the first step was to appoint a committee which should then engage an adviser for preliminary discussions. A few years later, in 1479, the chapter of Westminster Abbey called in three master masons to make a brief survey and report. As well as their fee, the masters were given a 'rich' lunch at the abbey's expense. Nor were the masons the only master craftsmen with bright career prospects. In 1457, the prioress and convent of Nuneaton commissioned the Lichfield master, Thomas Carver, to build and carve forty choir stalls for a total fee of £43 6s 8d. This did not include the design of the stalls which was to follow 'the form of a picture in the keeping of the Prioress'.

During the century many of the country's great monastic institutions were engaged on large building projects. The priory of Durham seems to have been in almost constant upheaval during the abbacy of John Wessington, who commissioned an extensive series of extensions and renovations to the abbot's lodgings. A decade or so before, the bishops of Durham had run an ambitious building programme at Oxford when Durham college was provided with a new gatehouse, chapel and library.[13] The bishops and priors financed such works from the massive endowments of see or priory. The building of a new parish or town church depended largely on local subscription. St Mary Redcliffe in Bristol would never have been started without the huge contributions of William Canynges, five times mayor of the city. As the work continued other merchants came in. The initial impetus could be decisive. In the nearby township of Bishopstone in Wiltshire, Henry Berwyk had left 20 marks in his will to the building of the church tower 'when the parishoners begin to build anew'. At Chesham William Duffield directed that £6 13s 4d (or 16 marks) should be paid from his estate to the building of the new church, but only when the other subscribers honoured their commitments.

The immense costs of building meant that even the modest programme for a parish church might falter. The chief cost was labour – about one-third of the total. The second heaviest charge was generally transport though some building committees were fortunate. The oolithic limestone used for the cathedral at Wells came from Doulting quarries only

about eight miles away. Others were less fortunate, or more
ambitious. The architect's specifications for the buildings at
Eton required a variety of stones from Merstham and Maidstone in Kent, Taynton in Oxfordshire and even as far afield
as Huddlestone in Yorkshire. Wherever possible, waterways
were used. The stone from Merstham was taken the twenty
miles to Kingston-upon-Thames at a cost of 20d per load.
From there it was floated up the winding river to Eton –
about twice the distance of the most direct land route but
also about half the price. From Merstham to Eton was a long
haul, about fifty miles, and the savings from using water
transport correspondingly large. Yet even on the twenty-
mile journey from Bramham quarries in Yorkshire to York,
the water route was preferred. The stone was taken by cart
from the quarries to Tadcaster, then up the River Wharfe
to York and from the quays there dragged by sled up to the
minster site.

A quarry was a profitable business which could be run in
various ways. The builder with a large job on hand sometimes opened up a new quarry, if one was conveniently near
the site. The first job was to clear the earth and top soil down
to the rock face, called the freebed. More often, stone was
taken from an existing quarry and the quarry master either
sold stone as required to the builder or leased the whole site
for the duration of the job. Wells Cathedral rented the Doulting quarries for 20s for the twelvemonth, 1457–8; Henry VI's
agents obtained a long lease on the quarry at Huddlestone
from the owner of the land Sir John Langton. When the
college of All Souls was being built, on land cleared of many
small halls of residence and houses in the centre of the city,
the foundation leased one of the Taynton quarries from
Master John Howes. The stone was taken the mile or so to
Burford where a large bench of masons had established themselves on contract to the college. The finished sections were
taken down to the Thames and thence by barge to Oxford.

England's dense network of inland waterways was fully

exploited. The winding lazy rivers, particularly of the south and Midlands, provided comparatively cheap transport deep inland. To the small river craft of the day, the Cam was navigable as far as Cambridge and some of the little villages off the main river, linked to it today by insignificant rivulets, were way stations for a busy distributive traffic, remembered now only by little water inlets that come up to the backs of the houses on the main streets. Such private wharfs were to be found in the great merchant houses of many a market town where today the river has silted up or altered its course. The river systems draining into the Great Ouse and the Trent served the east coastal belt and the east Midlands. On the west the great River Severn carried traders up to the wharfs of Worcester and from there up to Stourport on Severn. Here the Stour joined the main river and it was used up to Stourbridge and beyond.

On the borders of England's central counties and with cheap water transport to the Severn Estuary, Stourport was one of the greatest inland ports in England. On the other branch of the system traffic continued up the Severn to Shrewsbury and beyond to Welshpool in the Marches. So advantageous was water transport that parts of Somerset, only thirty miles from the great port of Bristol, were served by small inland docks, long since decayed. At Radclive (modern Rackley) on the River Axe, cargoes of salt, iron and fish came from Dartmouth and even Brittany. It is surprising enough to find this Somersetshire village engaged in international trade – still more remarkable is the presence of ships from Dartmouth in Devon. The sea route round the Cornish peninsula is more than three times as long as the land route.

But although road travel was expensive it was not so atrocious as it was to become in the eighteenth century. Scientific indications are that the climate of England was drier during the later Middle Ages. More important, there was far less wheeled traffic on the roads, and virtually no passenger wheeled traffic. Even the greatest in the land travelled on horseback, though rich and fashionable ladies sometimes used luxury 'chariots'. Richard II's exchequer had paid out £400 for the making of the queen's chariot, a sum that would have purchased a herd of eight hundred cattle. The fourteenth-century Luttrell Psalter has an illustration of a heavy and luxurious travelling carriage used by the ladies of the family. A generation later we find a noblewoman bequeathed to her daughter 'her great carriage with the couvertures and cushions'. But these were exceptional cases; a passenger vehicle was so generally unfamiliar that the language did not yet have a specific word for it. Richard Neville, Earl of Salisbury, asked for the loan of the Bishop of Durham's 'chariott and chariotour' to transport his armour to a muster against the Scots in Northumberland. In the nineteenth book of Mallory's *Morte D'Arthur* Sir Launcelot, dashing to the rescue of the queen, has his horse so badly wounded that he has to beg a lift in a passing 'chariot', which then 'drove on a great wallop'. When he eventually reached the castle where the queen was being held, one of the ladies-in-waiting observes languidly, 'See, madam, where rideth in a chariot a goodly armed knight; I suppose he rideth unto hanging.'

In the 1440s John Paston lay ill at London. Although his wife Margaret desperately wanted him back in Norfolk she did not imagine he could move until he was well enough to ride. Chaucer's prioress Madam Eglantyne, rode a horse like all the other pilgrims. Possibly she followed the new fashion among ladies of riding side-saddle, though it did not become widespread until the fifteenth century and the gentle prioress more likely sat her horse like a man. There was a wide variety of breeds of horse. The heavy war horse, or destrier, is still remembered in the sturdy lines of the percheron breed of the modern farm horse. There were the high-stepping palfreys of the ladies; hunters; cart horses; heavy sumpter pack horses; half-breed rounceys and the donkeys ridden by the poorer members of the clergy.

There was plenty of traffic on medieval roads though the

bulk of the population rarely travelled far from the town or hamlet in which they had been born. For them the most important people on the roads were, no doubt, the bailiffs, agents and receivers of the manorial lord making their rounds from manor to manor in pursuit of revenue. The vast estates of clerical and lay landlords consisted of scattered holdings over many shires run by an increasingly professional group of estate managers. During Caxton's lifetime the training of these experts expanded considerably and the centre of their studies shifted, over the century, from the business schools at Oxford to the inns of court and chancery in London. A shift which underlines the increasing laicisation of literate culture at this time.

These Oxford 'management courses' were outside the traditional clerkly curricula. In the 1430s these private grammar schools and fringe seminaries had become so numerous that the university authorities attempted to regulate the position of those 'teachers in the arts of writing Latin composition, the speaking of French, the drafting of charters etc and the keeping of courts for laymen and pleading in the English manner'.[14] The master of a grammar school was permitted to contract special terms with students who wanted instruction in more than the basics of Latin composition or who were older and therefore assumed able to pay higher fees. Some parents it seems, hearing of a promising job prospect for their son, might order him to drop his academic degree course and go instead to one of these masters teaching writing, composition and accounting. Thomas Sampson, one of the most successful, had been charging as much as 100s for such a course in the late fourteenth century; at the end of it the boy would be qualified to enter the estates office of a nobleman.

Sampson, like others of his profession, did not himself bother to complete the arduous bachelor's degree, which might take up to ten years to complete. The successful master could supplement his income from teaching and, more important, extend his own reputation with treatises on conveyancing and related topics. Intended in the first instance for the students of his own courses, they inevitably reached a wider audience and so further enhanced his reputation. Even when the centre of business studies had moved away from Oxford these treatises remained standard texts and even went into printed editions in the early sixteenth century.

A favourite teaching aid was the specimen letter. One of these purports to come from a young man who, while travelling in France, has been asked by a nobleman to enter his household. Keen to get the job, but unqualified, the young gentleman accepts and then writes home to his young brother, urging him to take a crash course at an Oxford business school so that he can give a hand in the office. The job the elder brother had landed could lead to the position of estate steward, the senior post in a great aristocratic establishment. Its responsibility was the profitable running of the numerous, often far-flung manors, and its job prospects were good, leading in some cases to the royal service. The household steward, on the other hand, had a more restricted function, as the name implies, and was usually a man of humbler birth who regarded such a job as the fulfilment of his highest ambition.

The estate steward travelled from manor to manor, haggling with bailiffs and agents, inspecting their books, keeping a shrewd eye open for the real prosperity of the lands he passed through to be compared with the account he received from his lord's agents. He would be followed up by the receiver who, within a grouping of manors called a 'bailiwick', was responsible for collecting all cash payments due and sending them in sealed sacks and under armed escort to wherever the household might be at the time. There they were enrolled by the receiver general for the whole honour. Estate management was big business.

The hand of the improver was to be seen in all parts of the country. The monks of Canterbury pushed back the

limits of Romney Marsh along a line between Appledore and
Aldington. The reclamation took decades to complete and
cost the immense sum of £1500 but the returns were on the
same scale. The 1480s saw an increase of some twenty-five
per cent in revenue from this area alone. Each new water mill
for fulling or an iron bloomery meant large-scale excava-
tions. A mill leet carried water off from the river to the mill
pond reservoir. From this it ran in the head race to the wheel
where the speed of flow was regulated by a sluice; beyond
the wheel it drained back to the downstream river course
along a tail race. On exposed uplands the tower and sails of
windmills dotted the landscape. On the estates of nobles and
clerics rivers were systematically exploited for food as well
as power. All but the smallest streams were potential fish
farms. A series of dams retained the main fish pond with
smaller secondary ponds which were fed by culverts and
drained by overflow channels back to the main stream.
Stocked with fish from neighbouring estates, the ponds were
intensively farmed to yield far larger, more varied and more
accessible supplies than the river could have yielded in its
natural state.

The red meat diet was supplemented by venison and this
too, was, in a limited sense, farmed. The deer park was a familiar part of the landscape. An area of the manorial woodland
and pasture was enclosed with a bank and ditch topped by
a wooden paling, hedge or stone wall and broken at widely
spaced points by 'deer leaps' so designed that the deer from
the surrounding open country could get into the park but
not out. But like the fish ponds, the park sometimes needed
replenishing with new stock. In September 1490, we find
Jegon the parker receiving his expenses from the household
steward of the Earl of Oxford, for a journey to fetch a buck
from a neighbouring estate.[15]

The enclosing of a park sometimes meant the destruction
of homesteads or even whole villages within the boundaries –
a case in point is the village of Steeton in Yorkshire which

was demolished in the 1480s for a park by the Fairfax family. Today it is hard to grasp the absolute rights the landlord could exercise over his tenants. But since the Norman conquest the areas of England designated as royal forests had been subject to draconian legislation. Over the centuries kings had assigned their rights in more and more of these areas to private landlords who acquired, along with the right to hunt the royal game of the red and fallow deer, the royal right to exclude others. Destruction of villages in the course of emparkment was by no means new, but the fifteenth century brought disaster on a far larger scale.

As early as 1414 the village of Chesterton in Oxfordshire petitioned against the lord of the manor who had 'made a great waste...of housing, of halls and chambers and other houses of office that were necessary in the same manor...and none housing left standing there but if it were a sheep cote or a barn'.[16] At the end of the century the archivist and chronicler John Rous made a list of 580 villages and hamlets which to his personal knowledge had been depopulated in as many square miles. Rous was writing in the year of Caxton's death (1491) and in that same year Gabriel Armstrong cleared the village of Thorpe in Nottinghamshire to make way for his sheep runs. The people 'left their houses weeping' and walked away into unemployment and destitution.

The pattern was already well known elsewhere. It was once thought that the ruin of the village of Stretton Baskerville, near Bosworth, was the work of looting soldiers from Henry VII's victorious army. In fact it was achieved in the normal processes of profitable land development, four years after the battle. Thomas Twyford, the landlord, having enclosed 160 acres at the cost of a mere seven houses then sold to a certain Henry Smith 640 more acres which, since time immemorial, had been under the plough. In the search no doubt for commercial viability and following the soundest contemporary investment policies, Smith abandoned arable farming and systematically cleared the land for pasturage. When he had finished, twelve houses, with their gardens and closes, and four adjacent cottages stood desolate and ruined. There were also eighty people, who had worked here, who 'went away sorrowfully to idleness, to drag out a miserable life and so to die in misery. Animals shelter in the church from storms and feed among the graves of Christian men.'[17] Nor was it only a case of the local gentry dispossessing their hereditary tenants. The manor and houses of Cestersover in Warwickshire, a flourishing enough place with well-stocked fish ponds, was depopulated by its new owner Henry Weaver, a London draper, who received permission to enclose for sheep runs in the 1460s.

Of course, once sheep had been introduced, not only were the former dwellings irritating obstructions to their runs and tumbledown buildings hazardous to their safety, the services of the village were no longer needed. In the place of a flourishing community there was only one man to guard the flocks and his, the shepherd's, house was often the only one left in the parish that was inhabited. There were some contemporaries who were genuinely compassionate for the evicted tenants, left to starve or fight their way to survival in the rugged fringe society of medieval wayfaring life. Posing as pardoners, friars or pilgrims when they were not involved in highway robbery or starving in the hedgerows, they and their families sired the scores of beggars and vagrants which plagued the legislators of the next century. The unholy twins of greed and 'enlightened economic policy', which we have long since recognised as the incestuous parents of Progress, were identified very early. Rous records that he had presented a request for legislation against enclosure as early as 1459.[18] The attempt was doomed. Sheep, and the wool they yielded to the burgeoning cloth industry, were too profitable for even a religious foundation to be diverted by the thought of homeless families. Ten years after Rous had failed with his petition to parliament, Leicester Abbey was enclosing the village of Ingarsby to provide cattle and sheep pasturage.

Even the government was powerless. Oddly, or perhaps characteristically, it first identified the problem of enclosure as one of national defence. The first statute on the subject, in 1488, was a special bill for the Isle of Wight, which had 'late decayed...by reason many towns and villages be let down and the fields dyked and made pastures for beasts and cattles'. If nothing was done to stop the threatened depopulation of the island it would lie 'open and ready to the hands of the king's enemies'. Since the king in question had come to the throne barely three years before with the support of French money and French mercenaries he, better than most, saw that it was 'to the surety of the realm that the Isle of Wight be well inhabited by English people'. The same theme crops up in the following year. But the preamble to the great 1489 statute on enclosures, to be the basis of all future legislation on the subject, saw a good deal more deeply into the matter. Because it lists so fully the consequences of enclosure and, in so doing, reveals the grave social problems that were emerging from the agricultural and industrial movements of the fifteenth century, it is to be quoted at length.

It lists the 'inconveniences' caused by

desolation and pulling down and wilful waste of houses and towns and laying to pasture lands which customarily have been used in tillage whereby idleness, the ground and beginning of all mischiefs increases. In some towns where 200 persons were occupied by their lawful labours, now there be two or three herdsmen; husbandry is decayed and the churches destroyed; the service of god withdrawn; the bodies of those buried not prayed for; the patron and curate wronged; and the defence of this land against our enemies outwards feebled and impaired.[19]

The complaints were to be echoed many times in the years ahead. To many the desecration of the churches seemed almost worse than the homelessness of the villagers, though it is difficult to see why. Such things were not at all new. As will appear in the next chapter, fifteenth-century churchmen had to fight almost every inch of the way to keep the public at large interested in them and their doings. The people of influence in lay society generally treated the Church and its institutions with deference or contempt as suited their purpose. Where one rich man off-loaded his debt to piety with a handsome chantry at a remote crossroads, another of a later generation, observing that it was little used and stood conveniently close to his lands, took practical advantage of the situation. In the middle of the century a chapel, which had been built some time back on the 'waste of the village of Baston, for the convenience of wayfarers and the benefit of tenants', was claimed by John Witham of Boycote Green to be on his private estate. Accordingly 'in this same chapel...long consecrated...he held his courts secular and for the purpose of profaning the place...ordered a stable to be made therein for his horses'.[20]

Enclosure and its attendant depopulation brought misery to isolated, though increasingly numerous, parts of the country. But it has been suggested that for the majority of England's peasant population the central decades of the century were a high point of prosperity. These were the years of Merrie England; a period in which the institutions of serfdom were dying in most parts of the country; when the depopulation caused by two generations of plague had reduced the labour force and so raised the level of wages; when land was everywhere coming on to the market and hard-working peasants were amassing sizeable holdings which were the basis of the yeoman holdings of the Tudor period. A survey of the manor of Gillingham, made in the 1440s, revealed sub-letting, exchange and land sales on every hand and parts of the demesne enclosed by palings to mark the boundaries or to protect young corn.[21]

From the beginning of the century people had been astonished at evidences of wealth in the most unlikely and improper corners. Parliament passed repeated statutes in an attempt to keep the lower classes in their place; in a 1483 Act of Apparel Edward IV specifically excluded eleven favoured members of his household from its provisions.

It was a short-lived prosperity. The peasant farmer who had a freehold on his land was fortunate in having an almost inalienable right to his land. He was also rare. The great majority of peasants had a much less secure legal status. The traditional labour services had been commuted for money rents in many parts of the country in the late fourteenth and early fifteenth centuries. This produced a new form of tenure called copyhold, from the copy of the manorial roll entry which had set out the new money obligations. When the original copyholder died his heirs had to pay a fine to enter into possession of his lands. Since this fine was often at the discretion of the landlord it is obvious that when economic conditions changed he was able to force his peasant tenants to compete among themselves to meet his ever-increasing demands.

In the first decades of the century English society was in a turmoil, the increasing lawlessness of the upper classes was matched by the surging confusion of the ambitious peasantry. In these years a cluster of northern folk heroes came to grip the national imagination. Adam Bell, Clym of the Clough and William Cloudesdale roamed the woods of Cumberland and Northumberland to the discomfiture of baronial oppressors and royal sheriffs. The achievements of these fictional champions of the underdog sometimes show a surprising similarity to stories from other parts of Europe. William Cloudesdale, for example, like William Tell, won his freedom by shooting an apple from the head of his little son. But the most popular of them all was Robin Hood and his merry 'meynie' in Yorkshire's West Riding and then in Nottingham and the neighbouring Sherwood Forest.

Recently scholars have argued about the exact nature of Robin's appeal to contemporaries. It has been pointed out that not one of the stories shows him robbing a secular lord though opulent clerics were often his target, and it has been suggested that his generosity to the poor was not intended as altruism as such but rather to demonstrate his Christian charity to the discredit of his prelatical victims. It has even been proposed that he was the hero of the yeoman class who saw themselves embattled against the cruel forest laws and the oppressive corruption of the central government represented in the shires by the sheriff.

In fact, like all best-sellers, the Robin Hood stories appealed to the widest possible readership. In the Kentish risings of the 1430s his had been one of the fanciful soubriquets adopted by the anonymous leaders. The 'stupid multitude', we are told by another commentator, regaled itself with 'tragedies' and 'comedies' of Robin Hood, and another observed:

> Each [ploughman] had two bushels of wheat that was good,
> They sang going homeward a gest of Robin Hood.

In short he was a hero for anyone with a grudge against the system and the sheer violence and brutality of the stories, bowdlerised in the nursery versions of later rewrites, guaranteed them success. After defeating and killing Guy of Gisborne Robin, as befitted a fifteenth-century hero, cut off his rival's head and spiked the grisly trophy on the end of his bow so as to have a workmanlike grip while he mutilated its features with his knife.

The central point about the stories was outlawry. Given the corrupt and partial justice of the time, many chose to become outlaws, rather than face certain conviction. In theory it was a fearful state – the secular equivalent of excommunication. Banished from the friendly commerce of human society, debarred the chance of seeking the good lordship of a powerful patron, unable to own property and fair game for any who could take or kill him, the outlaw should have been a pariah. Yet in fact many flourished, though often they were undoubtedly criminals. A woman who murdered her husband in 1425 was charged and convicted and then managed to escape. She was at large for twelve years and was able to take advantage of the general pardon of 1437, when she was still living close to her home town of Kingston-upon-Thames. Another who saw no need to seek the safety of the greenwood was one John Scotland who lived as an outlaw for more than twenty years and for most of that time continued to trade in London itself. Agnes Fish, convicted as a thief in 1426, also went into outlawry in the capital and did not bother to take advantage of the 1437 general pardon though she did take advantage of a second one nine years later.[22]

In view of all this it is not surprising that some looked on Robin Hood as a menace. When Richard Venables of Derbyshire and his followers were terrorising the county and 'in manner of insurrection went into the woods of that country', the local gentry petitioned parliament to put a stop to the menace, 'like as it had been Robin Hood and his meynie'. One's views on the ballad hero very much depended on how one happened to be standing at the time. While Derbyshire gentlemen excoriated the outlaw, Sir John Paston regularly paid one of his servants a special fee for performing the roles of Robin Hood as well as St George and the Sheriff of Nottingham. The man must clearly have been the original quick-change artist.

Such home dramatics were a favourite diversion in the mansions of the wealthy (see below, p. 191). But the venerable tradition of the mumming play, with St George and the Turkish Knight, were common property. London's city fathers tried, without much success, to stop the city's apprentices from using false beards or 'disformed or coloured visages' in their Christmas mummings.[23] The English love affair with the theatre began in this century; drama, for centuries domiciled in the church, moved decisively into the street and on to the green. At Lincoln, towards the end of the century, the dean and chapter continued to foot the bill for the 'play or ceremony of the Assumption of the Blessed Virgin, performed in the procession in the cathedral nave by the citizens, according to the custom'. Voluntary contributions were taken but the bulk of the costs was left unpaid and was borne equally by the common and fabric funds. Out in the diocese, however, the local troupe of players was much more enthusiastically supported; each of the larger villages had its own and took its play round the hamlets of the neighbouring parishes at its own expense.

More exciting, even, than this neighbourhood entertainment was the occasional visit of a professional troupe. It was heralded a few days before by the arrival of the two *vexillatores*. Taking their position on the town green they soon drew a crowd with a dazzling display of banner-swirling – still to be seen in Swiss and south German folk festivals. Sure of their audience they then 'read the banns', an announcement and outline plot of the forthcoming show. They were followed by carpenters and stage hands who erected a ring of scaffolds and raised booths to provide boxes for the wealthier patrons and also tableau stages for the main scenes of the action. In the popular *Castle of Perseverance* the centre of the acting area was occupied by a wooden tower raised on stilts, giving space for action below as well as on the mock battlements. It was girdled by a shallow ditch to represent a moat.[24]

The play portrays the siege of a man's soul by the Devil, the World and the Deadly Sins. The castle of perseverance is surrounded by its enemies in strongholds mounted on four of the scaffolds in the ring and the action involved movement between this outer circle and the centre. This open space also provided cheap standing room for the bulk of the audience. Marshals kept the lanes of movement open for the actors and controlled the crowd as it surged from one area of the arena to another, following the shifting action. This medieval theatre in the round involved the audience in a way not found again until the experimental theatre of our own generation; the sense of community participation was heightened by the fact that the marshals were recruited from among the local worthies, men with sufficient standing and authority to control the boisterous and excited crowd. Nevertheless, unlike the great cycles of mystery plays put on by the guilds of the major cities, travelling shows like the *Castle of Perseverance* were performed by troupes of professional actors and, following a tradition that stretched back to the classical world, the leading characters wore masks. Contemporary illustrations show us Devils and Sins with the grotesque features which the audience would have immediately recognised from the wall paintings in their local church. Stage machinery was sometimes used for still more startling effects; in the play of *Mary Magdalen* a ship was drawn on to 'the place' of the action.

No doubt the 'comedies' and 'tragedies' of Robin Hood were received more enthusiastically than the moral themes of the 'legitimate' theatre, but a play of any kind was rare enough to ensure a packed house. More rare still, in England at least, were the market place jousts – the most brilliant public spectacles the age had to offer. Horse racing was another aristocratic diversion that might sometimes provide popular entertainment and a glimpse into the glitter and incredible luxury of the ruling class. The memory grew with the telling. That medieval super knight, Beves of Hampton, built Arundel castle with his winnings on a single race.

> In summer, about Whitsuntide,
> When knights most on horses ride,
> A course they cried upon a day
> Steeds and palfreys to assay
> What horse that best might run.
> Three miles the course was then
> Who first came to the end, should
> Have twenty pounds of ready gold.

No apprentice could hope to buy a horse, but the world of 'high life' set the style then as now. From boyhood the young noble was learning to handle the lance in the saddle by tilting at the 'quintain'. This was a target on a swivel arm with a sandbag at the distant end which tumbled the novice off his horse if he did not score a direct hit. The apprentice had to make do with a wheeled hobby horse hauled by his mates, but the sport was good enough and open to many variations. In one the 'jouster' took up position in the stern of a boat and was rowed at the target; in another he and his mates, stripped to the buff and grasping a pole, charged a full water tub on a post with the clearly forlorn hope of avoiding a drenching. Statutes and guild regulations, passed with ineffective frequency, testify that during the middle decades of the century the lower orders were far too well off and far too prone to enjoy themselves. In the 1470s we find the Lord Mayor of London grouching against 'labourers, servants and apprentices...playing tennis or football or cards or dice'. The penalty was six days without the option.[25]

Tennis and cards are surprising prohibitions. The one, requiring expensive equipment, would be expected to be beyond the reach of the poor, the other seems to have been introduced only a decade or so before, yet had already lost the privileged status of a new fashion. Football, however, had a long tradition. Played with a leather-covered pig's bladder, sometimes stuffed with dried peas, it involved huge and riotous teams. The aim was 'with foot and with hand the bladder for to smite' through the streets of the town to the opponent's goal – some agreed landmark. The outcome was generally a running brawl which lasted as long as the teams had strength or until the authorities dared intervene. Broken bones were expected. At the Calais peace conference of July 1439 one of the commissioners was so badly injured at a friendly between the sessions that he had to miss one of the discussions. Death was not uncommon. Dice and its variants such as backgammon was found in ale houses throughout the land, the poor saving the price of the board by scratching it out on the nearest bench – in the monastery, the nearest stone seat.

In the villages the time for sport was more limited as was the range, wrestling being among the most popular. The dawn to dusk working day meant that Sunday and holy days were about the only times a man had for relaxation. 'For of all the days in the year, the holy days be most cursedly dispensed in the Devil's service in despite of God and all his saints in heaven',[26] and the Dominican friar John Bromyard inveighed against the bull-baiting sessions that were standard Sunday entertainment in the larger towns.

But in both town and country the ale house was the chief leisure centre. To the delight of the wives, preachers attacked 'husbands who spend their goods upon the ale house' while other priests were generally to be found 'not in the temple of God, but rather in the tavern or the ale house, where they often drink so much that they can hardly get through vespers or matins'.[27] And what they drank there would often have done credit to a prohibition speak-easy.

Guild regulations did something to maintain the standards of professional brewers. Taverns, like the famous Tabard of Southwark where Chaucer and his friends stayed on their way to Canterbury, were regularly visited by the ale-conners who were directly responsible to the mayor. The landlords were up time and again for diluting or adulterating their ale; but even this was an advance on the conditions in the thousands of small ale houses that served the bulk of the population outside the towns. Brewing was traditionally the work of women, as it is still in most 'primitive' tribes. They had a poor reputation. The poet John Skelton's portrait of Eleanor Rumming and her brewing vat, reinforced by the droppings of the pigeons that she kept roosting above it, rang all too true to his contemporaries. But even as he was writing, the good ale of old England was in the throes of a far more serious pollution.

In the 1420s some brewers in the London area began

adding hops and other bitter herbs to their ale after the Flemish fashion. Protests against this new form of adulteration were soon flooding in to the city authorities. Half way through the next century the new-fangled 'beer' was still being condemned as the 'natural drink for a Dutch man'. The traditional ingredients for ale were water, barley malt and yeast; the English drinker did not like the taste of hops and suspected that the brewers used the flavour to mask a weakening of the brew. He was probably right since a royal writ of 1436 commending the 'new drink called biere' described it as 'notable, healthy and' – here came the rub – 'temperate'. The brewers' battle with the drinking public lasted out the century. Eventually, as always, they won and Henry VIII himself had to abandon the attempt to stop his brewer from using hops.

Monasteries and manor houses all brewed their own ale and so did most well-to-do villagers, from barley, wheat or oats – the poorer peasants could not spare the grain. But in general the poor lived better than ever before and for a long time afterwards. Sixteenth-century critics of enclosures complained that the countryman was now so impoverished that he could no longer afford even the occasional dish of beef or mutton or veal. Few peasants, it is true, ate the finest white bread. Known as *paindemagne*, it was made of wholemeal flour, refined as far as possible by being bolted through linen mesh. White bread was a status symbol and as such preferred, by those who could afford it, to the coarse black bread made from rye flour. This was the villager's staple but in addition he had a varied diet of vegetables – peas and beans, onions, leeks, parsnips, turnips and cabbages – cheeses, the occasional dish of meat, eggs and bacon when the pig was killed. These long-snouted, ridge-backed pigs of the medieval village scavenged their own food on the byways and common and grubbed up roots in the woodland. Most families kept a pig, the better off peasant farmer might even have a cow and a few sheep.

During the summer of a good year the villager, while he ate less meat and fish than his neighbour in the town, could live well enough. But when the harvest failed, as in the disastrous years of 1437 and 1439, famine was bitter. When heavy rains made the roads impassable it was perfectly possible for hamlets only twenty miles from a flourishing market town to face the threat of starvation. During the winter months everyone except the rich had an unbalanced and tedious diet of salt meat, bread and peas. The manor's fish ponds and pigeon lofts provided fresh proteins but the gentry, like everyone else, were desperately short of essential vitamins so that by the end of a hard winter most of the population was on the verge of scurvy.

April was then truly the cruellest month, a time when the siege rations of winter were exhausted and new crops were still awaited. Cold and hunger had killed off the weakest people in the community, generally the very young and the very old. The fearfully high rate of infant mortality dragged down the average life expectancy at birth to barely forty years for the bulk of the population, though those tough enough to survive the danger years of childhood could expect to better this considerably and the privileged compared well with modern standards. Edward IV died in his forty-first year, an age when many of his poorer subjects would have reckoned themselves getting on in years, yet his death was quite unexpected and was attributed not to old age but to a lifetime of debauch. The Good Duke Humphrey of Gloucester was fifty-eight when he met his death, by murder as most believed; Henry VI was in perfectly sound health when he was murdered at the age of fifty; that tough old warhorse Sir John Fastolf died in his bed aged eighty. William Caxton himself lived the full biblical span of three score years and ten. Longevity was not the exclusive preserve of wealth. A well-regulated life, insulated from the violent fluctuations of bread-line existence and the hazards of unhygienic town life, could expect a longer span than most. It has been estimated that the average monk in the priory at Durham lived as much as ten years more than the average man outside the walls.

The fact is that those fortunate enough to be able to feed themselves properly and keep clear of the worst infections stood a good chance of long and active life. For the rest, weakened by recurrent malnutrition, cold and damp, even the slightest disease was likely to prove fatal. As for he great killer epidemics, they were completely beyond the medicine of the day while the only known cure for the grotesque and slow death of leprosy was to isolate the victim as far as possible. Considering the callous crudity of public morals, the leper often enjoyed remarkable consideration. Exile from the community was a cruel but necessary precaution; the leper was also expected to sound his bell or wooden clapper to warn others of his approach. Yet food was put out for him and a person could be forced out of the community only when the accusation of leprosy had been confirmed by a careful examination.

Sometimes the fear of the disease was used by unscrupulous relatives or neighbours who wanted to dispossess or victimise a wealthy or unpopular enemy. It was not easy. Johanna Nightingale demanded a legal enquiry when her neighbours tried to force her out of town because she had been 'infected by contact of a foul leprosy'. After testing her for no fewer than forty symptoms and getting a negative reading on each one, the commission declared her 'utterly free and untainted' and their willingness to confirm as much in chancery.[28]

5
♣♣♣
Church, Churchmen and Dissent

During divine service on Sunday, 1 January 1434, the congregation of Chesterfield parish church in Derbyshire saw
Henry Longford and William Bradshaw murdered before
their eyes, and Sir Henry Pierpoint foully mutilated. It was
the most recent act in a gentry vendetta which had harried
the district for months past and neither Pierpoint nor, one
suspects, the parishioners themselves were totally astonished
by the desecration. The enforced respect paid to the churches
of England today would have surprised Caxton and his contemporaries. The Chesterfield murders outraged opinion in
more settled parts of the country, but everywhere the nave
of the church and the churchyard were treated with cavalier
disregard.

Go! little bill, and commend me heartily
Unto her that I call my truelove and lady
By this same tokening
That she saw me in a church on a Friday in a morning,
With a sparrow-hawk on my hand...[1]

Assignations for love or for business were commonly made
at church, the general meeting place and the greatest building
in the town. It was the despair of the clergy, this indifference
to the house of God, and it was one of the many signs that
the religion they taught touched all too rarely on the confused but powerful religiosity of the people at large.

The Church was the richest institution in the country. Its hierarchy wielded great power in central government and local affairs; its courts were an important part of the legal system; and it was accorded a moral leadership in the nation's life today long forgotten. Yet it is doubtful whether the medieval Church answered the spiritual needs of the population any more satisfactorily than does its modern counterpart. This chapter starts with a look at those aspects of religion that did interest the people before turning to the institution of the Church which bulked so large in their daily secular lives.

A mid-century treatise on the state of religion confidently observed that 'few of the common people knew even their Paternoster, Ave or Creed'. Formal liturgy was little listened to and less understood for the focus of popular interests was the cult of the saints. The great shrines of England were Canterbury, Walsingham, the Abbey of Hailes in Gloucestershire, which claimed to have a miraculous phial of the blood of Christ, St Albans, Bury St Edmunds and the shrine of the beloved St Cuthbert of Durham. They drew pilgrims from all over Britain. In the West Country, Glastonbury Abbey held the remains of St Joseph of Arimathea and down in remote Cornwall St Michael's Mount remembered a visit from the archangel himself. But almost every town had its revered local patron, sometimes canonised within living memory. When Margery Kempe visited the Augustinian Priory of Bridlington in Yorkshire, some of the older townsfolk would have been children when the saintly Brother John was still alive. In many other places, too, the traveller could ask the intercession of some local man or woman, in their day the inspiration of their neighbours and now with the heavenly host.

But if the Church's doctrine of the Communion of Saints did fire the popular imagination, there was a dark side. At Lincoln, the cult of Bishop Hugh, founder of the cathedral and canonised in 1220, was neighboured by the popular devotion for 'Little St Hugh'. In 1225, discovery of the murdered body of a nine-year-old boy had started a witch hunt against the Jews of the town, accused of using the child in some supposed religious ritual. Twenty were tortured and killed. At Norwich a parallel outbreak of ignorant mass neurosis spawned the cult of St William.

Such superstitions were the penalties paid by a religion that attempted to mesh with common life, and they were willingly paid. To the towns themselves the influx of pilgrims

One of the first English best-sellers, Chaucer's *Canterbury Tales* survives in numerous fifteenth-century MS copies. It also had many continuators, recounting the doings of the pilgrims in Canterbury and on the return journey. Here we see the pilgrims setting out from the cathedral city on their return. *The British Library*

meant business. St Winstan's Church in Leicestershire was maintained solely on the proceeds of pilgrim traffic; at Glastonbury the trade was so heavy that the abbot built a special hostel for pilgrims in the 1470s. To churchmen waging a constant battle for attention and respect, popular superstition was too important to be denounced out of hand. The Bishop of Durham accepted fees for marking cattle against the murrain, with the signet of St Wilfrid, and many a peasant priest authorised periodic distributions of holy water so that the pious might sprinkle themselves or their cattle.

People believed fervently in the power of spiritual forces. In anthropological terms, the Church was a vast reservoir of spiritual *mana*; its rituals and attributes were seen by many as potent magical tools. The Host of the Communion, if it could be smuggled out of the church, could be used to cure human and animal disease; to put out fires; as a love charm; to increase the fertility of the soil; and even in the charms and spells of the necromancers. At the end of communion the priest drank the holy wine to the lees and locked up every crumb of the sacred wafer to protect the transubstantiated body of Christ against such profanation. But there was little he could do when a communicant left the church with it still unswallowed.

The line between faith and superstition was often blurred beyond definition by the clergy themselves, nervously anxious to bring the folk traditions of their parishioners under their own control. They regularly presided over what were clearly the remnants of pagan customs. Under their auspices the ploughs were dragged round the fire on Plough Monday 'that it should fare the better all the year following'; the bonfires of Midsummer were lit in the name of St John the Baptist's Eve and, as the fifteenth-century treatise *Dives and Pauper* loudly hints, some priests even practised black magic in their own churches. For 'they do sing mass of requiem for them that be alive, in hope that they should fare worse and the sooner die'. Keith Thomas, from whose magnificent book *Religion and the Decline of Magic* much of the above is derived, concludes: 'The rural magicians of Tudor England did not invent their own charms: they inherited them from the medieval Church.'[2]

The parallels between such beliefs and the sorcery of 'primitive' tribes is apparent. And there are deeper similarities. Medieval people, too, accepted accident and chance far less readily as explanations than we do. Mishap and catastrophe, especially to important or unusual people, were seen as part of the intervention of the divine in the ways of men. People looked for it. On the Friday before Whitsun Margery Kempe was at mass in St Margaret's Lynn when part of the roof above her gave way and came crashing down. To the astonishment of the congregation she was virtually unhurt except for shock and some bruising where the masonry had struck her a glancing blow.

For years Margery's exaggerated exhibitions of piety had been a subject of local controversy. Now, those who accepted her claims to a special relationship with God believed he had given her a miraculous deliverance. Her opponents saw it as warning of divine anger at her presumption. No one doubted that it was a sign of some sort. A Cambridge doctor of divinity, called in to investigate, weighed the fragments of stone and timber work and pronounced that they should have been lethal. Undoubtedly Margery had been spared by a miracle. There was no need to inspect the roof. Everyone knew that faulty masonry and rotten timbers were liable to collapse and these could be repaired in due course. The important question was why did they collapse on Margery Kempe.

The immanence of the spiritual in the world was part of common experience. The cults of the saints appealed precisely because they were the interceders with the unseen powers. Among the most potent demonstrations of popular discontent was the paying of saintly honours to victims of the regime in power. Throughout the fifteenth century the

Canterbury shrine of Thomas à Becket, considered a martyr to royal tyranny, was the most visited in England. From 1405 the northern province of York could boast another such hero. In that year, Richard Scrope, the highly political archbishop, was executed for his part in the rebellion against Henry IV. Royal edicts could not prevent his tomb in the minster becoming a centre of pilgrimage. In the 1420s the cathedral chapter earmarked the offerings made there for the building of one of the great columns in the nave. In the 1450s the shrine was a rallying point for popular discontent and as late as 1459 a York lawyer bequeathed a book which 'the blessed Richard Scrope had and bore it in his breast at the time of his beheading'.[3]

The burning of Richard Wyche as a heretic at London in June 1440 seemed, for a time, to threaten an insurrection. Wyche was a Lollard priest who had had connections with Sir John Oldcastle and had been imprisoned for his views though later released. Successively vicar of a number of livings in Kent and Essex, he won a large following for the goodness of his life. The site of his martyrdom immediately became a place of pilgrimage. People found that the ground and the ashes of the dead man were sweetly perfumed and claimed to have seen miracles. The next month a cross had been erected on the site and candles were being burnt there. The authorities issued a ban on pilgrimages to the place and then, in desperation, turned the site into a dunghill. Yet the people still came and a watch had to be kept for the next two months.

Lollardy sprang from the basically anti-clerical teachings of John Wyclif. In addition to attacking the hierarchy of the Church he denied the doctrine of transubstantiation and claimed the right for all believers to hear the scriptures in the vernacular. He was condemned as a heretic after his death in 1384 and the group of academics who had gathered around him at Oxford quickly pulled in their horns. Some, by careful conformity, rose high in the church, like Philip Repingdon who became successively, chaplain to Henry IV, Bishop of Lincoln and, in 1408, a cardinal. The ideas of Wyclif had also spread to the gentry and for a time it seemed this might burgeon into an important movement. The parliament of 1406 debated a proposal to disendow the Church and during the next ten years, under the leadership of Sir John Oldcastle, Lollardy became associated with revolution. Oldcastle's eventual capture and execution for treason and heresy broke the movement. It lost what support it had had among the gentry and became a scattered underground sect of craftsmen, labourers and lesser tradesmen.

There was no 'Lollard's creed' as such but all shared the basic Wyclifite tenets – criticism of the hierarchy, denial of transubstantiation and devotion to the English Bible, based on Wyclif's translation. Those indiscreet or brave enough to let their heterodoxy show were liable to examination before a Church court. The records of these heresy trials are a window into the minds of ordinary men and women struggling against an oppressive orthodoxy to assess for themselves the conventional wisdom of their age. Many earned an independent living in the burgeoning new cloth industry, as weavers, wool combers, winders and fullers and dyers' servants. Others – smiths, wiredrawers and carpenters – were employed in the building trades and industrial maintenance. The ties of deference and obligation which bound the peasant farmer and labourer to his lord were loosened as were those of the priest and the Church. For the growing army of wage earners Lollardy offered a religious experience that matched the kind of self-sufficiency demanded by their working lives.

In this primitive industrial society a man's status depended not on his 'station in life' but on what he could do as a craftsman. Lollardy extended this principle to the priesthood by denying the automatic validity of ecclesiastical orders. Without virtue no man, priest or lay, could exercise spiritual functions. With it any man could. Even the powers of St Peter had terminated with his death; his successors had the right to claim them only if they were as good as he. Any good Christian could consecrate the bread and wine, but no one had the power to turn the bread into the body of Christ. The attack on transubstantiation was a fundamental attack on the exalted position the Church accorded to its priests. In the same way confession could be made to laymen or even to one's own conscience – in fact confession had been ordained simply so that priests could have an excuse to pry into the sex life of women. Christening, the child's first encounter with the superiority of the priestly office, was said to be unnecessary for the children of Christian parents. Images were idolatrous and the Lollards went to the extreme of denying the spiritual value of pilgrimage and the whole of the saints and relics system. William Carpenter of Newbury, who 'believed that if the faith of the Lollards were not, the world should be soon destroyed', held also that the Church had no right of canonisation since it could not know with certainty whether its 'saints' were in heaven or hell.[4]

By rejecting the one religious element that was genuinely popular the Lollards ensured that they would remain without any real influence. Their claim that Wyclif was a greater saint than Thomas of Canterbury met hostile contempt; their devotion to Wyclif's Bible made them automatically suspect in an age when literacy was rare. Their more extreme views ran from the pietism of those who held that the Church of God was within every man, to outright paganism. A butcher of Standon averred that there was no god but the sun and the moon. The view of Thomas Taylor of Bristol that the faith of the pagans was better than that of Christian men and that Christ was merely a good prophet was matched by Richard Gryg, a weaver, who held that Englishmen were 'worse than Jews and Saracens for these make no oblations to images as Englishmen do'. Both reflect the pervading influence of Mandeville's account of Islamic beliefs.

Such ideas belonged to the fringe of the fringe, but the stream of Wyclifite–Lollard belief and practice was so strong that evidence of Lollard converts is found in Kent into the beginning of the next century. It is a tenuous thread linking the revolutionary doctrines of Wyclif to the age of the Reformation. What little we do know of this fifteenth-century pattern of protest comes from the careful combing of the bishops' registers by John A. F. Thomson. He concludes that the Lollards represented only a small minority even in the areas, in the south of England, where they were strongest. However, although there were heresy trials throughout the century, they were not numerous and the campaign against heretics was sporadic and rarely intense. And this was true even though the lay authorities were interested in the suppression of the heretics. Oldcastle's political threat was never forgotten. One of the duties required of the sheriff by his oath was 'to destroy and make to seize all manner of heresies – commonly called Lollardies'.[5] The fear was justified in 1431 when riots and anti-clerical demonstrations broke out in the south of England from London to Salisbury and northwards to the Midlands. The centre of the troubles was in the counties of Berkshire and Wiltshire – the growing centre of the new cloth industry. The chief platform of the rebels seems to have been the disendowment of the Church in favour of the earls, knights, gentry and almshouses. It may well be that the upheaval was engineered by members of the lesser gentry or was a purely secular movement. The links with Lollardy are extremely tenuous and the charge against them may have been government propaganda. Whatever the facts behind this outbreak, they show the link in government thinking between heresy and treason.

From the fact that many of the people brought for interrogation admitted to having been helped by friends or for their own part to having aided heretics, it can be deduced that there was quite a ground swell of popular opinion in favour of the dissenters in some parts of the country. A still larger number of people read the Lollard scriptures or listened to readings while continuing to attend the parish church so as to allay the suspicions of the neighbours. Seven found guilty of heresy at Salisbury at the end of the century had continued to attend church 'Only for dread of the people and to eschew the jeopardy and danger that we dread to fall into if we had not done as other Christian people did.' Thomas Boughton of Wantage admitted, when finally brought to book, that he had privately rejected the doctrine of transubstantiation for twenty-five years past, without ever having confessed this sin against the Faith to his priest. It was the kind of testimony to make the blood run cold in the veins of the conscientious churchman. How many other such silent protestants there might be in every country parish did not bear thinking about. But if many lay discreetly low, a few went to the fire for their beliefs with stalwart courage. John Goose, burned at Tower Hill in 1474, dined off a dish of meat on the scaffold commenting to the crowd below: 'I eat now a good and competent dinner, for I shall pass a little shower ere I go to supper.'[6]

London, Bristol, Coventry: these were the typical centres. From them the new teachings spread into the countryside, along the natural routes of trade. Considering the regular commerce in cloth and dyes between Coventry and Bristol, it was natural for the two heretical communities there to be in close contact with one another. From Bristol north and west contacts spread into the strange and independent world of the Forest of Dean. At this time it was probably the most industrialised area of England. The traditions of mining there stretched back into neolithic times and by the fifteenth century the free miners of the Forest had won the status of a privileged and, as far as this was possible in the medieval rural community, independent status. It was fertile soil for Lollardy.

Sometimes it seems from the records as though the ties between London and the provinces were kept up on a semi-organised basis. The Coventry group, for example, which had established a colony in the neighbouring market town

of Birmingham, had firm ties with the capital. Joan Washingby of Coventry, who was later to be burnt, was able to
arrange hospitality for herself in the house of Joan Blackbyre
of London who was also a heretic, though her husband
apparently was not. This same Joan had dealings with another
Coventry woman, Agnes Johnson, from whom she received
a book. The prominence permitted to women among the
heretics was another charge against them. Among the forty-
seven people brought to trial along with Joan Washingby,
twelve were women; to the horror of the orthodox the
heretics even allowed their women to preach.

Between the soft-centred credulity of the pilgrim shrine
and the narrow fervour of the Lollard Bible class, the bulk
of the English were indifferent to Church religion. Where
John Willis the Lollard saw the woods and the fields as being
as much the temple of God as any church, most of his fellow
citizens saw them as the place for hunting, poaching and
sport, and Sunday the time for it. The great processions of
the Church festivals were attended by fewer and fewer
people and these were mostly members of the clergy and
members of the lesser bourgeoisie. The nobility ignored
them. 'Does it not seem abominable that, if there should be
a duel held tomorrow in the city of London...so many rich
men and nobles would congregate there, that there would
scarcely be room enough to hold them? But if a procession
is arranged at London for prayer...although the bishop be
there with the clergy, yet scarcely do a hundred men of the
populace follow him.'

Sermon after sermon complains about lower attendance
figures and even the people who did come were depressingly
inattentive. The preacher who tried to win his congregation
with jokes and vivid instances found that while these 'were
retained in the memory well enough' and repeated 'again and
again with glee' after the service, the 'good things' were forgotten. Any distraction was enough to lose the vicar his
audience and of all the distractions a pretty woman was the

worst. Not even the twelve apostles could compete with the modern coquette as she stands in the aisles of the church with her painted face and fluttering eyelashes. The men 'take nothing of God's word; they run to the dancing strumpets. The priest can stand alone in the church for all they care; but the harlot is hired for good money.'[7] Even the ladies of the manor do not escape. Their long toilet makes them late for the services and when they do finally arrive it is more 'from pride in entering the holy church with pomp and vain glory and noble attire, to be looked at by the people, than for any devotion to God'. Once in their places they do not sit still for long 'but ever as any man comes into the church or goes out, they look after him and forget their prayers'.

Yet then, as now, women far outnumbered men in the congregations. No doubt this was partly because there were fewer other public places where a woman of any social standing could be seen. The men that did come too often dozed off to sleep though, exclaims the parson apparently surprised, they stay awake for hours when they go drinking in the ale house. At other times they ask the priest to let them out of church early because one of their friends is giving a feast. One can imagine the request was readily granted in the country parish. Desperately poor, often ill-educated and ignorant and inevitably in the lower reaches of the social order, the priest would have needed a particular brand of foolhardy courage to stand up to any request from the manor. These country parsons, though they found their champion in Chaucer, struck most observers as much by their brutishness as the great clerics did by their opulence.

The fundamental problem of the medieval Church was not its ridiculous excess of wealth so much as the fact that as the largest, the best organised and the most influential institution of its day it was the obvious career ladder for the ambitious. The medieval rat race, in short, was run by the self-styled servants of God. The contrast between Christ's doctrine of humility, poverty, and love and the grotesque wealth and luxury and arrogance of his chief ministers on earth is one of those simple dilemmas which the sophistication of the prelate may dub simplistic but which has always seemed unanswerable to lay minds. As early as the twelfth century one heretic had dated the decline of the spiritual power of the Church back to its fourth-century alliance with the Roman state under the emperor Constantine. In the age of Caxton such criticisms were commonplace. Sometimes also they were highly ingenious as in the following 'punctuation' poem. The author's written punctuation is shown; the punctuation that would be supplied by the average contemporary reader is indicated by the obliques.

> Trusty; seldom/to their friends unjust;/
> Glad for to help; no Christian creature/
> Willing to grieve; setting all their joy and lust/
> Only in the pleasure of God; having no care/
> Who is most rich; with them they will be sure/
> Where need is; giving neither reward nor fee/
> Unreasonably; Thus live priests parde.[8]

Every preacher facing a bored or unruly congregation knew that, short of following the example of the German Abbot Gerard who on one memorable occasion electrified a crowd of dozing gentry with the inspiriting cry: 'There was once upon a time a king called Arthur!', the shortest way to immediate attention was to attack his own profession. Once he widened his field of fire the response became patchier. 'When their own sins are spelled out they get angry; but when those of others, they are delighted', wrote John Bromyard the Dominican. And he added with somewhat laboured sarcasm, 'It seems that in spiritual matters at least, they consider the welfare of others before their own.' So much so in fact, that the vicar sometimes found himself approached during the week with a request to touch 'on other men's faults in his sermon'. Even so, he had to go carefully. Finding themselves under attack from the pulpit, members of the congregation were quite liable to answer back and 'decry the preacher, attacking either his person or his profession, thus, "I have never known worse, prouder, or more greedy men than the churchmen." '9

Thinking members of the clergy were well aware of the problem and equally depressed about it. 'Today our priests are as dissolute, as greedy, as ambitious as are the common people: when they are not worse.' Sometimes a voice from the episcopal bench is heard fulminating against the inarticulate ignorance of the parish priests, but the chief indictment of the secular clergy, priests and bishops alike, comes from the regulars, notably the friars. Established at the beginning of the thirteenth century as mendicant evangelists, they were the traditional enemies of the parish priests who were, perhaps understandably, unwilling to give these fire-eating hot gospellers permission to exercise their talents in their parishes. The charge sheet drawn up by the Dominican Bromyard, therefore, may be less than objective but the tenor is supported by other sources. He begins with the bishops themselves and their 'swarms of bastard children' and concludes with an excoriating denunciation of the secular clergy as a whole, 'a profession into which more insufficient and ignorant persons find their way than any other in the world'.10

The organisation of the Church made it virtually certain that this should be so. More than a fifth of the land in England was owned by the Church and its best talents spent most of their time supervising its administration or fighting in the courts to maintain their tenures. The bishop's functions were largely administrative and supervisory and he need have little part in the pastoral care of his diocese. The ambitious opened their career by reading law at Oxford and then moving as quickly as possible into diocesan administration, preferably in Canterbury. Theology had little appeal to candidates for the secular ministry and was the preserve of members of the monastic orders. Royal service was as good an avenue to advancement as the ecclesiastical civil service; John Stafford, who became Archbishop of Canterbury in the 1440s, had become Keeper of the Privy Seal in his early thirties (1421) and ten years later was chancellor.

For all its faults, the Church was open to talent from all social classes. Stafford himself was the bastard son of Sir Humphrey Stafford and Emma, a local girl from Sir Humphrey's manor of North Bradley in Wiltshire.[11] A noble father was more of an advantage than illegitimacy was a drawback and at the age of twenty the future archbishop received a papal dispensation to enter holy orders and was soon collecting benefices. Thomas Bekynton, Bishop of Bath and Wells, was the son of a weaver; Walter Lyhart, Bishop of Norwich, was a miller's son. Men like these served on an equal footing with aristocrats like Richard Scrope or George Neville, Bishop of Exeter, the brother of the Earl of Warwick and therefore one of the most powerful men in the land. And like their aristocratic colleagues they soon joined the ranks of the absentees who drew the contempt and condemnation of the high-minded. Thomas Bouchier, who succeeded Stafford as archbishop, was said to have visited his previous diocese of Ely only once and that on the day of his installation. Half way through his reign at Canterbury Archbishop Chichele confessed that the royal service had so monopolised his time that he had been absent from the council only thirty-three times in eleven years.

The rich benefices of the Church were used as salaries for state officials and as perquisites for royal or baronial favourites. William Booth, successively Bishop of Lichfield and Archbishop of York (1452), was attacked as 'but a common lawyer who confers benefices on boys and youths'. Only the poorest sees could look forward to true pastoral care from their bishop. Llandaff, the most impoverished in the kingdom, went to an obscure friar named Wells in the 1420s; unlike his wealthy colleagues he remained in his diocese, if only because he could barely afford to pay a suffragan to take over his spiritual ministry and a vicar-general for his administrative work.

The bishop also needed the help of an official to preside over the diocesan consistory court and another to make visitations of the parishes. Here too the real work was all too often performed by deputies. The income from such a benefice or rectory depended on the endowments it had received during the centuries and the value of the tithe. Sometimes this could be as low as £10 a year, little better than the wage of a skilled craftsman working a full week all the year round. Because career men regularly received the income from several parishes from which they kept the chief tithe revenues, the vicars they appointed lived in abject penury and had to supplement their living by farming the glebe, or freehold land, attached to the parish. In many an English country community, the priest was little more than an ordained farmer who had to fit his parish duties into the agricultural calendar. Even the vicars of rich livings neglected their priestly duties for a second job. The pseudonymous pamphleteer 'Jack Upland' knew of many a priest who rather than 'study in God's law', preferred 'other diverse laws for the more winning'.[12] The clerk who had been to Oxford or Cambridge was a valuable professional in the rural community and could generally find work in the accounts office of the manorial lord.

A priests' handbook warns them against being too drunk to say the holy office without stumbling over the words. Jack Upland even accuses them of selling the sacraments. Some thought their greatest failing was in the pulpit. But the official clergy had become wary of preaching since the indictments of the Lollards. In the 1450s the monks of St Albans, questioned by a newly appointed abbot about any internal reforms that might be needed, replied that one of the things that had been for long neglected was 'the preaching of the sacred word by the brothers in the pulpit'. By this time, the friars had lost their original high reputation and were being accused of 'preaching the people fables, to please them'. And 'in token of this chaffering they beg after that they have preached, as who should say – "Give me thy money, for I am worthy, by my preaching." And this chaffering is the selling of preaching.' The activities of the pardoners also had corrupted the once respectable office of the pulpit – for they 'preached publicly and pretended falsely that they had full powers of absolving living and dead alike from punishment and guilt'.

In fact the pardoners and the friars often seem to have come to blows, contesting the right to use a parish pulpit. The parish priest, once obliged to give these travellers the hospitality of their pulpits, had been relieved of the duty by the papacy because of abuses by the mendicant preachers. Yet friars were barred from few parishes. Those who dared refuse them permission or were too strict in examining their authorisations, found their mass held up or their church invaded by the angry mountebank, loudly calling for alms or denouncing the hard-hearted charity of the official clergy.

The friars' criticisms of the secular clergy were preached in the popular pulpit. The measured reproof of a bishop or prior within the solemn context of abbey or cathedral church was far less subversive than the wayside pulpit denunciation spoken in English to the rabble at large. Since it was their trade, the friars naturally emphasised the role of preaching, even suggesting on occasion that it was more important than the mass itself. Many laymen who took religion seriously shared the view, foreshadowing one of the themes of the Reformation. Many a parish church was fitted out with a new carved wood or stone pulpit and some, as the one in Burnham Norton, Norfolk, were proudly embellished with the portrait of the donor. At the same time pews, which had been available for the gentry since the thirteenth century, came to be installed for the whole congregation. 'The extensive series of pews, sufficient for all, which fill the naves of many churches by the second half of the fifteenth century, reflecting much of the carven beauty of clerical stall, pulpit, and screen, are testimony in themselves to the place which preaching has come to take in the religious life of the people.'[13]

It also, no doubt, reflects the interests of the new merchant class of church builders, the 'open plan' effect of fifteenth-century buildings, in which the divide between nave and chancel is marked only by open-work wooden screens, expresses the growing unwillingness to accord the clergy the privacy and cult secrecy of the enclosed chancels of earlier centuries. Handsome stone pulpits, like the one in the fine wool church of Northleach, stand outside the sanctuary in the people's part of the building. But if the audience was there for good preaching, it is clear from the complaints of churchmen that the clergy were mostly unskilled in the art. As a result it was hard work to get the average man to come to church. 'He will make his excuse and say "I am old and sickly", or "I have a great household" or else he has some other occupation.' Yet despite all this, if the priest could hire them and say, ' "I will give good wages", they would lay their excuses to one side and come to divine service according to their duty.'[14]

The friars, however, were colourful and compelling speakers. Their open-air congregations, in the churchyard or at the preaching crosses on market square and village green, revelled in their tirades against the clergy and their indictment of tithes which they presented as the extortions of an over-rich church from poor Christian folk. Most notorious were the sermons of William Russell, warden of the London Greyfriars. In the 1420s he was delighting congregations at Stamford in Lincolnshire with the message that tithes were contrary to the law of God; later, in London, he somewhat modified this to the unexceptionable comment that the payment of tithes was not enjoined by divine law. Possibly Russell was thought a little unbalanced for he also held that it was permissible for a religious to have carnal knowledge of a woman.[15] But the anti-tithe campaign had a considerable response. In the province of Canterbury, there were many who were 'striving to withdraw such tithes; many who already had withdrawn them; and...it is feared that more will be hindred from payment...to the...injury of curates and particularly vicars'.

Nowhere was the opposition to tithes more persistent than in the city of London, though its basis was simply a dislike of paying any tax and was not specifically anti-clerical. A test case came up in 1451 when Robert Wright appealed to the papal curia against a tithe assessment and demand made on him by the court of the dean of St Paul's. The city reckoned the issue so critical that they subsidised Wright's defence costs. The embassy was something of a fiasco, it should be said, nevertheless, two years later, the city's authorities passed an ordinance 'whereby the duties of the Church be withdrawn'. Over the next twenty years or so city and Church extracted a succession of conflicting bulls from the papacy which in fact left matters more or less where they had been at the start of the row.

The merchant complained that as he was not a farmer he could not be expected to pay a tithe on crops. The attempt by the Church to commute this to a cash rate on property and, in addition, to levy personal tithes on the proceeds of business was strongly resented as yet another example of ecclesiastical avarice. It is not surprising that the friars found support for their attacks on clerical wealth. Yet they themselves were still more vulnerable.

Founded by St Francis and St Dominic as orders of poor, self-denying preachers and evangelists, they, more than any other body in the Church, were committed to Christ's doctrine of poverty. But within the century they were building great hostels and churches that made a mockery of their ideals. The Spiritual Franciscans broke away from the main order in the fourteenth century against the opulence which was swamping it, but they remained a minority. When Jack

Upland launched his attack it was a long time since the friars in general had had 'nothing in this world in proper neither in common, but to beg with Christ'. Their revenue in alms was too tempting and there were too many other ways of supplementing it. The least disreputable was the granting of 'letters of fraternity' to lay benefactors which, in return for endowments, gave them a vicarious share in the spiritual rewards the friars supposedly won for themselves by their good works. But they were also charged with selling prayers and masses and persuading parishioners to be buried within the precincts of their houses rather than in the parish churchyard so that the endowments for the necessary masses for the dead soul would go to their funds.

> Friar, why may you for shame lie to the people, and say that you follow the apostles in poverty more than other men do; and yet in curious and costly houses, and in fine and precious clothing; delicious and lusty feeding, in treasury and jewels and rich ornaments, friars outdo lords and other rich worldly men.[16]

Upland's complaint was unanswerable but it had to be answered. The reply, by a friar under the pseudonym Daw Topias, is a tissue of special pleading. When 'Jack' metaphorically claims that many a friary is larger than the king's palaces the answer takes him literally: 'Where saw you Jack a friary like in any royalty to the Tower of London, to Wyndsor, to Woodstock...to Westminster?' Refuting Jack's claim that there are too many friars he falls back on sophistry. 'Thou sayest that God has made all things in measure, weight and number; and that a friar is something thou mayest not deny: and thou sayest friars be made against God's will. Then hath God made something that he wished not to make.'[17] All good clean fun, of course, but convincing neither to Upland nor to most of his contemporaries.

Perhaps because they had been on the scene far longer than

the friars and their relaxed corruption and high living were consequently generally accepted as part of the order of things, the monastic orders were less harshly condemned. But Upland had a word for them too and questioned the validity of the cloistered life even when lived according to its own principles. They were another 'host against Christ's ordinance, closed from the world in walls of stone, cloisters and cells, and whereas they should have laboured in the world in help of all Christ's Church, with meek love and low livelihood, now they live in idle life and secure from all poverty'.

That security made the monastic life highly attractive to many a poor country lad. There is statistical evidence, mentioned above, to indicate that people lived longer in monasteries. That being the case, entry on a religious vocation was a shrewd career decision for the rustic or his father, with the additional bonus that he could consider himself on the side of the angels even if others accused him of sponging on the welfare system. Certainly the life of the cloister was no hardship, though the slipshod discharge of the half-understood daily office could become boring. Yet with ale and food in good measure this could be borne and even in the most decrepit rural monastery, the living was infinitely better than in the villages round about.

Nor, except under the stern rule of the seven Carthusian houses in England and a handful of others, was the monk cut off from his old friends and the community at large. Most monasteries had side doors opening into the streets of the adjacent town or village; it was a simple matter for Humberstone's sacrist, John Gedney, to don his hunting clothes and slip out for a morning's wild fowling after he had rung the bell for matins. At the great monasteries, the brethren were provided with pleasant holiday homes on outlying manors. The Benedictines of Christ Church Canterbury, could choose between rest houses at Caldecot and Hendon. The prior of Durham held four 'ludi' or holiday periods of a fortnight at his country seats of Pittington and Beaurepair.

Elsewhere the monks drew a regular salary from the abbey's endowments, leaving considerable sums of money to the refectory or books to the library. The house's income could be increased in various ways even though the level of voluntary lay endowments had fallen off. At Fosse in Lincolnshire, Sir John Pyggot of Doddington made a handsome cash payment in return for the use of a hall and a chamber in the monastery estates as a dower house for his mother.[18]

In fact the flood of money which had launched and floated the early stages of monasticism was running dry during this century. Few younger sons of the nobility took vows and their families increasingly preferred to invest either in church building or chantries. The fashion had been growing since the middle of the previous century. Its chief attractions to the investor were versatility, value for money and personalised service. The cheapest form was an endowment yielding a yearly stipend to a priest for saying a specified number of masses for the soul of the founder on specified days. Even if the family could not afford a stone tomb, the terms of the endowment might provide for the erection of a gabled timber 'hearse' on the days of the mass. This was then draped with a black pall and surrounded with a metal frame carrying candlesticks. A little further up the scale a wrought-iron 'hearse' could be fixed over the tomb permanently, to be brought into use on the days when the masses were to be said. A richer man could afford the building of a special altar for his masses and the really wealthy a special chantry chapel built either into the aisles of the church or as an extension. Beyond this the endowments tended to become less exclusively concerned with the mere saying of masses for the dead and more with charity.

The most magnificent chantry endowment in the country – undoubtedly popularising the whole system among the nobility – was the commemoration of Edward I's queen, Eleanor, in Westminster Abbey. Every abbot was bound by an oath to observe the exact and complete order of the ceremonies so that every St Andrew's Eve, from 1292 to the Dissolution of the Monasteries, the great church conducted one of the most impressive rituals to be seen anywhere in western Europe. One hundred wax candles, each weighing twelve pounds, were burnt from the evening to high mass on the following day. All the bells of the abbey church were rung throughout the day, the divine offices were chanted hour by hour and all the nobility and chief clergy in town were expected to be present.[19]

One of the great sights of medieval London, this royal chantry inevitably impressed the nobles who were able to attend. But the main chantries of the fifteenth century were more than mere pomp and ceremony. The Church was the focus and often the sponsor of such altruism and welfare as there was in this harsh age. The chantry priest often had the job of distributing alms from a specially provided fund. Or, in the case of richer foundations, served as the chaplain and manager of the almshouse established by the founder. The scale of such endowments is instanced by the attractive and comfortable almshouses of Ewelme in Berkshire. Set up in 1450 under the terms of the will of the unlovely and grasping Duke of Suffolk, they were modernised in the early 1970s at a cost of thousands drawn entirely from the revenues of the foundation and they provide twelve self-contained maisonettes housing twenty-four pensioners.

The pattern of the traditional English almshouse – terrace or court of self-contained cottages, each with its own fireplace and separate offices – was the invention of the fifteenth century and the standard design for old people's homes up to this century. To many of the 'bedesmen' the accommodation must have seemed a miracle of opulence. After a lifetime's penury in a leaking smoky one-roomed mud hovel shared with family and animals they found that each 'have and hold a certain place by themself within the said house of alms. That is to say a little house, a cell or a chamber with a chimney and other necessaries in the same, in which any

of them may by himself, eat and drink and rest, and sometimes among attend to contemplation and prayer.'[20]

This 'contemplation and prayer' was rarely optional. At
Ewelme matins was at 6 am; mass at 9; bedes at 2 pm; even-
song at 3 and the bidding prayer said round the founders
tomb and in his memory, at 6. A hard schedule with stiff
penalties for any breach. 'And if it so be that any of them
be so slowthful that the first psalm of matins be begun ere
he come into his stall he shall lose one penny.' There were
other fines for 'rebelliousness', failing to sweep the courtyard
or weed the gardens at one's turn of the roster or even coming
to church without one's tabard. In return for secure accommodation and food such a regimen could well be borne. And
these working retirement homes expected of their inmates,
work. The religious services which the bedesmen pensioners
had to discharge were a form of work which even old age
could bear and which the community recognised as valuable.
The psychological advantages of such working retirement
homes over the often demoralising 'dying homes' of our own
age do not need stressing.

While some founders made the living work for them after
they were dead, others funded more positive social services
as the fee for their souls' salvation. The full scope and provision for medieval education is still unsure, but it is clear
that the chantries had an important role. Along with scriv-
eners in the towns and curates and parish priests in country
districts, the chantry priest taught the elements of reading,
writing and sometimes Latin. At the little Oxfordshire market town of Deddington the town's Holy Trinity Guild,
formed in 1445, set up a chantry to the memory of Richard
Andrew. A native of the nearby township of Adderbury, he
had risen high in the service of Henry VI and his chantry
priest had the additional responsibility of teaching the village
boys. For a century they had better educational chances than
they had ever known. When the chantry was disendowed at
the Dissolution of the Monasteries in 1548 the commissioners

reported that the then chantry priest, William Burton, was a 'good school master and bringeth up youth very well in learning'.[21]

At Chipping Norton, just a few miles distant from Deddington, the Holy Trinity Guild soon followed their neighbour's example and in 1450 a teacher was attached to the staff of St Mary's Parish Church 'to give instruction in Latin to any boy who came to the town to learn'. In fact, all over the country the merchant community was becoming more involved in education. Robert Chirche, a London businessman, contracted to send one of his apprentices to school for two years to learn grammar and writing. When he stopped paying the fees half way through the course, the boy's friends raised a formal complaint. Most masters found it worth giving their apprentices a rudimentary education and as the century advanced more and more people were learning to read, sometimes in the guild schools, though more often in establishments founded by the church.

The monasteries played little part in this. Their bursars and management officials may well have taken a course in business studies at Oxford, but the monks' own teaching was confined almost exclusively to candidates for their orders. By contrast, the secular cathedrals and collegiate churches did run schools for the laity. The system reached into the remoter localities, thanks to enlightened bishops and patrons. When the parish church of Wotton-under-Edge was reorganised as a collegiate foundation, Lady Katherine Berkeley endowed a master and two scholars of grammar with the duty to teach at least two candidates for the Church and any others who came, free of charge. At Tonge in Kent, a college based on the parish church also offered free elementary education to the boys of the neighbouring towns. In the 1460s the Bishop of Worcester appropriated the revenues of the parish church at Clifton to the maintenance of a grammar master at the nearby college of Westbury on Trim. The royal foundation at Eton originated in the same way. The first step was conversion of the parish church of Eton into a collegiate establishment governed by a provost and ten priest fellows. The rest of the establishment was made up by four clerks, six choristers, twenty-five poor grammar scholars and twenty-five poor men. A master in grammar had the job of teaching any poor boy who offered himself, free.

The Church was the only institution capable of providing anything like mass education. Even when the funds came from lay patrons the teachers were men in clerical orders. But instruction was not confined to religious or even academic topics. When Thomas Rotheram, Archbishop of York, founded his Jesus College at Rotheram in 1483 he made provision for the teaching of writing and accounting there as well as Latin. At the universities the business schools of the lay masters competed for students with the colleges and even in their precincts the study of theology came a very poor second to the arts courses, philosophy and law. Vocational theology for candidates for the Church was concentrated largely on the monastic foundations such as Durham and Canterbury Colleges. Though when William Waynflete founded his new college of Magdalen at Oxford in 1448, of the three lectureships one was in theology. He also provided for the training of two or three students in the humanities so that they could instruct others.

At the end of the century William Grocyn introduced the teaching of Greek at Oxford. Early in the next century Erasmus was a visiting lecturer at Cambridge and John Colet at Oxford. Until then, Italian humanism made little impact on the conservative authorities in either of the English universities. At Oxford this was in part because of a fear of overloading the already heavy arts curriculum. In addition to the traditional seven liberal arts – music, grammar, rhetoric, logic, arithmetic, geometry and astronomy – this included natural, moral and metaphysical philosophy. The teaching was largely oral – the university library based on the princely gift of some three hundred books by Duke Humphrey of

Gloucester and housed at the university's church of St Mary's was open just three hours daily. In consequence Latin grammar was essential for the student whose examinations were in the form of public disputations in Latin.

To complete the full arts course might take the best part of a decade and be stretched further by absence to avoid the almost endemic 'sweating sickness'. Peter Talbot lost two terms and the long vacation – virtually the whole academic year of 1450 – rather than live in the plague-ridden city. Forty years later the fellows of Merton College moved out to the village of Islip for the same reason. In fact the death rate from this and other causes was a barely credible ten per cent. Given the pressures of work and the uncertainty of residence, many looked for ways of reducing the load. Dispensations from some of the prescribed academic exercises were commonly granted 'on account of plague'; the examining authorities agreed to accept vacation work towards the degree – a concession made use of by William Browne who spent the final year before his master's degree in the country. Despite strict regulations to the contrary it was even possible to exchange parts of the course. In 1451 Thomas Bury was permitted to waive two disputations by offering to make two in another discipline after he had been awarded his master's degree.[22]

The traditional course was increasingly by-passed in favour of specialisations. Typical combinations were grammar with rhetoric – an ideal combination for prospective lawyers – astronomy, arithmetic and geometry – the nearest equivalent to a modern science course – and music. And there were fringe opportunities for exploring the modern humanistic theories of Italy. About the time that the first of Magdalen's 'two or three students' in the humanities were completing their qualifying degrees, the Italian scholar Stefano Surigone settled in Oxford. He taught rhetoric in the official curriculum but was able to pick up a useful second income by taking private students in humanistic studies. Some of them must have been Magdalen men and others may have been members of the humanist group which had begun to meet in the rooms of Thomas Chaundler, Warden of New College, in the year Surigone arrived (1454).

But the general interest in humanism was slight. Far more important was the study of astronomy and its attendant art of astrology, though the two were not strictly distinguishable. The astronomical tables produced and systematically revised at Oxford were valuable aids to the work of the astrologers, the most important of whom seem to have been working at Merton College. The warden, Richard Fitz-James, who built the great arch at Merton with its frieze of zodiacal signs, used astrology to calculate the most auspicious time to start the building. During his time as bursar he had used the same methods, investigating *per talos et cartes*, in an attempt to trace some lost college property. His rough calculations still survive in a manuscript of astronomical and astrological studies. A few years later we find the bursar of Magdalen hiring an astrology expert from Westminster to divine the whereabouts of £112 which had disappeared from the vaults.[23]

But fascination with the occult could lead down dangerous ways. When Eleanor, Duchess of Gloucester, was charged with an attempt on the life of the king, her co-defendants were Thomas Southwell and Roger Ballyngbroke, both Oxford graduates. By luck or good management Southwell died in the Tower but Ballyngbroke was duly hanged, drawn and quartered after having first been exhibited, with his astronomical instruments, in the public pillory. In the 1470s two more Oxonians, this time from Merton, were charged with having 'worked and calculated by art, magic and necromancy and astronomy' to bring about the death of Edward IV and the Prince of Wales. One of them, Dr John Stacey, had already been suspected of advising Joan, Lady Beauchamp, in her attempt to cause her husband's death by melting a leaden image of him.[24] The same 'wasting' principle of sympathetic magic was reckoned a potent weapon against faithless lovers, though a burning candle was more commonly used. 'As the candle is consumed, so will a man waste away.'

There was nothing 'folksy' about magic. When Henry VI gave his physician John Faceby a licence to investigate the possibilities of the transmutation of metals the secrets of the alchemist were as mysterious to him as the work of the astrologer. Experts in both, however, were expected at the country's leading centre of learning, and the university magician was more to be feared than the village practitioner because he was better informed. At her trial Elena Dalok, witch, averred that she 'cared nothing for any heaven to come. All she wanted was heaven on earth.' She hoped to go to Hell where, she had heard, a certain John Gybbys was, with whom she had a few old scores to settle.[25] Some may have been shocked by her blasphemy, few doubted that she was a true witch.

To the people of her village Elena Dalok was a more potent agent of the spiritual world than the priest, just as magic was more real than religion. The same was true even at the most sophisticated level of society. Accusations of witchcraft could make convenient political weapons and they were potent precisely because people believed they could be true. George, Duke of Clarence, whose instability at times seems to verge on madness, went to the extreme of accusing his brother the king that 'he wrought by necromancy and used craft to poison his subjects' and had intended 'to consume him in likewise as a candle is consumed by burning'.

6

The Woman's Place

Attitudes to women were coloured by a religious mythology both potent and ambivalent. Eve, created from Adam's body, caused his fall from God's grace; the Blessed Virgin Mary bore Christ, the second Adam, and so brought the possibility of redemption. Eve is excluded from the first dawn of Creation; St Joseph takes no part in the conception of the New Creation. The Pauline theology of the celibate clergy condemned sex and by implication women. But if they were subjected to small-minded hectoring from the pulpit, they were not gainsaid their place in the churches. The Christian denial of the female principle never went to the length of segregating the women of the congregation behind a grill, as was the case in the synagogue. At least one friar must have wished that it did and considered that in this matter at least the despised Jews had something to teach. Delivering what he no doubt felt to be a magisterial rebuke to a chattering woman in the congregation, he was met by the outraged reply: 'Marry, sir, I beshrew his heart that babbleth the most of us both! For I do but whisper a word to my neighbour here, and thou hast babbled there all this hour.'

A woman had once used equally forthright language to the pope himself. In 1370, St Bridget of Sweden wrote to Pope Clement VI that he would be struck dead if he dared desert Rome again for Avignon. The pope ignored the warning and, within the month of his return to Avignon, was dead. Bridget, canonised soon after her death, already had a reputation which outshone even fireworks like this. Margery Kempe, housewife and mystic, consciously modelled herself on the saint who had a wide reputation throughout northern Europe.

The Brigittine convent founded at Sheen by Henry V was one of the few religious establishments in the country to hold to its vows. Elsewhere the nuns, so far as we can tell from the scant references to them, matched the lackadaisical corruptions of the monasteries. Dame Pride, Dame Envy, Dame Sloth, Dame Lust and Dame Wanton were just some of the inmates according to one critic. At Gokewell in Lincolnshire the ladies had long since abandoned the plain fare and demure communal mealtimes enjoined by their rule. Instead they ate in their rooms with their friends, drawing ale and bread from the kitchens but filling out the meal with meat and delicacies bought from local traders. It was one of the richer of England's 130 or so nunneries, getting a healthy income from running a boarding school which took girls up to the age of ten and boys up to eight. Most houses supplemented inadequate foundation endowments by demanding 'doweries' from the fathers of rich novices. It was, of course, forbidden by their rule.

Of the fewer than 2000 nuns in England at this time, only a very small number followed their vocation with the devoutness envisaged by the founders of the houses. Apart from the unfortunates placed there against their will while children, the inmates were widows seeking a retreat, the unmarriageable daughters of the wealthy who preferred the comforts and dignity of the nun's status to the ambiguous social standing of the spinster, and very occasionally some great lady sent away by her family or the king into honourable house arrest. Soon after he had seated himself firmly in the throne Henry VII dispatched his mother-in-law Queen Elizabeth Woodville to a nunnery on the charge that she had been on unduly affable terms with Richard III, the reputed murderer of her children.

The only formal function allowed to women by the Church was as the member of a nunnery. Priests found, however, that the bulk of their congregations were women. They welcomed them as ideal sermon fodder; among the heretical Lollards, by contrast, women seem to have enjoyed full equality. Joan Smith of Birmingham learnt Lollardy from her husband but after his death she became an active teacher and preacher with converts to her own credit. Joan Gest, also of Birmingham, converted her husband to the sect and many other women played a positive role, acting as messengers between the conventicles and conducting Bible classes. They showed the same adventurous theorising as the men. Margery Goyte, widow, of Ashbourne in Derbyshire, was one of the many Lollards who denied the doctrine of the Virgin Birth, claiming that Joseph was physically the father of Christ.[1]

A few virtuous hermits or churchmen kept their vows of chastity but they did not impose an undue strain on the consciences of their fellow clergy or on lay society. We know from John Bromyard's testimony that clerical bastards were commonplace; a Lollard suggested, as a cure to the poverty and immorality of the clergy, that they should marry and take jobs, conducting divine worship only every other Sunday so as to have time to earn their families' keep. Love poems tell us the sad tales of virtue lost to Jankin the priest and of nights of love with a holy water clerk. Pulpit denunciations of the lechery in the lay world and faithless wives receive confirmation from many sources—the authors of the Coventry Miracle Play of the Annunciation give nearly a fifth of the dialogue of their short play to Joseph's accusations of Mary when he finds she is going to have a child.

Infidelity was expected of any lusty young wife of an old husband because sexuality was enjoyed. The congregations who took so little heed of the churchman in his church, took no notice at all in their private lives. St Paul's notion that sex was for the procreation of children only, and the modern notion that medieval people were ashamed of their sex are equally absurd in the face of the poems, plays and journals of the period. Margery Kempe, that passionate and strange spirit, tells us that before she got religion, she and her husband John had 'great delectation either of them in using of other'. For a time after her great renunciation of sex her husband was still able to tempt her back to the old happy ways. The point about Margery is that while a few churchmen approved her commitment to chastity, most of them and all her neighbours wrote her off as an eccentric.

When the merchant's son John Kempe married Margery, daughter of Mayor Brunham, the young couple were as pleased with each other as much as their families were with the match. Of course it was an arranged marriage; it could not be otherwise when the families were members of the town's little ruling oligarchy, but arranged marriages too could be happy. The fact that twenty years and fourteen children later Margery felt the call to a life of religious chastity can hardly be laid at the door of her father. The fact that she was able to force John to resign the marital rights awarded him by the law of both God and man is the measure of her wayward and overbearing personality. The odd new contract between man and wife was ratified in a ceremony before the Bishop of Lincoln.

It was John Kempe's misfortune to be an ordinary man married to an extraordinary woman. 'Woe is him that is bound, for he must abide.' The second shepherd in the Townely cycle is talking good Church doctrine as well as for generations of men. The fifteenth-century husband could beat his wife with the sanction of Church and society, could expect a full housekeeping service as of right and was the woman's lord and master in the most literal sense of those words, but as John Kempe found, personality has a way of ignoring right. The home life of Mak, the sheep stealer in the Townely Shepherd's Pageant, was no bed of roses. Returning with a fine ewe which he has rustled from his

friends' flock, he calls his wife to come and look and is met
with a tirade.

> Why, who wanders, who wakes? Who comes, who goes?
> Who brews, who bakes? What makes me thus hoarse?
> And then
> It is pity to behold –
> Now in hot, now in cold,
> Full woefull is the household
> That wants a woman.

'Woe is him that is bound, for he must abide.' But who
in fact was bound and what precisely constituted a binding
marriage? For the vast majority, a church service followed
by consummation. But the archaic pagan rites of betrothal
were still powerful enough to constitute a prior commitment. To her fury, the imperious Margaret Paston discovered her wilful daughter Margery had secretly plighted
her troth to the totally ineligible Richard Calle, one of the
family's estate stewards. In desperation, having failed to
browbeat the girl into a public denunciation that this private
oath had ever been made, Margaret called in the family. The
situation was pressing because the Bishop of Norwich, having got wind of the secret betrothal, was insisting on an inter-
view to establish the facts. He refused to accept Margaret's
assurance that nothing had passed between the two and that
her daughter was still free to choose. The Pastons finally ran
out of manœuvres and the bishop was able to question Margery. After he had urged her to follow her mother's wishes
and warned her that she would be disowned if she did not,
he asked for the exact form of words she had used to Richard
for he would 'understand the words, whether it made matri-
mony or not...And she rehearsed what she had said, and said
if those words made it not sure she said boldly that she would
make it sure ere than she went thence; for she said she thought
in her conscience she was bound, whatsoever the words

were.' After this Calle was examined 'apart by himself' to see whether his story matched Margery's. But the lovers held firm and the bishop had to tell Margaret that, though they might not have been married in a church, the two were married in the eyes of God.

Margery's steely courage won her the husband she loved and her mother's unyielding hostility. Such courage was rare indeed – few girls attempted to change the system of the arranged marriage. Margery had only been saved by the convention of the betrothal and the Church's insistence that the girl's consent must be given to a marriage. Usually it was an easy matter for the family to force a daughter to give this 'willingly' – by getting herself betrothed Margery had established a strong position. Generally a girl, no matter how spirited, had to submit to her parents' arrangements. 'As for Stockton's daughter,' wrote John Paston to another member of the family, 'she shall be wedded in haste to Skeerne as she told, herself, to my silk maid, which maketh part of such as she shall wear, to whom she break her heart, and told her she should have had Master Paston.'

But for the girl who could keep her emotional involvement in check the conventions of marriage and the lottery of death offered possibilities. After the first marriage she was free of her family and could choose her husbands where she pleased. Life expectancy was lower and women tended then as now to live longer than men. Few marriages lasted more than twenty years, most a good deal less; the very fact that family politics might force an old rich husband on the girl could work to her advantage. In a society where love and sex were not the decisive criteria of marriage, women could and very often did, go on marrying with advantage – deploying the initial capital brought in by the first unwanted match to the best possible advantage. John Stokker's death left his widow Joan a fabulously rich heiress – thanks to his legacy and those of two previous rich merchant husbands. On her fourth trip to the market the lady, whom Adam of Usk dubbed 'the modern Jezebel', joined the ranks of the nobility as the fifth Lady Abergavenny. It had taken her just three years of good marrying and fortunate dying.[2]

In the city, in the absence of an effective merchant banking system, the heiress was an important source of capital. William Nightingale, draper, acquired £100 and a thirty-four-year lease on a valuable dock-side site on his marriage, not to mention a thoroughbred Irish horse. A few years later the court of the Mercers' Company formally congratulated one of the young candidates for the company membership who had persuaded a rich widow to marry him. In their view it was 'a worship to the fellowship for a young man out of the livery to be preferred to such a rich marriage'. He was duly inaugurated a full member.

This was a love match, nevertheless. Unless she had a young family in need of a guardian, the widow could dictate her own terms if indeed she married at all. Elizabeth Kirkeby, left a considerable fortune as well as a flourishing goldsmith's business under the terms of her husband's will, was, in city eyes, a highly desirable property. She was also a shrewd woman who had no intention of making a second marriage but every intention of exploiting the marriage market. Her suitors included George Bulstrode, a draper whose business needed capital for expansion; Elizabeth accepted his advances and even, so he claimed later, signed a marriage contract with him. Over the next three years he showered her with gold, silver, jewellery and, as he bitterly noted, a 'popinjay which I might have sold to my Lady Hungerford'. He spent a good deal of time on her affairs 'intending it should have been for his own weal and profit in time coming'. Yet when he got back from a business trip to Spain (where, incidentally he had spent £400 of his own money on her behalf), she had found herself another friend. She held them both at bay and died without remarrying, leaving a personal fortune estimated at £2000.[3]

Wiser men than Bulstrode were careful to research the

market before committing themselves and might pay as much as twelve and a half per cent of the expected dowry for the services of a good marriage broker. His job was to convince the father that the applicant would, in due course, be able to guarantee the girl and her children a good settlement. It was a harsh environment for young love. But the Kempes' marriage shows how successful even these arranged affairs could be, and, once married, the talented woman found there could be considerable scope for her in a city business community.

In fact one trade was almost exclusively in the hands of women, from manufacture to distribution. Although the finest silk came from Italy and the East, there was a growing market for cheaper home-finished products made from raw imported silk. In 1368 the London Silkwomen had presented a petition to the Lord Mayor against a 'Lombard' merchant who had succeeded in establishing a monopoly of the raw product. A century later the Guild of London Silkwomen was petitioning for protection against Italian imports of finished goods – by the 1450s silk was a specialised and profitable business.[4]

There were three basic craft processes involved. The spinning of the raw silk into yarn; weaving this yarn into the coarser types of silk fabric, and making the material up into garments. The work was done on the putting-out system and the set-up was ideally suited for exploitation by a merchant's wife. Gossip with neighbours and even the servants meant that she could easily raise a list of addresses where the woman would be interested in part-time work, and her husband's business made for easy contacts with foreign importers and English traders. The working capital was often a loan from the husband but the businesses were firmly in the control of the women. Occasionally an unmarried woman went into trade on her own account. Agnes Langton, launching her business on a legacy from her father, travelled in the provinces to sell her goods and died comparatively young while attending the Stourbridge fair. She left debts to Genoese merchants totalling £300 15s, which were taken over by her mother.

Agnes, a confident and established business woman, dealt direct with the Italian importer – others might prefer to use an English broker. The size of her debts, which her mother was able to honour, shows the extent of her operation. The London Silkwomen were not engaged in a pin-money operation. Guild members regularly made bulk contracts with Italian and English dealers up to £50 and £60 in an industry where skilled workers reckoned to earn between 4d and 6d a day; most of the women engaged their own apprentices.

The terms of service were regulated by standard forms of indenture between parents and mistress. Boys as well as girls were occasionally taken on and, like apprentices in every trade, they were liable to find themselves exploited by harsh employers as general household skivvies. But the job could be interesting and even responsible. Joan Woulbarrow, apprenticed to Katherine Dore, was in charge of distributing the commissions and materials to the 'costumers and workers in Soper Lane and elsewhere' and paying for the completed jobs as she picked them up. Apprentices are often mentioned in wills. Isabel Fremely left a valuable green silk girdle garnished with silver to one of her girls and Agnes Brundyssch, who proudly described herself as 'citizen and silk woman', remembered to make a formal remission of the indenture period her apprentice still had to run at the time of her death.

There is no reason to think that Agnes exaggerated in ranking herself a citizen. The fact that she and most of her fellow guild members were, or had been, married, had little bearing on their business status. The articles of apprenticeship between mistress and parents named the mistress's husband as a matter of form, but it was made clear that he had no active part in the transaction. Women are often named as creditors and debtors in their own right without reference to husbands and, to enjoy the full privileges of a London trader, it was only necessary for a woman to be recognised as a 'fem sole'–i.e. independent. Occasionally someone appeared before the mayor to vindicate her claims to the status but others, like William Horne's widow, simply did not bother with the formalities.

There were 'fem sole' entrepreneurs outside London. A preamble to a statute of 1482 refers to 'the men and women of the whole craft of silk work of London, cities, towns, boroughs and villages of this realm of England'. But women were by no means confined to the silk trade. Joan Lister of Nottingham was a wholesale dealer in corn; Dame Alice Andrew of Orwell is registered as the owner of the *Bartholomew*, though whether she decided matters of cargoes and sailings or merely took her share of the profit is not clear. Dame Ellen Sturmy, on the other hand, was well established as a 'fem sole' during the life of her husband, the famous Bristol merchant Robert Sturmy. No doubt to ensure her independence, Ellen preferred to trade through Southampton and often worked in partnership with William Needham there. Another Bristol widow, Alice Chester, continued her husband's import business bringing in iron from Spain and extending the range of the operation. Her benefactions to the city included the building of a loading crane down on the docks and a magnificent new rood screen for the church of All Saints. Husbands did not discount the obvious abilities of such wives. Sturmy directed that the disposition of his large assets should be in the hands of his wife.

Ellen Sturmy was probably the most successful career woman of her generation but there were many other widows who improved the family business. Alice Bacon, continuing her husband's dockyard stores and depository, won the important contract to store the gear salvaged from Henry V's navy when it was disbanded in the late 1430s.[5] On the same waterfront women handled one stage of Southampton's most important export commodity. Once the clumsy and bulky sarplers of fleeces from the Cotswolds and elsewhere had been weighed by the Italian agents they were handed over to the woman's guild of woolpackers to be made up into compact bundles for stowage.

Women are found in many other jobs which today we would reckon men's work. A girl was apprenticed to a carpenter by her father, who complained that the carpenter was not teaching her the craft as he had promised to. Robert Parys of London left 20s to 'Eleanor, the woman who runs my garden across the Thames'. Before she turned religious, Margery Kempe had revelled in the conventional outlets for feminine excess and her husband eventually had to point out that her expenditure on clothes and jewellery was bringing the family to the verge of bankruptcy. 'Shrewdly and shortly', she retorted that her father had been mayor and she had a position to keep up in the town; her assets were in any case bigger than her husband's. But her indignation was followed by a more practical response and, with her husband as a nominal partner, she went into brewing. Three years later the venture was obviously tottering so Margery bought herself a horse mill. The technology had been known for at least half a century (in the 1360s a carpenter at the Abbey of Glastonbury had been sent to make sketches of the one at work on the estates of Lady Elizabeth de Burgh), but under Margery's management the experiment was more disastrous than the brewing had been. Perhaps the machinery was at fault; perhaps, as the miller declared, the Devil had got into the horse or, of course, he may have been cheating her. Margery failed, not because she was a woman affronting the conventions of a man's world, but because she was no good at business. Alice Chester and Ellen Sturmy had shown what could be done while at Coventry Margery Russell's import operations were on such a scale that on one voyage alone she was freighting cargoes worth £800.[6]

Margery Kempe simply was not in the same league, while as a brewer she may have been too honest for success. A comic epilogue tacked on to the Pageant of the Harrowing of Hell, performed by the Cooks and Innkeepers of Chester, shows how, when Christ liberated the souls in torment, only one was left behind – an alewife. 'Welcome, dear darling,' leers Satan, 'though Jesus be gone withour menie, Yet shalt thou abide here still with me.' Too late, too late, the wicked woman repents. 'Of cans I kept no true measure: …With hops I made my ale strong; …Selling small cups, money to win, Against all truth to deal.' She was, she admits, in league with 'mighty Mahomet' and many a time came near to poisoning her customers.

> With all masters, minglers of wine in the night,
> (I Brewed) so, blending against daylight;
> Such new made claret is cause full right
> Of sickness and disease.

She had begun her sorry career as a barmaid, a job rich in opportunities for the medieval fallen woman. The town pub was in most cases the local whore house and in the absence of evidence to the contrary it could be assumed that the girl behind the bar was fair game. One of the many fifteenth-century continuations to Chaucer's *Canterbury Tales* begins with the Prologue 'of the merry adventure of the Pardoner with the Tapster at Canterbury'. While the other members of the party are out sightseeing the Pardoner makes a pass at the Tapster. She shows him her bedroom, 'where she sleeps naked each night' and while the rest visit the cathedral, she goes out shopping for supper. More ambitious than his brother cleric, the Friar makes a play for a nun, but cannot even get a glimpse of her face behind her cowl. His attempt to get hold of a holy water sprinkler and so confront her face to face while he blesses her, is also baulked. With a sounder grasp of tactics the Pardoner is still at the inn and when the Tapster has settled down for her afternoon rest 'surprises her sleeping'. 'You should have coughed as you came in, said she, Where learnt you courtesy?'

The public baths, or stews, were the favourite territory of the capital's good-time girls. The baths were concentrated in Southwark, where the Bishop of Winchester was the major landlord and the girls were universally known as Winchester geese. Europeans had discovered the decadent luxury of the Turkish-style bath during the Crusades and had taken to the idea with uninhibited speed – a twelfth-century Arab diarist describes the shock with which he first saw a naked Frank in the baths, while the Franks were highly amused by the quaint Islamic conventions of modesty which required the wearing of loin cloths, even in the steam room. By Caxton's day the bathhouse was well established. One of Sir Launcelot's adventures, described in Malory's *Morte d'Arthur*, was the rescue of a lady who for five years had been boiling in 'scalding water' by the enchantment of Queen Morgan le Fay. 'And so Sir Launcelot went into the chambre that was as hot as any stew.' And there he found 'the fairest lady that ever he saw...naked as a needle.' Given Sir Launcelot's track record the lady was lucky to escape with a mere rescue; there were moralists among Malory's contemporaries who were shocked by the promiscuity of the mixed bathing in London's baths, though it is not recorded that the Bishop of Winchester was of their number.

Cabaret may have provided an occasional and profitable sideline for the ladies of the town, though this kind of show may have been the preserve of professional dancing girls. It was such a conventional part of the between-course entertainment of any smart banquet that one of his noblemen provided topless dancing girls during a dinner at which the young Henry VI was guest of honour. The king was scandalised and turned on his host with the strongest oath he knew: 'Forsooth, forsooth, ye be to blame.' We hear nothing of such strictures during the reign of Edward IV. Across the Channel, Louis XI's *entrée* to Paris in 1461 was accompanied by a series of tableaux, among them 'three very handsome girls, representing quite naked sirens so that one saw their beautiful breasts, which was a very pleasant sight, and they recited little motets and bergerettes'. Despite pulpit invective and the repressive theological view of sex as merely the means of procreation, it was an age of unbridled sexuality. Family politics, of course, determined the marriage partner of most well-to-do girls and for them the chances of physical fulfilment in their first marriage were something of a lottery. Yet even in this strait-jacket arrangement many husbands and wives learnt to love one another, and with passion. When his beautiful and adored wife died, Thomas, Lord Berkeley was only thirty-eight and still in need of a male heir, yet he did not marry again though he lived another twenty years.

In Italy, if we are to believe the passionate moralisings of San Bernardino, the early decades of the century were a time of permissiveness to surprise even our own enlightened age. 'Be always watching your daughters.' A warning which would have been fully appreciated by any English squire calculating on a good match. 'Let them have nothing to do with servants.' How Margaret Paston would have agreed. But she might have raised her eyebrows at what follows. 'Let them not have too much converse even with their relations; for if you find them pregnant, you need not ask how it happened...Never, never, never let them sleep in the same bed as their brothers as they begin to grow bigger...Hardly trust her even to her own father, when she has reached the age of marriage.' English ecclesiastical court records show that adultery was common bordering on the commonplace, but incest was not the English vice.

Nor were the English of Caxton's day renowned for sodomy – to eighteenth- and nineteenth-century Europe *the* English vice, with sado-masochism. Homosexuality there was. We have seen that Dame Lust and Dame Wanton were to be found sometimes within the convent walls – but since fifteenth-century nuns were also human beings it is barely surprising that their membership should show instances of all human traits. But whereas San Bernardino warns against allowing girls to be left by themselves and paints lurid pictures of 'boys who paint their cheeks and...practise sodomy for gain' these 'unnatural vices' are not targets we find in the English sermons of the day.

What did astonish the foreign observer, at least, was the open display of affection he found in England and particularly among the women, who, according to one Italian, were said to be 'very violent in their passions'. The most ordinary social encounters were framed with kisses. 'When the guests first arrive at an inn the hostess comes out with her whole family to receive them, and they have to kiss her and all the others.' For Erasmus England was populated with 'goddess girls, divinely fair...They come to see you and drink your health in kisses...whomsoever you meet, there are kisses in plenty, and wherever you go the world is full of kisses waiting.' It is not surprising, in such a country, that even the earnest-minded Lollards believed that celibacy was impossible and led to unnatural vice and that the profession of religious vows by widows encouraged infanticide and abortion. A Venetian was surprised at the easy way these 'most beautiful ladies, and most pleasant' kissed all and sundry, and a German was astonished to find the custom as freely practised in the street, even the church, as in the home.

Affable, hot-blooded when roused, and with a forceful independent spirit, the English woman was not the oppressed tool of lust in a man's world that clichéd accounts of medieval life sometimes suggest. There was little the peasant girl could do against the gentleman lecher yet, from the way they often treated their bastard children, it is clear the men concerned also loved their mistresses. Archbishop John Stafford's natural father had given the boy his own name and promoted his career; Richard Bamme of the city of London left £20 to 'Thomas Bishop my bastard son', and many a peasant girl was put in the family way by many a peasant, without benefit of gentry and without any great show of reluctance on her part. The clergy were shocked by some of the 'disgraceful sports', especially on 'Hok' days, but the young men and women who took part were not greatly concerned.

The law barred a bastard from succeeding to the family lands, which was hardly astonishing when lineage, property and prestige were indissolubly linked. The social pressures on bastardy and the unmarried mother were not especially stringent by later standards. Girls who gave birth out of wedlock suffered comparatively small penalties in the manorial courts and at St Bartholomew's Hospital in London they were positively well cared for. William Gregory, who visited it in the 1430s, thought it 'a place of great comfort ...in special unto young women that have misdone that be with child. There they be delivered, and unto the time of purification they have meat and drink of the place's cost, and are full honestly guided and kept.' If the mother died in child-birth her child was brought up at the hospital until the age of seven. Nor was it always the girl who was censured. When one of Edmund Paston's servants 'in plain terms' did 'swive a quene' and had the misfortune to be 'espied by two ploughmen of my mother's', he was dismissed.

Marriages were arranged between peasant families as they were among the gentry. Here too a matchmaker, mediator or marriage broker, was generally employed though in this case it might be a relation – uncle or cousin – if the village had no regular or reliable matchmaker. The idea that marriage is a matter only for the individuals is recent and restricted to industrialised countries and culture. Medieval Europe, like the primitive tribes which still survive today, saw it as an association of kin groups and, because it involved the interests of so many more people than the couple, regarded it as an important institution. Setting up a new home meant the assignment of land or funds from the families' assets, at all levels of society. Since this by definition meant the depletion of other rights it was necessary to bargain closely and to explore the available possibilities so as to ensure that the mar-riage of a son or daughter did not disadvantage the kin but,

on the contrary, improved its position if this was at all possible. As in all poor and underdeveloped societies, people were
too valuable to be wasted and too important, among the
sparse assets that the average kin could boast, to be allowed
to follow their personal preferences in such vital matters.
When Margery Paston held true to her betrothed her mother
called on the whole family for assistance and advice.

Property and marriage were so closely identified that the
link is recognised even in the romances of chivalry. When
Alice la Beale Pilgrim 'said openly in the hearing of many
knights, that "what knight may overcome...shall have me
and all my lands"...many of the knights of the Round Table
were glad, for she was passing fair and of great rents'. But
Alice was fated to fall in love with Sir Alisander and there
was 'great love betwixt them'. As described by Malory it is
love at first sight and mutual, yet when they have exchanged
names Alice proposes that when they 'be more at our hearts'
ease, both ye and I shall tell others of what blood we be come.'
It was an entirely proper subject for discussion. Few individuals wished, any more than did their families, to lower their
social esteem by their marriage. For Alice and Alisander we
may assume that the exchange of genealogical personalia was
merely a pleasant diversion. In real life there were few girls
who would have followed the headstrong Margery Paston
in marrying below their station. Indeed her own cousin,
Clare, considered it would be 'folly to forsake [one of her
suitors] unless you know of another as good or better...if it
is really so that his land is unencumbered'.

Once she was married a girl's station in life was one of subjection to her husband; she exchanged the obedience she had
owed to her father for the obedience she now owed her husband. This at least was the theory, but even in the humblest
household the woman had real responsibilities and independence. In Mak the Shepherd's cottage, the household budget
owed a good deal to the money his wife Gill earned by her
spinning and when he disturbs her, just as she is settling down

for her evening's work, she gives way to her exasperation as many a woman since. 'Any woman who has been a house-wife knows what it means to be got up continually from her work. Thanks to the interminable chores one has no real work to show.' And in the great merchant or noble house-hold the woman's responsibilities as housekeeper were heavy. Paying the servants, buying in provisions for a household of a dozen or more people, keeping an eye on the children's education and tutors, as well as making, mending and buying their clothes, were among the standard 'chores'. In troubled Norfolk, as we have seen, a good head for military tactics and logistics was also a vital asset.

Medieval women were undoubtedly second-class citizens. Entry to the intellectual elite, the priesthood, was denied them. Religious and social theory defined them as inferior to men. Social convention obliged them to submit to mar-riages arranged for them and was generally less tolerant of their sexual adventuring than it was of male philandering. The arts and crafts were almost exclusively the preserve of men. It was a picture unchanged in its general outlines for centuries. Yet in the English fifteenth century that picture had numerous unexpected details. Whatever social or religious convention might prescribe on the theoretical subjection of women, society was simply too poor to ignore half its human resources. The peasant woman laboured as an essential partner with her husband; the noble woman ranked with her male peers and could be called on to discharge typically 'masculine' roles, often with outstanding success. While in the middle ranks of society women could and did compete efficiently in male activities.

It is not proposed that an Ellen Sturmy or a Margaret of Anjou were typical of the women of the fifteenth century; it is proposed that such careers as theirs were not considered freakish by contemporaries and are vital to a full understand-ing of the woman's true place in the age of Caxton.

7

♠♠♠

The Life of Privilege

As he lay dying at his manor house of Rye in Hertfordshire, in the year 1454, Sir Andrew Osgard could look back with pride on a career of service to the crown, profit and prestige. His fortune was founded on the war in France. Among other posts, he had been captain of the garrison of Caen, and he had amassed lands which, at one time, brought him an income of £1000 a year. But the expulsion of the English from their French territories just the year before his death can have caused Sir Andrew little more than a twinge of nostalgic regret; for some years past, he had been busily investing his war profits in England. The castle of New Buckenham and other lands in Norfolk had absorbed £2330; rebuilding his manor house of Emneth near Wisbech £1330; the manor of Rye £1100; and the house there a further £2660. His rent rolls provided a handsome English income while his liquid assets amounted to more than £4600, held in the coffers of a friend.

The figures come from the notebook of William Worcestre, secretary of Sir John Fastolf who had risen from the status of an esquire worth £46 a year, to the rank of baron in France and a knight banneret in England with a rent roll of more than £1450. Worcestre's cash and balance-sheet approach reflects the fact that England was in the slow, socially disruptive process of becoming a money-based economy. Noble households received a large part of their rents in kind; the court, too, lived off the produce of royal manors and one of the most strident complaints against the government of Henry VI was the extortion of the purveyors, the royal officers with the job of commandeering accommodation, transport and produce. The Church received tithes in kind which might consist of manufactured goods as well as crops: in the 1440s, 5000 large bricks were supplied as tithe by the kilns of Tattershall Castle for the rebuilding of the Lincolnshire abbey of Edlington. Peasants all over the country did boon work on the lord's land in return for 'feasts' of barley and wheat bread, oatmeal and ale by the gallon. But in the economically more sophisticated branches of society it was money that greased the wheels, as contemporaries were well aware.

> Man upon earth, whatsoever thou be
> I warn utterly thou gettest no degree,
> Nor no worship will abide with thee,
> But thou have the penny ready to take to.
>
> If thou be a yeoman, a gentleman would be,
> Into some lord's court put thou thee:
> Look thou have spending, large and plenty,
> And alway the penny ready to take to.
>
> If thou be a gentleman and would be a squire,
> Ridest out of country as wild as any fire:
> I thee warn as my friend thou failest of thy desire
> But thou have the penny ready to take to.
>
> If thou be a squire and would be a knight,
> And darest not in armour put thee in fight,
> Then to the king's court high thee full tight,
> And look thou have the penny ready to take to.[1]

Sir Andrew Osgard was one of those who had taken the message to heart. Arriving in England in the 1430s, a penniless

Danish nobleman, he had taken himself at once to the king's court and had, in addition, dared in armour to put him to fight. The reward had been not only money but also that most treasured of all fifteenth-century possessions, 'worship', for as well as his knighthood he could boast service as Member of Parliament for his adopted county of Norfolk. With Sir John Fastolf and a few others, he represented the class of new men who had raised themselves close to the ranks of the nobility and well into the ranks of privilege. That neither of them left a male heir to succeed them was the one bitter failure of their careers.

They demonstrated what was possible in an age when the English social structure was more mobile than it had long been. The rags to riches dream, so much a part of our more recent heritage from the nineteenth century, was well known to the contemporaries of Caxton. The middle decades of the century, we have said, were a period of well-being and prosperity for the lower orders of society. In the Wakefield Shepherds' Pageant Mak's friends, before they realise that his new 'baby' is in fact their lost sheep, offer the 'bairn but sixpence' as a birthday present. It was a labourer's day wage and even between the three of them would have been an act of impossible generosity in a community of peasant paupers. The comparative prosperity of all the social ranks below them, even the poorest, was an unsettling factor in the lives of the privileged and in part explains the cut-throat rivalry between them.

Sumptuary legislation, attempting to regulate this sorry state of affairs, had been passed from the late fourteenth century by successive parliaments, a fact recognised by an act of 1463. Preparing yet again to stop people wearing what they wanted to, though now in the name of economics and the restraint of imports, it comments that earlier 'statutes and ordinances notwithstanding, for lack of punishment and putting them in due execution, the commons of this your said realm, as well men as women, have used and daily do use, excessive and inordinate arrays'. It was too true; merchants' wives dressed themselves like noblewomen and immortalised their shameful presumption on the brass or alabaster monuments on their tombs.

What Osgard and Fastolf and others like them aimed for was a life of luxury and respect enjoyed by so small a fraction of society that it has been estimated that fewer than a thousand families enjoyed an income of more than £100 a year. The comforts and independence that such wealth conferred put its possessors into a category different in kind rather than degree from the rest of society. Either side of the £100 a year boundary stood the extensive class of gentry and merchants who aspired to scale the ladder of degree and aped the manners of the richer. The spectrum ranged from the £50 a year squire like the young Fastolf to the incredible wealth of a man like Ralph, Lord Cromwell, whose household at Tattershall Castle numbered a hundred or so, whose London stables alone housed 120 horses and whose annual outgoings were reckoned in the region of £5000.

Such oriental extravagance rested on inherited land, pensions and perquisites from the royal exchequer, the plunder of one's neighbours and, of course, wholesale extortion. When he died in 1455 Lord Cromwell's executors 'full greatly moved' in their conscience, restored lands to the value of £5500 to their lawful owners. But this takes no account of the constant petty extortion of money and goods from any who were too weak to resist and the steady oppression of the peasantry. The conscience money paid out by Cromwell's executors was matched by others in church building and charitable foundations but there were even churchmen honest enough to recognise that many of these good works were built on the proceeds of injustice. Observed one sermon writer: 'I am sure...that either they must be strong thiefs to rob their neighbours in the country, or wrongful extortioners, to maintain their proud estate, or must fall into debt for borrowing to that proud array.'

Account books and household records fully bear out the accusation. John Pickering, receiver general to the third Duke of Buckingham, meticulously noted his diligence in his lord's affairs; disciplining parkers who pilfered green and dead wood for their own fencing or fuel, or tenants who hunted in the lord's warren with greyhounds or ferrets. And if, by a lucky chance, a tenant managed to prosper undetected it was not for long. John Dyx of Padbury, who had quietly amassed chattels valued at some £18, was duly seized and a surety for his body of £40 extracted from his family until he agreed to compound for his liberty in the sum of 4 marks (£2 13s 4d). The duke, who personally scrutinised every page of his own accounts, kept his servants tightly under control, encouraging them to spy on one another as a further precaution against losing his money.

This Scrooge-like figure, with his money-bag avarice suited in the conventional scheme to a city merchant, was the scion of one of the most ancient and noble families of England. Such behaviour might be expected of a newcomer like Fastolf, 'Cruel and vengeful…and for the most part without pity or mercy', but contemporaries lamented the trend in their days when 'lords be led all out of kind' for 'law they learn' and 'knights be made customs men'. But it was a time when wealth grew with careful management and a man could be robbed by his servants if he was not business-minded. The seigneurial administration was a scaled-down model of the royal, with its chancellor, receivers, estate stewards, bailiffs and 'officers…to attend sufficiently to all the worldly needs of their lands' and as with the royal government, where the king was the initiator and prime decision-maker, if the lord let things slide, 'their servants made their own profit'. Commines, that sardonic observer of the French court, had often seen it happen: 'Lords, who have not thirteen livres in rents, puff themselves up and say, "Speak to my men", thinking that by these words they imitate the very greatest men.'

It was, in Commines view, 'right and proper' that lords should surround themselves with 'clerks and lawyers...when they are good men', but essential that the lord himself should be able to deal with them on equal terms. 'For they have some precedent or story on the tip of their tongues for every occasion which they distort in order to present it in the best light.' There were few English aristocrats in the fifteenth century who did not follow the advice. The time was long past when the lay nobility were the illiterate thugs and popinjays beloved by historical romance. Thugs and popinjays there often were but, as will be seen later, some were also talented writers and all were quite able to keep abreast of their household affairs if so inclined and could pen a well-turned letter if a secretary was not to hand. There were few gentlemen of birth who had not been to Oxford, Cambridge or one of the Inns of Court in London. The landowners' necessary enthusiasm for law was a prime factor in the rise of the Inns to the status of secular near-universities during this century. Precedents, titles and papers of all kinds were vital in an age of endless law suits and sharp contention over property. Already in the 1400s those without the money or the power to corrupt it, were criticising the English system of unwritten case law.

> In all kingdoms, their law is written;
> For whim or fear they change it not.
> In England, as all men witten,
> Law, like cattle, is sold and bought.[2]

What is now England's 'proud heritage' of the common law was, in the age of a Sir John Fastolf, a curse to many a poor and protectorless litigant. The expense account of any gentleman's agent worth his salt was peppered with such entries as '...to Clough and Forster to labour the jury', 'Item delivered to Clough to drink with the jury'. And the juries sold their honour dear. Early in the century a case in Wiltshire

cost Ralph Green a total of £2 3s 4d in this kind of 'hospitality' alone. The nub of the problem was the sheriff and
sometimes it required a more deeply laid strategy than simply
a drinking session. If the 'labour...to the sheriff for returning
of such panels as will say for me in my right', failed, the
under-sheriff might be approached to delay the action. If this
too drew a blank there was a sequence of tactics, against
which only the most upright of under-sheriffs would resist.
'If that will not be, entreat him to make a good panel; if that
will not be, to return an indifferent panel...if that will not
be, to get a copy of the panel he will return, and entreat as
many of the inquest as you can...that they will not appear;
and those that appear not and they be not seen in the town,
they shall never lose money there for it.' Small wonder that
the poet urged 'And look thou have the penny ready to take
to.'

The only protection possible against this kind of thing was
the lordship of a great and influential man. The network of
patronage is traced in the letters of the period; small men
looking for patrons and great men looking for clients.
Friendship and relationship, even of the remotest kind, were
the cement of security and influence in a society without
corporate organisations of a reliable and uncorrupt system
of law. As in the societies of the primitive world, the kin
group and the affinity were the natural and crucial organisations of social structure. As a member of the Stonor family
put it, 'it is reasonable [for] a gentleman to know his pedigree
and his possibility' – the writer was complaining that one of
his third cousins had recently cut him.

Good relations with one's own family were a first step.
The wealthy extended their protection and recruited their
supporters from less wealthy members of the nobility or the
gentry. These retainers were the successors to the feudal
menies of an earlier age and ultimately the war bands of the
Germanic nobility; in the disturbed decades of the fifteenth
century the retainer's military function was still important

John, Duke of Bedford, the English regent in France, shown in a characteristic role for a patron of the arts, receiving the dedication of a book
from its author.   *By permission of the Archbishop of Canterbury
and the Trustees of Lambeth Palace Library*

and when a conflict was brewing in the locality short-term indentures, for the duration, were made with those who wished to serve. Between campaigns such men were laid off. But the life-retainer was expected to serve in peace as well as in war and was a full member of the household even if his attendance might be only occasional. The statutes against livery and maintenance, which had been passed in the reign of Richard II, had attempted to stop the casual recruitment of short-term retainers. In the prevailing conditions of the mid-century civil turmoil such laws were often breached and the recruitment of life retainers, permitted by law, continued.

The wearing of another man's livery conferred two distinct advantages: money fees and protection, at law or against the illegal pressures of other lords. The advantages of livery were available from the bottom to the top of the social scale. The shepherds, in remarkably outspoken criticism of the oppressive system, complained that they were 'hammed, fortaxed and rammed, made hand-tamed with these gentlery men'. The complaint was not simply that life at the bottom was hard, but that it was especially so for those who were not 'lord-fast' men.

> Such servants as I, that sweat and works,
> Eat our bread full dry, and that me irks.
> We are oft wet and weary when master-men wink [sleep];
> Yet come full lately both to dinner and drink.

These lord-fast masters' men enjoyed the security of a regular wage and the petty power of the master's agents in the rural community; but there were knights and even noblemen willing to supplement their income by retainers from others. The dowager Duchess of Buckingham paid fees to the Earl of Shrewsbury and Lord Hastings, among others, as stewards of certain of her manors. Sir Humphrey Stafford of Grafton, in the West Midlands, a distant relation of the Buckinghams, received annual retainer fees from the duke and six other lords. In his own neighbourhood Sir Humphrey was a man of considerable influence and as such was a useful agent for those noble patrons with interests in the locality.

A man who was well placed to do others service could expect to receive offers, and the best placed of all were those at court. Lord Hastings, the friend and confidant of Edward IV, earned himself a fat living from fees paid by other men to use his influence on their behalf; Ralph Alygh, who was just one of the squires in the household of the chancellor, agreed in return for twenty shillings a year to support Fastolf's tenants in the Southwark district. Good lordship was not just a question of fees; the tenant and retainer expected his patron to be able to further his interest at court or in the county and the patron was as anxious to do so, for it increased his prestige and thus his influence if he could deliver.

Fastolf died a few months after engaging the services of Ralph Alygh: the weeks that followed were a scramble to secure the large inheritance. 'There is laboured many mediators to entitle the king in his good,' wrote William Paston. Two years later the family is still on the war-path, this time after the manor of Dedham and again the arena is the court. This time the younger John Paston is in town 'labouring daily my Lord Essex...every morning ere he went to court'. For a time it looked as though Essex 'was not willing to move the king therein', and John began to wonder whether perhaps the noble lord had plans of his own. From Essex's point of view, however, this country gentleman's daily pestering was as misplaced as it was irritating. The courtier's art lay in choosing the right time to broach a subject and in the fullness of time the Pastons did get their manor.

They had a strong case, having been loyal Yorkist supporters and so having a claim on the new king. Eventually Essex was able to report that he had raised the subject at court and 'rehearsed the king's answer therein: how that, when he had moved the king in the said manor of Dedham, beseeching him to be your good lord therein, considering the service and true heart that ye have done and ought to him, and in especial the right ye have thereto, he said he would be your good lord therein as he would be to the poorest man in England'. A promise of good lordship from the king himself was the nearest one could get to a guarantee.

The power to provide good lordship, or good mastership – the two were not equally prestigious as Lord Scales had occasion to remind the overweening Sir John Fastolf – was the highest exercise of his 'worship' open to a nobleman or, at the somewhat lower, Fastolfian level, a gentleman. A man's 'worth'-ship was his most vital attribute in a world where prestige was the ingredient of success and the two were often synonymous with survival. Something of its potency lingers in the fossilised honorific 'his worship, the mayor', but the nearest modern equivalent is the semi-magical power of the word 'confidence' in the financial world. When a wife addresses her husband as 'right worshipful' or a son writes to his 'right reverend and worshipful mother' it is not a matter of empty formulas. A contemporary traces the ancestry of the Dukes of Suffolk back to William Pole, a merchant of Hull, who had grown to be 'a worshipful man...by fortune of the world'. The Lord Chancellor lets it be known that he would have Sir John Fastolf 'buried worshipfully' and within the city boundaries and at its functions the Lord Treasurer himself is reckoned second to the worship of the mayor.

In the year 1464 the serjeants at law invited the treasurer to their annual banquet at Ely House held to celebrate the admission of new members to the order of the coif – the equivalent of taking silk. The mayor, Matthew Philip, a noted member of the Goldsmiths' Company, was naturally the principal guest, but when the guests went in to dinner he found that the seat of honour had been reserved for the lord treasurer. Without another word, the mayor's party left the hall. Too late the marshal of the feast recognised his breach of protocol. Stewards and servants were hurriedly dispatched to the lobby with 'meat, bread, wine and many diverse sotelties [pastries]', but the mayor was not to be placated. The offence against his 'worship' and, by extension to the city itself, was not to be atoned by scullions and pastry cooks; he left Ely House and 'made dinner at home with his aldermen'.[3]

If umbrage taken on this scale strikes us as ridiculous the fate of Sir Ralph Gray, in the same year, may help to adjust the perspective. Clearing up the Lancastrian opposition in the north had taken the Earl of Warwick the best part of three years; the capture of Bamborough castle after a stubborn siege concluded the operation. The commander, Sir Ralph, was not only condemned to death for his contumacy but singled out for an exemplary death. The execution was preceded by elaborate and humiliating preliminaries, designed 'so that thou shouldst be degraded of thy worship, noblesse and arms, as of the order of knighthood'. A man's worship was rated on a par with his nobility.

Nevertheless, worship was not an inherent quality like nobility; it had to be constantly buttressed and demonstrated. It is in this context that we should understand the conspicuous consumption, the egregious feasting and extravagant dress of the medieval magnate. Underlying such sophisticated interpretations of the modern observer there was, no doubt, an exuberant, half unbelieving delight that, in a world of grinding scarcity, the rich man could actually eat more than he needed and waste where others wanted. Sir John Dinham's family relished the fact that their father hunted with arrows bound in gold and that he and his lady slept in a bed which would have cost a poor esquire four years' income. When Sir Andrew Osgard made an annual allowance of £100 to his chapel or Henry Scrope amassed more than ninety copes among the vestments of his chaplains, they were not simply concerned with the well-being of their souls. It was a competitive world where the prizes went to the great or the apparently so. 'Every lord beholdeth other, how he is arrayed, how he is horsed, how he is manned' and very often 'to perform this, their own livelihoods will not suffice'. For many, even in the highest ranks of society, debt was the reverse of the coin of 'largess' – that quality which the man of worship was expected, above all, to display. When his nephew's wife died, William Harleston of Denham in Suffolk wrote to the young man whose income had largely depended on the lady's lands, to warn him against running up debts. 'For god's sake be ware, for now you may break your household with your honour and worship, now after the decease of my good lady your wife, and stabilise, now wisely with a convenient fellowship so as you may keep within your livelihood.'

But if he advised a 'convenient', that is sufficient, fellowship Harleston would not for a moment have recommended dispensing with retainers altogether. A man's household was the outward sign of his worship. When the Duke of York went to dinner with Richard Beauchamp, Earl of Warwick, at Rouen in the spring of 1431, his retinue consisted of four knights, twelve esquires and fourteen yeomen. Forty years later, a correspondent reported that the Duke of Suffolk could not come to London himself 'at this time to his worship' because too many of his servants were at home for the Christmas festivities. Worship is the attribute which, more than any other, marks the privileged classes in society out from the rest. Once the thriving yeoman or citizen could afford to worry about his social standing and others came to accept his pretensions, he had entered the bottom grade of that elite category headed by the aristocracy. In the tight little community of Lynn, Margery Kempe, the mayor's daughter, had a recognised status, however absurd and insignificant it might appear to the local nobility. For them the notion of worship was still governed by the antiquated but fascinating code of chivalry.

To us it seems obvious that the high ideals of honour, loyalty, liege homage and knighthood have little place in the moneyed self-interest of fifteenth-century society. Many contemporaries thought the same and lamented the passing of former virtues. Thomas Hoccleve, who died in mid-century, had dedicated his *Regiment of Princes* to the young Henry V in the hope that he would restore the old values:

> For that I would that the high degree
> Of Chivalry universally
> Bare up his head and bend not awry.

But another poet saw that the foundation values of honour were too far eroded:

> Winter's weather and woman's thought,
> And lords' love changeth oft:
> This is the sooth if it be sought,
> For service is no heritage.[4]

When the lords themselves could not be trusted to deal honourably with their servants it was small wonder that a steward 'would forsake his master and get him a new, if he thought he should...' and that 'much of all the country is so disposed'. 'What he commandeth, they be obedient to do, while that he of good is abundant'; the solvent power of money was seeping at the foundations and weakening the whole social fabric. As always, when people lament the passing of 'the good old days', the problem is to locate them. In the mordant words of one historian, 'those who wish to believe in a golden age when men's appetites were subdued by simple faith are well advised to seek it...in the period before 1066, for which there are practically no records'. In the later Middle Ages: 'If public duty was ever remembered, it came at any rate second to a man's over-riding duty to his family and friends.' Far more interesting than the invectives against decadence, the background hiss of virtually every society, is the tenacity of the knightly values and assumptions.

The code of chivalry had been born in the murderous
mêlées which had become a popular diversion for the warrior
gentry of the later eleventh century. These friendlies to the
death involved scores, sometimes hundreds of combatants;
men were killed, ransoms were taken and fortunes made and
lost. William Marshall, the most famous knight of all, had
risen from penury to be one of the greatest landowners in
England and the honoured adviser of King John and guardian
of his boy successor, Henry III. But he was the last to build
his fortune on the spoils of the tourney which was being
disciplined by rules and conventions. By the 1200s men were
no longer willing to risk lands and prestige on the chances
of a mock battle. The tournament was becoming part of a
courtly culture with a tradition, code and ethics to rival the
spiritual values proclaimed by the Church. At its height,
chivalry was almost a lay religion, enjoying a more ardent
commitment than its devotees paid to the religion of the
clerics.

Its holy books were the Arthurian legends which had
swept Europe from the Cheviots to the Apennines within
years of the publication of Geoffrey of Monmouth's *History
of the Kings of Britain*, in the 1130s. Later writers introduced
a spiritual content lacking in Geoffrey's supposedly historical
narrative and this, in amalgam with the conventions of
courtly love and the still more important conventions of warfare, gave the military aristocracy a mythology for its life
style and real aspirations. Christ himself was sometimes por-
trayed as the paragon of knighthood and the Harrowing of
Hell as a great exploit of chivalry. The institution of knighthood was as venerable as the orders of the Church. Heralds
traced the origins of their office to its institution by Julius
Caesar, just as clerks traced their orders through the Apostolic
Succession back to St Peter and through him to Christ. It
was held that the Romans had won the empire of the world
because of their 'valour and warlike skill' as the 'votaries of
chivalry'. The Chronicles of Waurin attributed the victories

of Henry V to his revival of Roman standards, for 'well he kept the discipline of chivalry, as did the Romans in former times'. In certain circumstances this noble and ancient institution could take precedence over the Church itself. A clerk who took up arms was to be treated as a soldier, according to a precedent of the 1370s, and if he offended against the laws of war he was to be tried before the Constable and not in the ecclesiastical courts.

The Court of Chivalry, the name for the military court which was presided over by the Constable of England, and its French counterpart were very important tribunals during the wars in France. Their deliberations concerned both honour and profit. A prince who committed himself to war made himself vulnerable to the humiliation of defeat and the strict regulations which in theory governed the conduct of war, were to protect the general's honour as well as the rights of the combatants. When Philip the Good of Burgundy was forced to withdraw from before Calais in 1436, he had a proclamation read through the army that he had never laid formal siege to the place but had merely, as it were, bivouacked before it. A state of siege was adjudged to exist when the attacker had sent a herald to summon surrender and, on refusal, fired his cannon against the walls. For the besieged the convention was weighty; until the formalities were concluded they might honourably resist without fear of unrestrained sack and pillage in the event of capitulation. Philip had good reason to remind his troops of the formula to protect their morale from the dishonour of retreat.

London's ballad-mongers were not in the least impressed by the duke's huffing and puffing, but we can at least recognise some practical point behind Philip's action. Chivalry for its own sake, however, is the only explanation for a somewhat startling episode in Henry V's historic and dangerous march from Harfleur to Calais. On the night of 23 October 1415, with the French army known to be close by, the king overshot the rendezvous point for the night's camp by two miles. Nevertheless he and his entourage pitched camp beyond the protection of the main army because the king considered it a dishonourable retreat to move back once he had donned his coat armour.

Such gallant play acting no doubt raised the morale in the ranks, but for many of the knights in the army it was also a correct and laudable act of chivalry. Nor was the world of honour forgotten in the time-serving calculations of the civil wars in England. After Tewkesbury, Edward IV dubbed new knights on the field of victory, among them the sheriffs of Staffordshire, Devon and Herefordshire. In planning the disgrace of Sir Ralph Gray after Bamborough, and through him the whole Lancastrian cause, Edward's advisers drew on all the still potent symbolism of chivalry. Gray's adjudged treason was the worse because he 'had taken the order of knighthood of the Bath, and any so taking that order ought to keep the faith the which he makes'. In the ceremony as at first devised and promulgated, Sir Ralph's spurs were to be struck off with the hand of the master cook and his own proper coat of arms to be torn off his body by the kings and heralds of arms, 'and another coat of thine arms reversed, the which thou shouldst have worn of thy body, going to deathward'. It was a terrible warning of the penalties that the Court of Chivalry could impose. The mere proclamation of the sentence meant total disgrace. Sir Ralph was spared much of the ceremonies but not public penance. 'Thou shalt go on thy feet to the town's end and there thou shalt be laid down and drawn to a scaffold made for thee and thou shalt have thy head smite off thy body to be buried in the friary, thy head where it please the king.' Lord Audley, convicted of treason in the reign of Henry VII, was led to his death wearing 'a coat armour of paper upon him all to-torn'.

Such public and humiliating penalties had a very practical function, for honour was one of the most important sanctions in the business aspects of war. On 12 July 1421, Nicholas Molyneux and John Winter entered into a contract in the church of St Martin at Harfleur which made them sworn brothers in arms. The ceremony between these two modest esquires was much the same as the solemn exchange of sealed letters between the Duke of Brittany and the Count of Charolais years later or the agreement pledged by four French soldiers on the field of Montreuillon in 1475 who swore 'all four to be brothers-in-arms and live and die by one another'. The high-flown language of chivalry decorates what are essentially business contracts.

Molyneux and Winter, promising to be loyal to one another without dissimulation or fraud, agreed that if either were taken prisoner, the other should find ransom money up to £1000; that they would pool their surplus loot which was to be held *pro tempore* in the coffers of a London church; that the first to return to England would invest it to mutual advantage. Fifteen years on the two were still in business, buying English manors with their proceeds of the wars and the famous Boar's Head tavern in Southwark.

The esquires held faith to their mutual advantage but the bonds between brothers in arms sometimes transcended mere business interests and could even be forged inadvertently. In the year 1420 the Seigneur de Barbasan commanded the gallant defence of the town of Melun. During the siege he fought hand to hand with Henry V in the mines which had been driven beneath the town walls. When the place fell the Seigneur, who had been party to the murder of John the Fearless of Burgundy, the father of Henry's ally Duke Philip, was put on trial for his life and was condemned in the king's court. But, we are told, he appealed to the judgement of the officers of arms and 'his appeal was by them...approved' on the following grounds:

...that no man having his brother-in-arms in his possession...[might not] put him to death for any displeasure or occasion, and that he [the Seigneur] was brother-in-arms to the king by arms; and approved that he had fought with

the king hand to hand in the mine...; which battle was
held by the heralds of arms in like strength as if he had
fought with the king body to body within the lists.[5]

Thanks to a technical point in the code of honour, Barbasan
found his sentence commuted to life imprisonment and nine
years later, when the French recaptured Château Gaillard
where he was being held, regained his liberty.

In no aspect of warfare were the laws of honour tighter
or more binding than in the matter of ransoms. The first
point to establish was the identity of the captor. In the confusion of the battlefield, with the victorious side 'running and
making prisoners' wherever they could find them, it was not
uncommon for a noble to yield himself to a succession of
'captors' who then dashed off to secure another profitable
prize. Dismounted and probably unarmed in combat, a
knight was easy prey to common foot soldiers and might
pledge his word to any opponent who seemed able to protect
him until the killing was over. To make good his claim, the
captor had to be the first to receive the pledged word of the
captive; he had to be the first man to seize the captive's right
gauntlet and to shake him by the right hand; and then ensure,
either in person or through some reliable lieutenant, that the
prisoner's life was secure. If this was done, and the gauntlet
produced as proof, the prisoner was bound by his word of
honour to be subject to his master until the ransom was paid.
This promise given in the heat of war was considered so binding that, according to the lawyers, 'even if he is rescued by
his own side while the battle continues, he is not freed from
his captivity or from the faith he has pledged' – even so the
wise captor drew up a written deed for signature. In it the
prisoner promised obedience in all things reasonable; to
renounce any right he might have or attain, by judgements
in any court whatsoever whether church or secular, to dispute his master's title; and invoked the most humiliating
sanctions against his honour if he broke the articles. Dis-

honour was a valuable weapon against a defaulting prisoner. The captor might have a painting made of the defaulter's arms reversed, or of the man himself hanging by his heels or in some other such humiliating posture. Alternatively, the defrauded captor might find a merchant of the prisoner's side in the war, who was willing to pay the ransom in part in return for a receipt which he could use in a prosecution of the ex-prisoner as a common debtor. An English merchant called Bernard conducted a flourishing trade in ransoms during the 1430s and 1440s in Paris.

There were handsome profits to be made even from negotiating the exchange in a case of ransom. Lady Margaret Hungerford paid a ransom of £6000 in return for her son and heir Robert Lord Moleyns who had been wounded and taken prisoner in the 1452–3 Gascon campaigns. But in addition she had to pay £1100 in interest on the borrowed money and £600 as a ten per cent fee to the merchant who handled the transaction. Lord Moleyns' capture began a series of disasters which sadly depleted the family fortunes so that when, in 1476, Lady Margaret drew up her will she felt obliged to set out in detail why 'mine heirs have none occasion to grudge for that I leave them not so great inheritance as I might and would have done, if fortune had not been so sore against me'. Her son's ransom money had forced the family deep into debt and mortgage, but a still heavier blow was his attainder as a Lancastrian by the Yorkist regime in 1461. The unmortgaged estates he had inherited from his father were confiscated by the crown and his mother was forced to sell two of her own manors to meet her obligations to her creditors.

Yet on balance the Hungerfords as a family did not do badly from the French wars. Lord Moleyn's father, his uncle and grandfather all took rich French prisoners – it was said that Sir Walter, the uncle, had built his castle at Farleigh on the proceeds of Agincourt. Stretlam, in the bishopric of Durham, Sudely in Gloucestershire, Ampthill in Bedfordshire, and many other great houses were attributed to the profits of the French wars by later generations and on balance the English took far more out of France than they lost. Even in the last months, when the military situation was against them, they were able to negotiate terms by which the French abandoned immense ransom claims in exchange for immediate English withdrawal. Rents from French lands and official fees must be included with ransoms in any final assessment of the yield of the wars and even important French victories, such as Baugé in the later stages, were offset by the fact that the English were able to pillage piecemeal in a hundred minor expeditions. Insignificant in terms of military history, they yielded large plunder to those who fought in them and were taken correspondingly seriously by contemporaries. 'Liketh your highness to wit that, the Saturday before the date of this,' wrote Richard Beauchamp, Earl of Warwick, to Henry V on 21 June 1421, 'I...came home from a Journey, which I made into Anjou and Maine, where as I had assembled with me great part of the captains of your land; and blessed be God we sped right well; for your people is greatly refreshed with this road; for they say in common, they were never more in no such road. And we brought home the fairest and greatest prey of beasts, as all they said that saw them, that ever they saw.'

Of all the many Frenchmen held in English castles from 1415 to the 1450s, the most famous was Charles, Duke of Orleans, nephew of Charles VI and father of Louis XII. Captured at Agincourt he was held for twenty-five years. His release for £40,000 was negotiated in 1440 on condition that he help secure truce terms for the English. Most of this huge sum was paid, as was £35,000 to redeem his younger brother John, Count of Angoulême. Count John had not been taken in battle but had been surrendered by Charles himself as a hostage for the payment to an English expedition of 1412 to withdraw from France. The pay-off was divided between scores of English captains and the count was freed, after thirty-three years of captivity, only when the last account had been settled. His detention, like that of his brother, had been far from arduous. As the enforced house guest in the castles of a succession of gentlemen warders, they lived in considerable style which was paid for out of their French revenues.

One of the century's finest poets, Charles begins one of his English pieces somewhat strangely for a prisoner:

> O! sely anchorite, that in thy cell
> Enclosed art with stone, and goes not out,
> Thou mayst be gladder so for to dwell,
> Than I with wanton wandering thus about.

Yet free though he was to move in the society of his guardian host, the duke, in the absolute obedience which as a prisoner he owed his master, emblemised the fall from high estate by revolution of the wheel of fortune, which is one of the classic themes of the contemporary view of life. A generation later the reversals of the civil wars provided Frenchmen with the refreshing spectacle of English gentlemen brought low. Commines describes how he saw 'some of them before the duke knew of their plight in such great poverty that beggars could not have been poorer. I once saw a Duke of Exeter walking barefoot behind the duke's train, begging his livelihood from house to house without revealing his identity.' The plight of Edward IV after his hair-breadth escape from Warwick's invasion was very little better. He was 'completely penniless and gave the ship's master a robe lined with fine marten's fur, promising to reward him better in the future. There never was such a beggarly company...' Even reduced to such straits, Edward did not forget the essential kingly attribute of largess. He and his party had to rely on the generosity of the Lord of Gruithuis for transport to the Burgundian court and decent clothes, but the sea captain received his present.

For the average English man and woman the one

compensation for the turbulence and injustice of the times
was the ruin it sometimes brought to the haughty oppressors
themselves. In November 1449, John Cockayne of Ashbourne in Derbyshire, sent a hundred men to Oakeover Park
after its owner had dared arraign him, himself a gentleman,
before the king's bench for poaching. Cockayne's ruffians
hunted the park until nightfall, killing all but five of the deer
and breaking down the fences; they then converged on the
house where they 'broke up the doors, bay windows and
other windows of the said manor, with forms, tressels and
tables and burnt them there and by the said fire roasted part
of the said deer taken in the said park'.[6] Rather than suffer
such damage to one of his manor houses at Rey, near Castle
Rising, Thomas, Lord Scales pulled it down and razed it to
the ground 'although grand and nobly built'. When the
gentry were so effectively their own nemesis Dame Fortune
had little work to do. But more generally the locality had
only her intervention to trust to and meanwhile watched
with awe and envy the luxurious life style of these great
houses.

The focus was the great hall and the epitome of etiquette
and opulence achieved in the serving of a ceremonial banquet. The greater houses modelled their procedure as far as
possible on that at court – during the reign of Edward IV that
is; under Henry VI the aristocracy would have disdained to
offer a table as meagre as the king's. The most important
official was the marshal or usher who 'must know all estates
of the Church goodly and greable, and the excellent estate
of a king and his blood honourable'. The occasion could be
made or ruined by his seat placings and it was also up to him
to ensure that the decorations and hangings were both tasteful
and, where symbolical, apt. During the proceedings a
company of tipstaffs under his direction kept order among
the cluster of hangers-on at the bottom of the hall and cleared
gangways for service to the tables. The lord of the household
and his family and guests of honour sat at the high table on

the dais, the other guests taking their places at tables ranged down the walls according to their rank.

The meal generally consisted of three courses, each comprising scores of dishes. To a modern palate the combinations seem quite arbitrary, though they did allow each guest to build his sequence if he so wished. A first course of pike in a thick sauce, poultry and roast haunches of venison; a second course of bream in thick sauce, poultry and baked venison; and a third course of baked venison, tench in jelly, rabbits and singing birds, were rounded off by the serving of sweetmeats and spices with wine. Each course was ushered in by a steward perhaps to the accompaniment of a flourish of trumpets, while harps and lutes played during the meal. The intervals between courses were marked by the display of 'sotelties', pastry and sugar confections of various allegorical designs, and on great occasions the climax was provided during the third course with the solemn entry of roasted peacocks recased in their skin and plumage. With ceremony at almost every stage, the art of the carver was a high mystery with its own jargon. The *Boke of Kervynge*, written in the middle of the century, tells how to 'splat' a pike; to 'spoil' a hen; to unbrace a mallard; fin a chub; barb a lobster; to 'thigh' the small birds; 'display' a crane, and so on. When they were about eight or nine, the sons of the nobility were sent as squires to the household of a friend or relation to learn, among other things, the arts of serving and carving at table. There was a whole literature of books of courtesy to help them prepare.

To prepare, in fact, to be the most insufferable little prigs. 'Go forth your way,' advises one author, 'demeaning your behaviour, In sober wise that men may of you say, A goodly child there passeth by this way.' But there was also a heap of practical hints which indicate the kind of table manners that went with the gorgeous, gold-plated ceremony of the feast. Any belt-loosening for one's stomach's ease, should be managed discreetly before sitting down at table; avoid farting 'lest ye be shamefully found'; do not spit across the table; do *not* pick your teeth with your knife; and to maintain the reputation so carefully earned have nothing to do with 'ruskyn' gallants who serve unbelted at a table. Then, all one's lessons conned and learned, one may pleasantly reflect how

> ...glad may this child's friends be,
> To have a child as mannerly as he.

The young noble's apprenticeship in 'gentilness' was as arduous, to the horror of a visiting Italian at the end of the century, as the young craftsman's in his trade, for he was expected to do even the humblest chores. The day was a long one too. In the household of the Earl of Northumberland it began at four in the morning with the clerk controller making his first rounds. Having raised the clerks of the counting house, he then called up the cooks and settled the day's menus. While the rest of the household began functioning, the clerk controller took a cat nap before returning to the counting house. The family themselves were generally up soon after dawn to a breakfast of bread, ale and meat or fish, and the day's business had begun.

For all but a small minority, this generally meant some time spent on the business of the estate; perhaps an hour or two with the secretary dictating instructions to agents and bailiffs on remote manors; or a conference with the man at law arranging the fixing of the next jury; or supervising the progress of the building on the manor house; or discussing a report on work costs for a religious foundation. For it should not be forgotten that the church building of the wool merchants was matched by such great collegiate foundations as Leicester, Fotheringay, Tattershall and others founded by the aristocracy. In every age wealth and power have conferred independence of action and for this reason the lives of the medieval nobility were fuller, more exciting and generally more interesting than those of the average. More possibilities were open to them and they exploited them to the full.

Of course they hunted – Lord Scales wrote a book on the subject. Of course they indulged themselves – Richard of York owned a collar 'called in English "a White Rose"', valued at £2660. Of course they over-ate. The stewards, sewers, carvers and the rest would have little to do otherwise, and it is worth remembering that when Warwick the Kingmaker had six oxen roasted for breakfast at his London house, any citizen, apprentice or beggar who went round to the kitchen door could take as much meat as he could carry away on his dagger. But at Christmas, Twelfth Night and other high occasions, dinner was followed by entertainments ranging from the traditional mummers' plays to a new type of show, the 'Interlude', which held the seeds for the development of the sixteenth-century drama. Performed by troupes of professional interluders, the form had established an individual style of presentation by the 1460s when *Mankind*, the first one to have survived, was written. From hints in the text it seems likely that the company may sometimes have put on the play in an inn yard – at one point one of the characters calls on an 'ostler' to bring him a football. But other references make it clear that the action took place indoors rather than outside and the convincing reconstruction by Richard Southern, in his *The Staging of Plays before Shakespeare*, vividly depicts the scene in the hall of a great house when the interluders entered.

The lay-out of the hall itself determined the shape of the action. The public entrance was in the side wall in the far corner at the bottom of the hall. Opposite to it was another door leading to the kitchens and servants' area so that the bottom bay of the great hall constituted a kind of public throughway. By the fifteenth century this was partitioned off by fixed or movable screens to form an entrance passage or lobby to the hall proper. Two fixed screens projected from either wall a few feet to shield the entrance doors while a third screen placed a few feet in front of them in the body of the hall, gave two entrances, one either side. The main action of the interlude took place in the centre of the floor but the screen entrances at the one end, and the area in front of the high table and dais at the other, provided points of focal interest and exciting possibilities for dramatic tension.

A flickering pool of light floods out from the great fire-place half way down one side of the hall and the uneven glow is supplemented by torches in brackets along the walls. The host and his party at the high table lean forward looking down towards the screens, waiting for the action to begin. The guests at the tables along the walls turn round on their benches and the screen entrances are congested with standing servants and minor guests whose seats have been shifted to clear the acting area. A stately figure emerges from the crowd and walks the length of the hall to a chair which has been placed below the dais and takes his seat; another chair in front of the centre screen is taken by a second figure. Next enters Prologue and addresses the company, 'Ye sovereigns that sit and ye brothern that stand right up.' The play of *Mankind* has begun.

The first part of the action, at the centre of the hall, is a boisterous dialogue between three knaves, Newguise, Nowadays and Nought, who come tumbling in and plan their strategy for seducing Mankind. The figure seated below the dais is soon forgotten until drawn into the action by the dialogue when he stands revealed as Heaven. But there is a good deal of business to be completed first, notably the entry of the devil Titivillus. The entry of this comic monster character is carefully built up and prepared by the taking of a collection, for until the audience have paid up 'they shall no man him see'. When he arrives the attack on Mankind steps up, deploying all his infernal powers to get the poor innocent out of the way and while he steals his rosary, Titi-villus loosens his bowels.

'Arise and avaunt thee, nature compells', he orders and

finding himself unexpectedly caught short Mankind hurriedly obeys:

> I will into the yard sovereigns and come again soon
> For dread of the colic and also the stone,
> I will do what needs must be done.

While the audience is still holding its sides at this ancestral piece of English lavatory humour, Mankind returns and soon falls into a devilishly induced sleep.

At his first entrance, Titivillus has warned those in the audience with horses tethered in the courtyard to expect the worst and now he troubles his victim's sleep with a dream in which Mercy, the figure seated by the screens, is arrested for horse stealing. With confidence in his natural ally undermined, the harassment of the poor fellow continues. The entrances and exits through the screen accelerate as Nought, Nowadays and Newguise dash in and out with Mankind's seemly long gown which, by the time their off-stage tailoring is finished, has been cut down to the short, buttock-hugging doublet affected by the smart younger set. The actors make the most of the standing audience crowding the screens, ordering one to raise his torch higher to light their entrance or shouting through the crowd from off-stage so that Mankind is heckled and barracked by their disembodied, jeering voices. Mankind's damnation seems assured until at length, Heaven intervenes to bring everything to a happy conclusion.

Morality with a comic edge was good box office. The Church's morality plays were being progressively secularised and the solemn pageants of the town Mystery Play cycles were losing something of their appeal; it was probably to stop this drift away from the theatre that the cooks and innkeepers of Chester added the comic scene of the alewife to their play *The Harrowing of Hell* at about this time. The author of *Mankind* chose equally coventional targets for his wit. The moral theme of his play fitted contemporary attitudes and his attack on fashion might seem to derive from pulpit censures, but grumblings against Newguise and Nowadays have never been the prerogative of the clergy. A few years before *Mankind* was written, Peter Idley, an under-keeper of the royal mews and falcons, penned his *Instructions to his Son*. Beginning with a sharp indictment of the real corruptions of the law and religion he moves on to the precepts of the middle-aged in every generation. After a side swipe at long hair, which 'is not shorn but hangeth down to the brow beforn', he turns to the contemporary fashion in doublets:

> They be cutted on the buttock even above the rump.
> Every good man truly such shape loaths;
> It maketh him a body short as a stump,
> And if they shall crook, kneel or crump,
> To the middle of the back the gown will not reach.

With an English reticence one usually associates with later times, he says nothing of the aspect of the fashion which so horrified his Sienese contemporary San Bernadino. Warning mothers that even their sons may be one of those cheek-painted boys who practise sodomy for gain, he continues '...it is a grave sin to make them doublets that reach only to the navel, and hose with one small patch in front and one behind' for this is an outright invitation to the sodomites. But if Peter Idley kept off the subject there were English who agreed with the Italian and complained of 'newfangelness' ...'That makes the world so plainly transformate, That men do seem almost enfeminate.'

Not that the women were any better. The horned head-dresses which cropped up in one form or another from the early 1400s on to the 1440s were reckoned 'a thing contrary to femininity' so that wherever he looked, the moralist could find 'men arrayed as women and woman as man', and fashion 'disfiguring nature'. The obsession with fashion impo-

verished everyone, from the commons who observe no
'reasonable measure' in their dress to the gallant at whose
'girdle hangeth a purse', as fashion dictated though 'therein
is neither penny nor cross'. Small wonder that the kingdom,
once the envy of Europe for its chivalry, manliness and prosperity, had lost its French lands. There were some who
believed that the French connection was, in fact, the cause
of all the trouble.

> O France why did not these gallants abide there?
> England may wail that ever it went there.

For English culture was still heavily shaped by things
French. The heavy opulence of Edward IV's court, so
admired by foreigners, was modelled on Valois Burgundy.
Perhaps the only real difference was that the French style was
yet more opulent and 'wasteful' than its English counterpart.

In France and Burgundy, for example, every petty gentleman had his own pursuivant; in England sometimes the
greatest aristocrat was without. Lord Scales was not ashamed
to borrow the services of John Walters, the king's Chester
Herald, to carry a tournament challenge to the Bastard of
Burgundy. Other English noblemen, however, did consider
an officer of arms an important part of their 'worship'. Sir
John Fastolf, that flamboyant first-generation magnate,
maintained the Frenchman, de Fugiers, as his personal secret
pursuivant. But then the Beaufort and Holland Dukes of
Exeter, of the blood royal, maintained a Huntingdon Herald
in their capacities as the Earls of Huntingdon. John Tiptoft
had a Worcester Herald on his establishment and the house
of York a March Herald. When the family achieved the
crown he became for a time, a king of arms just as modern
Richmond Herald owes his status as a member of the royal
household to the fact that Henry VII was Earl of Richmond
before he seized the throne.

The upgrading of a herald's office to 'kingly' status was

a valuable advantage to its holders since the kings of arms—
the two principal were Norroy, with his province north of
the Trent, and Clarenceux—could authorise and register
coats of arms and receive the relevant fees. (The exact status
of Garter King of Arms, created by Henry V in 1415, was
something of a puzzle since although he was senior to the
two other kings, he had no specific province of his own and
had not been specifically given the rights of granting arms.)
All but the kings relied on irregular gratuities or 'largess' dispensed on certain feast days, at formal banquets, or in
payment for work as judges and umpires at tournaments.
Naturally, as members of the royal or a noble household,
they also had their lodging free. Edward IV's *Black Book of
the Household* lists the duties of the kings of arms, heralds and
pursuivants, and their perquisites at court, and in so doing
set the model for any great noble whose 'worship' required
the maintenance of heralds.

> ...if the king keep estate in the hall, then they walk before
> the steward, treasurer and controller, coming with the
> king's service from the serving board at every course; and
> after the last course they cry the king's largess, shaking their
> great cup. They take their largess of the jewel house, and
> during the festival days they wait upon the king's person,
> coming and going to and from the church hall, and
> chambre before his highness in their cotes of arms. They
> take...livery for their chambre, day and night, amongst
> them two loves, one pitcher wine, two gallons ale, and for
> winter season, if there be present a king of arms, for them
> all two great wax candles...and fuel. These kings of arms
> are served in the hall as knights, service and livery, for their
> horses near the court by the harbinger...[7]

The only mention of fees, as opposed to largess, comes at
the end of the paragraph. 'The fees that they shall take at the
making of the Knights of the Bath, it appeareth after the

chapter on squires.' Significantly, perhaps, it does not. But in the early years of Edward IV the royal largess made generous compensation for the uncertainty of income. Gabriel Tetzel, on a Bohemian embassy to London in 1466, commented on Edward's ostentatious distribution of largess to household musicians and officers, including twenty-four heralds and pursuivants 'who then told everyone how much they had been given'.

Nevertheless, a skilled herald could make a reasonable free-lance income as marshal at the numerous tournaments held all over northern Europe, provided he got his lord's permission. Widely travelled, and at the centre of aristocratic society, he was ideally placed for a wide range of ambassadorial and related work, for the royal government, noble patrons and even merchant corporations.

In the fifteenth century, diplomatic contacts throughout Europe multiplied many times and a specialist class of men to deal with them began to emerge. The humanist orators of the Italian city states, who from the late fourteenth century were shaping a rhetorical style of presentation to boost the prestige of their states and, almost as a by-product, launched the new Latinism that was to stimulate the humanistic studies of the early Renaissance, are the ancestors of the modern diplomatic corps. At the papal court, meanwhile, protocol and procedure were becoming increasingly formalised. And in English records there are some names which occur so regularly that it is plain there was a degree of specialisation here too. The most important single class of such men seems to have been the heralds, so that among the theologians, lawyers, noblemen and others who served on royal embassies, the heralds' college features so regularly that it has something of the air of a diplomatic service. During this period the heralds were winning a professional status far higher than ever before – a movement which culminated with their incorporation by Richard III.

When the government of Henry VI, using the order as a

diplomatic tool, invested the kings of Poland and Aragon with the Garter in 1453, Robert Legh, Clarenceux king of arms, carried the insignia to their courts. A fitting job for a herald. But one of his predecessors in office, Sir Thomas Hulme, was sent on numerous important missions to the courts of Burgundy, Scotland, France and Denmark. Likewise John Smert, Garter from 1450, was a constant visitor to foreign courts as was his contemporary William Tynedale, king of the Northern Province. But Tynedale's career shows that there could be more arduous business for a herald than the elegant longueurs of courtly diplomacy. In the disturbed months that followed Cade's rebellion, two horses foundered under him as he rode the country with messages to the local authorities.

Smert was a man of substance, holding family estates in Gloucestershire. Robert Machado, who rose to be Clarenceux in a mere ten years, controlled a flourishing wine trade. His numerous trips abroad, supposedly in the royal service, were almost all connected with his business interests and he left colleagues to deal with his work at the college. For men like this, the scanty, irregular income of the job was no great matter. But there were others of humble origins who had, perhaps, quitted minor Church orders for the lure of royal service or, like John Walters, had risen from the craftsman's status of heraldic painters. For them *ad hoc* commissions from virtually any source meant welcome cash. In the 1440s a group of London merchants lost a cargo of wine to Breton pirates. They reckoned their best hope of restitution was an embassy in due form to the ducal court at Dinan and they accordingly engaged the services of a herald. A few years later the royal court sent Chester Herald on a commission of enquiry into piracy in Cornwall. It was a delicate and dangerous business – the sheriff of the county was among the organisers of West Country piracy, and rumour suggested that a ship of the young Duke of Exeter, Lord Admiral of England, might also be involved. The herald seems to have

In England jousts were permitted by royal licence and were rare events; Henry IV held one for the coronation of his queen, Joan, in 1403. Her champion was the young Richard Beauchamp, Earl of Warwick. The mid-century illustrated life of the earl, from which this picture is taken, comments 'he so notably and knightly behaved himself as redounded to his noble fame'.

The British Library

been too successful for his own good. Soon after his return to London he lost his job and the next royal Chester Herald to be listed in the Chancery records is one William Whiting, formerly Huntingdon Herald to the Duke of Exeter.

Altogether safer was the herald's more conventional role in the tournament as marshal or judge. By the fifteenth century the tournament had rules for play and scoring which entitle it to be regarded as the world's first organised sport. John Tiptoft, Earl of Worcester, drew up a scoring system for jousts held in Smithfield in the mid-sixties and presided over by Edward IV. The highest points were for unhorsing an opponent; other good hits were a blow to the crest of the enemy's helmet and additional points were awarded for the player who broke the largest number of lances. One of the most difficult manœuvres was to catch the coronal (the rebated point of the lance) of your opponent with your own. Considering that lances were an average twelve foot this was certainly a considerable feat on a galloping horse.

Tiptoft's rules are something of an oddity since England, thanks to royal prohibitions, was not one of Europe's great jousting centres. During the 1440s a French knight had toured the country to the Scottish border issuing challenges as he went without any response at all. One Welsh gentleman, appalled at the shame the Frenchman had brought to the realm of Arthur, rode post to Dover just in time to miss the Frenchman's boat. Hiring a fishing smack he caught up with the challenger in mid-Channel. There and then on board ship, he ritually touched the gage which the French knight had bound to his leg armour as token of the challenge. The two sailed on to France to settle the contest of honour. There could be hazards in this kind of away match as another Welshman, Sir Thomas Key, discovered in his contest with the renowned Burgundian Jacques Lalain presided over by Duke Philip the Good. Key was soon dominating the contest and many spectators thought that Lalain was signalling the duke to stop the fight. He was bleeding heavily from his left arm and was in a bad way. But Philip affected not to see the signals. He had no intention of conceding defeat against the finest flower of Burgundian chivalry; Lalain would have to fend as best he could and save the honour of the ducal court.

Since the whole point of the joust was honour, the duke's action was clearly an unfair implied ruling. When Lalain, although disarmed, flukishly pulled the Welshman off balance, Philip immediately declared the 'fall' a good one and the bout went to Burgundy. Now it was Key's turn to appeal, and vehemently. Much in the style of modern wrestling, there were tournament regulations for determining a true fall. Key pointed out that he had merely fallen on knees and elbows and had been able to rise to continue the fight. The point was valid but bound to fail in front of a home referee and a home crowd. Sir Thomas was not only dishonoured but had to present his opponent and 'victor' with a ruby and a fully equipped horse.

The fifteenth-century joust was full of such technicalities to delight the *aficionados*. There was also good, old-fashioned foul play. At the tournament of Charlemagne's Tree, held near Mons by Pierre Baufrement, Lord of Charny, a Castilian entrant came into the lists with horse armour fitted with spikes concealed by the mantling. Before he could ram his opponent's horse the spikes were spotted by an observant herald and he was ordered to remove them. His plea that this was 'standard practice' back in Castile just saved him from disqualification by a panel of highly sceptical judges. Years later the incident was recalled at the Smithfield jousts. The combatants were Anthony Bastard of Burgundy and Lord Scales. In one charge their horses collided heavily and the Bastard's horse was killed outright. He was not satisfied until King Edward had come down from the president's box and inspected Scales' horse armour to confirm that it was as per regulations.

The tournament absorbed money: the Lord of Charny kept open house at three of his castles for two months during the

Tree of Charlemagne; it was overlaid with pageantry and the nostalgia of the Arthurian myth; it was good sport and it was *the* great cult of nobility. There were Englishmen who won European reputations – Richard Beauchamp, Earl of Warwick, on tour to the Holy Land attended tournaments in South Germany en route and was presented with the Heart of St George by the Emperor Sigismund. Others attended the great events in Burgundy and France. When Caxton published Malory's *Morte d'Arthur* he was sure of his market. If England had nothing to compare with the great European spectacles, her nobility were no laggards in the lore of chivalry, the rich man's sport and the preserve of privilege.

8

♣♣♣

Merchants, Mercers and Trade

English trade was given its first strong impetus towards expansion, during the reign of Edward III, when war, and the taxation and controls on wool exports it brought with it, encouraged the growth of the home cloth industry and then a corresponding growth in peace-time cloth exports. The export of wool sank from an average 32,000 sacks a year in the 1350s to 19,000 in the last decade of the century; in the same period the cloth exports rose from 5000 cloths a year to 37,000. The impact of the expanding industry on some of the towns and rural areas of England we know; the transformation caused by the changing trade pattern in the economic life of the country is equally important.

England's graduation to the ranks of industrial exporting nations took about two centuries. In the mid-fourteenth century, barely four per cent of the wool exported went out in the form of manufactured cloth. By the end of the reign of Henry VIII the percentage had risen close to sixty. During the same period, English merchants took over the bulk of the country's trade in wool and wine; though in cloth the Italians and other foreign traders continued to hold a place of major importance. English attempts to break into the Mediterranean markets made little headway and in the north they had to face the German Hanse cities.

The fluctuating pattern of England's fifteenth-century trade reveals an economy growing to maturity, hampered at times by foreign and civil wars and suffering from epidemics of piracy. Yet on balance the century was one of expansion.

There was something of a trading mania in the middle decades; shipowners came from all sections of society and from all parts of the country. Coventry owners had part shares in ships sailing out of Bristol on the Iceland run; at Harwich the parson was an owner, and elsewhere goldsmiths, butchers, soldiers, noblemen, apothecaries, innkeepers and even monks risked their capital at sea. Few operated on the scale of William Canynges of Bristol, who was sole owner of ten of the seventeen ships operating out of the port in the 1460s, and few as ambitious as John Taverner of Hull, who built a mammoth transport too big to put in at Calais so that Taverner was excused harbour dues there. The project, which took five years to complete, began in 1439 with the granting of a royal permission to take a hundred oaks from the king's forest in Yorkshire. The clerk to the navy in London apparently hoped that the ship would be useful for the royal service to Normandy. Only when it was finished was it seen that this would be impossible because 'he [sic] draweth so deep'.

The English shipping industry had had its first important impetus in the previous decade when the disbanding of Henry V's navy brought some twenty ships on to the market at bargain prices. John Morgan of Bristol picked up the *Christopher*, a Genoa-built prize of war, for £166; the 290-ton *Holigost of Spain* went to a Southampton consortium of John Radcliff, Ralph Huskard, Henry Baron and John Woodford; the 120-ton *Anne* to John Slugge of Saltash for £30. All these sales were completed in 1423, the year after the king's death; critics then and since have attacked this as shortsighted and wanton destruction of England's sea defences. 'Where be our ships, where are our swords become? Our enemies bid us put a sheep for the ship', wailed the author of the *Libelle of Englyshe Polycye*. The foreigners' jibe which

so pained him was a reference to the gold noble of Edward
III which depicted the crowned monarch standing in a ship.
Yet William Soper, the clerk to the king's ships who super-
vised the sale, had good reasons. In fact he was obliged by
the terms of Henry V's will to dispose of the late king's navy,
his personal possession, to meet his debts. Yet even without
this directive Soper would probably have urged the same
course. A navy was a luxury in peace-time – doubly so at a
time when England, now lord of Normandy, controlled
both the Channel coasts. In the two years before they were
sold, the *Christopher* and the *Holigost of Spain* had between
them cost £863 in repairs and maintenance. Fifteenth-century government finance was simply not geared to carry costs
like this with no definable return.[1]

Nevertheless, there were hazards to Channel shipping even
though the French navy was for the time being not one of
them. Piracy was endemic and during the 1430s and 1440s
became more serious than ever before. The need to 'keep the
sea' is a recurring theme and the failure of Henry VI's government in this matter was one important factor in its collapse.
The merchants of London were the most influential sponsors
of Edward IV's cause and all the south of England applauded
the victories over Spanish marauders in the Channel won by
the Earl of Warwick when he was captain of Calais. The idea
of England the fortress isle, defended by ocean walls, was still
a live and vivid metaphor when the author of the *Libelle*,
with a pre-echo of Shakespeare, wrote:

> Keep then the sea, which is the wall of England
> And then is England kept by God's hand.

Nor had the image of the ship of state yet become stale; the
author of a pro-Lancastrian political poem chose it as an eye-
catching title. The king himself is the ship, his heir Prince
Edward the mast, the Duke of Exeter the ship's light, the
Duke of Somerset the rudder, and so forth.

This noble ship made of good tree
Our sovereign lord King Henry,
God guide him from adversity,
     Where that he go or ride.
          .   .   .

Now help, Saint George, our lady knight,
And be our lode-star day and night,
To strength our king and England right
     And fell our foemen's pride.
Now is our ship dressed in his kind,
With his tackling before and behind;
Whoso love it not, God make him blind,
     In pains aye to abide.[2]

It was not unusual to refer to a ship in the masculine
gender at this time, but in describing the Prince of Wales
as the mast, rather than the main mast, the poet seems
to betray a clerk's ignorance of naval architecture. Progress
and development are not generally the characteristics we
attribute to the Middle Ages, but between 1400 and 1450
shipbuilding in northern Europe, inspired by Mediterranean
examples, made some important advances. The traditional
single-masted cog, with its one square sail, gave way to two-
masters with a square fore, or 'fukke', sail and then, early
in the reign of Henry VI, to three-masters with a lateen-
rigged mizzen sail. This was the crucial development that
made it possible to sail closer to the wind; but sail plans were
being continually improved – by the end of the century the
sprit-sail was to be seen on some new ships.

There were parallel advances in navigation aids and techniques. An improved compass with the thirty-two-point
'rose of the winds' had been in use in the Mediterranean from
the early years of the fourteenth century. But in the north
navigators stuck to the old system of 'needle and stone', a
suspended or floating iron needle magnetised by rubbing
with a lode stone when a direction or bearing needed to be

checked. The permanently magnetised compass needle with its direction card (which by now showed a rough value for magnetic north as distinct from true north) and housed in a lead binnacle was a valuable supplement to the basic tools of navigation. But these were still the sounding line and lead and the hour glass. In 1449 a Hanseatic Danzigman, bound for Lisbon, was put under arrest at Plymouth and to ensure that she did not slip out of harbour the authorities impounded the lead and line.[3] Perhaps even more valuable than the compass was the spread of reliable charts and portolans or rutters from the middle of the century.

Where the chart gave merely the coastlines, like a map, the portolan (Anglo-Germanic, 'rutter') was a compendium of sailing directions. The first one in English that has survived comes from the middle years of the century, though it was possibly based on an earlier example. The master had to calculate his longitude by dead reckoning but his rutter gave a series of depth soundings along the most important routes with descriptions of the bottom, the main headlands and currents. The main passages in the mid-century rutter are the coasting route from Berwick to Land's End; from Land's End to Avonmouth with information on the Irish coastal waters; the Scilly Isles to Beachy Head; Finisterre to the Severn; and from St Malo to Gibraltar along the Biscay Coast. The rutter has nothing to say on the Iceland passage, though at the very time it was being compiled this was one of the fastest-growing new routes of English commerce.

At the beginning of the century, Iceland was a remote land of myth and legend for the English; by 1500 it was again fading from their calculations. But for the middle sixty years of the century they had dominated international trade there and, in the words of C. J. Marcus the naval historian, it was the first really deep-sea venture for English shipping whose 'importance in our naval history can hardly be set too high'.[4] Once a Norwegian province, with its trade channelled through the port of Bergen, Iceland came under the Danish crown along with Norway at the Union of Kalmar in 1397. A remote outpost of European culture, the country depended for vital supplies on regular convoys from the Scandinavian mainland. The Norwegian failure to honour this obligation meant that the Icelanders were at first willing to accept the Danish royal monopoly. But it was very soon obvious that Copenhagen was interested only in taxes and the annual six ships stipulated in the agreement with Iceland arrived erratic-ally if at all. Any foreign shipping was bound to be welcome in Icelandic waters and the English were soon venturing there, with or without the necessary Danish permissions.

Cod, then as now, was the main attraction. In the last decades of the fourteenth century, English merchantmen were buying fish in Norwegian ports and English fishermen were beginning to work northern waters. In 1412, a year in which the annalist recorded no ships from Norway or Den-mark, the first English fishing boat appeared off the Icelandic coast and put in at Dyrholm. The following year a fleet of thirty came to the Vestmann Isles and then, in 1414, a merch-ant flotilla, with a ship owned by Henry V carrying letters requesting trading facilities, really initiated commerce between the two countries. The year before this an English captain had won permission from King Eric of Denmark to 'sail with his wares into the realm without toll'. But the expedition seems to have been too successful for the king's liking and he followed with a prohibition of the Icelanders dealing with any more foreigners.

Henry V's captain had been met with the news of the pro-hibition but in discussions the 'chief men of Iceland' to whom the letter was addressed waived their scruples. A pattern of Anglo-Danish disputes over trading rights in the area had been established. Next year, the governor himself returned with an English fleet, carrying with him a large cargo of dried fish and silver for a trade to pay, in part, for his pilgrimage to the shrine of St Thomas at Canterbury. Within these three years, English activity around Iceland exploded into an entirely new dimension and King Eric wrote to London protesting not only about the flouting of his Bergen monopoly but also against the unruly behaviour of the English fishermen. But the king still failed in his obligations to his distant subjects and before the decade was out they petitioned the crown to justify their dealings with foreigners. 'Our laws provide that six ships should come hither from Norway every year, which has not happened for a long time…Therefore, we have traded with foreigners who have come here peacefully…but we have punished those fishermen who have robbed and caused disturbance.'[5]

By the end of the 1420s Lynn had its company of 'merchants of Iceland', while Hull and Bristol were opening a thriving trade to the north. But they did not all come 'peacefully'. Anticipating reprisals from the Danish authorities on the island, which in any case they seem to have looked on as barely civilised, captains led their crews ashore in armed expeditions with drums beating and colours flying. Danish officials were killed and a governor captured and carried back to England. The men of Hull seem to have been the worst culprits, but there is evidence in the King's Lynn town records that some of its merchants bought young Icelandic slaves. The island's natives were caught between the grasping and oppressive Danish authorities (and glad to see them suffer at English hands) and the predatory foreign merchants who were happy to capitalise on their defenceless poverty.

For a time it seemed possible that the English merchants would have to abandon their highly profitable ventures (a single cargo could fetch more than £700). The council of the baby king supported the king of Denmark's proclamations, and in some towns the merchants who did regular business with Bergen and other Scandinavian centres put pressure on their fellow aldermen to stop the illegal ventures of the English which jeopardised their own legitimate trading. But here too there were obstacles. The power of the German Hanseatic merchants in the Baltic states made it easy for them to restrict and hamper the English. When representations to the royal administration failed to get action the citizens of King's Lynn sent an independent embassy to Denmark to plead their case, only to be met with angry reproaches for the misdemeanours of the English in Iceland. The merchants of York and Hull protested in the English parliament that they were 'greatly impoverished and undone and in part destroyed by the King of Denmark and his lieges, because they …take goods to the value of £5000 within a year, and of other lieges and merchants of England to the value of £20,000'. And there was no redress 'because none of the subjects of the king of Denmark come to England or have anything in England', whereas letters of marque could be issued to commandeer Italian property in event of defaulting by Italian merchants.

In these circumstances the English merchants soon took the law into their own hands again, trading irrespective of directives from either London or Copenhagen; fish cargoes were impounded at Bristol, Hull, Cromer and Scarborough and other ports by the authorities, while English pirates took full advantage of the ambiguous situation. Two Newcastle crews captured a Bristol ship on its way back from Iceland; the cargo was handed over to the Danes, the sailors were thrown into prison and the ship was sold to the profit of the captors and the king. An incident at Bristol itself showed another example of the possibilities open to the shrewd operator. John Wynche, at one time the surveyor of the customs, found his ship the *Mary* arrested by his successor in office. He calmly handed the cargo over to his friend and creditor the mayor and then sold the ship.

But many English merchants were able to trade quite legally; both the English and Danish authorities, as always chronically short of cash, granted privileges with little hesitation. The trade grew mightily. Between ten and twenty merchant ships came yearly to Iceland's shores and several more fishing doggers; the English, so Danish agents reported, 'build houses, erect tents, dig up the ground, and carry on fishery as if it were their own property'. With their larger boats and long lines carrying scores of hooks, the English were able to fish further out than the Icelanders and so catch the shoals before they came inshore. The island's fishing grounds were soon virtually controlled by the foreigners, a situation which continued well into the sixteenth century. The English fishing techniques, at least in the larger boats, were similar to the ones still used. Equipped with military arms in addition to some 3000 hooks, a ship also carried a large ballast cargo of salt; as the catches were brought on board they were salted down at once, ready for auction when the ship returned home. Many of the boats came from Norfolk ports like Cromer. Yarmouth, the other large fishing port on that coast, was famed for its herring rather than cod – the 'haraung de Gernemue' being ranked with the 'playz de Wynchelsee' and the 'merlyng de la Rye' as one of the staple fishes of the English diet.

The chief ports for the Iceland venture were Hull on the east and Bristol on the west. The east coast ports already had connections with the Bergen trade, and during the reign of Edward IV 'the mayor and burgesses of Hull' sent three or four ships annually, but, although a late comer, Bristol, England's second sea port, soon took the lead. London merchants took little direct part in the trade, using Hull-based shipping for such cargoes as they did venture north. Although the Germans were to develop a trade in oil, hides and various other items such as hunting falcons, the one thing the English wanted from Iceland was the hard dried codfish, called stockfish. In exchange they brought all the requirements of the comfortable life – metal goods such as needles, nails, swords, knives and kitchen utensils, together with garments and accessories such as girdles, gloves and purses; but the bulk of the English cargoes was linen and cloth.

The most surprising instance of English ascendance in Iceland was afforded by four trading privileges granted between

1427 and 1440 to bishops of Holar and Skalholt, remarkable because they were granted by an English king to men who were his own subjects. Both John Johnson and John Williamson were appointed bishops by the Danish synod, presumably because only Englishmen could be expected to keep some control of their unruly compatriots. The result was, though, that the lawless elements simply found themselves with powerful protectors. On one occasion, fleeing the anger of the mob, the English merchant community of Holar took refuge in the cathedral while an understanding Bishop Williamson declared them to be in sanctuary and their ships to be under his personal protection as the representative of the pope. They were heady years, but by the 1480s the English found themselves under attack. The rivalries of the civil war meant that privileges for the Iceland trade came to be granted as political bargaining counters and, rather than lose the support of influential commercial interests or the goodwill of allies, Edward IV, while making a treaty with Denmark which agreed English merchants should not trade without permission from the Danish king, at the same time continued to issue licences for evasion of the Bergen staple. But the real threat to English trade with Iceland was the emergence of new forces in the German Hanse, which was beginning to be disillusioned with the supposed advantages it enjoyed under the protection of the Danish king. In fact the monarchy had long been subservient to the powerful traders and when Edward was carried back to England for his 1470 restoration in Hanseatic vessels his debt to them was heavy. Added to this was the fact that an increasing body of powerful German towns was ignoring the monopoly exercised by others at Bergen. By the 1470s ships from Hamburg and Danzig were regularly sailing direct to Iceland and the English who had moved to Iceland to avoid the supremacy of the Germans in the Scandinavian area were forced to move once again. When the companions of Cabot returned to Bristol from their voyage to Newfoundland, they reported that 'they could bring thence so many fish that they would have no further need of Iceland'.

English rivalries with the German merchants of the Hanseatic League began in the 1380s when the resident English factors at Danzig were agitating for more favourable trading conditions. English cloth was flooding into the market towns of Prussia, and the Danzigers, anxious to keep their monopoly of their local market, tried, without much success, to mobilise the rest of the north German towns in their policy. Twenty years later the Prussian towns did win brief general support because of the depredation of English pirates. In 1405 the Hanseatic Council imposed an embargo on trade with England but it lasted barely a year, thanks to the smuggling activities of German traders in Prussia. The General Council could not hope to control individuals while the English connection was profitable. English trade in Prussia increased and by a new treaty in 1409 their trading and residential privileges were restored. They now set their sights on the markets of Livonia and West Russia and the right to form their own society in Danzig with the extra-territorial and tax-free status enjoyed by the Hanse merchants in London.

The Danzigers were outraged and perhaps genuinely fearful. Certainly they affected to believe that if the English got a firm base in their city, they would annex it and the whole of Prussia, just as they had once annexed Bordeaux and the whole of Gascony. The English were already being branded as empire builders and to this the Germans added the charge of hypocrisy. The great Hanse delegation to London, led by the Burgermeister of Danzig in 1434, reported back that its opening address had been met with 'many sweet words, after the old English custom'. They got little else, though by this time there was much to discuss and a mountainous backlog of German complaints to be answered.

The German merchants in London periodically asked for more support against the taxation and harassment at the hands of the English authorities. The English abroad were demanding parity with the Germans in London while the English at home were pressurising the government to restrict those privileges. When the Hanse's charter came up for renewal in 1427 the town council of King's Lynn, where the Germans had one of their provincial factories, authorised expenses for a deputation to parliament to lobby against it. English piracy continued and so did their refusal to complete compensation payments agreed in 1409. Danzig's attempt to mobilise another boycott was no more successful – Cologne totally ignored it as did Bergen. It was obvious they would have to negotiate and in 1437, to the horror of his fellow burgers, the Burgermeister of Danzig concluded an agreement which conceded to the English rights tantamount to those of the Hanse in London.

It promised a great future, but thereafter the English position in northern trade faltered and then declined in parallel with her political decline elsewhere in Europe. Her earlier successes had been built partly on the fact that, while Burgundy was her ally, and the Flemish fairs and markets easy, German embargoes were almost bound to be less than watertight. After the Burgundian turn-about at the Treaty of Arras in 1435, the access to the Low Countries was no longer automatic. The Hanse was necessarily more important in England's north European trade. But, flushed with the success of 1437, the English merchants who did go to Prussia, pushed their trade so aggressively and complained so vociferously about what they regarded as Prussian failure to observe the treaty, that ill feeling was certain. At home, while the Duke of Gloucester lived, anti-alien sentiment, so vigorous in London had a powerful ally.

During the forties, the merchants of Lübeck, Cologne and Danzig received reports of the increasing isolation of their people in the English capital and were warned that the Hanse's privileges were in jeopardy and that unless all the demands of the English in Prussia were met, German property would be confiscated wholesale. Yet as late as the spring of 1449 it looked as though the right compromise could be struck between a German community anxious for a settlement and an English government still able to resist popular anti-alien pressures. A new conference was arranged two years ahead and in the meantime private conciliation sessions were held. A month later the whole situation was transformed when English privateers, commanded by Robert Winnington of London, captured the salt fleet of 110 ships beating up Channel from Bourgneuf. The Flemish and Dutch ships and their cargoes were released, but the German ships, the majority, were confiscated and recognised by the London government as the lawful prizes of the privateers.

It was general knowledge that members of the king's council had profited from the outrage. The losers were the English in Germany (whose goods were confiscated to compensate the Hanse merchants with cargoes in the fleet) and the town of Lübeck, one of the few German cities without an English community. She now became England's implacable enemy, taking her first revenge on Thomas Kent and his embassy who had been dispatched to cobble a new understanding with the Prussians. Their ship was taken by a Lübeck vessel, its rich cargo confiscated in compensation and the ambassadors imprisoned. Soon afterwards he was released on parole to return to England and negotiate full compensation and when he broke his parole Lübeck's hostility was complete. When Kent coolly returned to the Continent as head of the English delegation to a conference at Utrecht, Lübeck understandably refused to deal with him. In league with Denmark the city closed the Sound to English shipping and, despite the pleas of other Hanse towns, refused to entertain English proposals for compromise through the 1450s. But Lübeck had to face reality and raise the embargo and even acquiesce in a truce made by the other towns with England.

In 1458 another Hanse fleet was seized in the Channel, this time by the Earl of Warwick, Captain of Calais. But even this second outrage was not enough to over-ride the value of the English trade to the Germans and the accession of Edward IV, who owed his throne largely to the support of the London merchant class, meant that the Hanse had to tread even more warily for fear that popular pressure would force the king to revoke their privileges. It looked as though, for all her high-handed actions, England was strong enough to force her terms on the powerful German federation; in 1467 even Lübeck, now virtually isolated, agreed to pourparlers. The English government, with a notable diplomatic and economic coup in prospect, sabotaged it the following year. An English fleet heading to the Baltic was captured by the Danes in June 1468, as a reprisal for English banditries in Iceland. Within days the council in London, remembering perhaps the part that Denmark had played in the closure of the Sound years before and claiming that there were Danzig ships in the Danish royal service, seized Hanseatic goods in London in compensation.

Protests flooded into Westminster, from the pope, the emperor and the Duke of Burgundy. A letter came from William Caxton, governor of the English community Beyond The Sea, and in Gloucestershire a demonstration of cloth workers, who relied a good deal on the trade to the east, was mobilised by the town clerk of Bristol, a well-paid friend of the London Germans. The council ignored the storm and, when the Cologne merchants broke with their colleagues, made the most of this split by restoring their property to them and reissuing the ancient privileges in their name alone. It was a brief triumph. The rest of the federation rallied round Lübeck and declared war on English shipping. More conclusive still was the fact that Edward IV was carried back to his restoration in England by Hanseatic shipping. In 1475 they were formally reinstated in their ancient privileges with the traitors of Cologne duly excluded. England's cloth manufacturers again had access to German and Prussian markets, but English merchants, through their own arrogance

Like many other nobles of the period, Richard, Earl of Warwick was closely involved in the management of his estates. Here he is shown supervising the loading of wool from his pasturelands on to one of his ships.

The British Library

and the mismanagement and misfortunes of the royal government, had less and less part in carrying it. Where once, in the great days of the 1430s and 1440s, more than a score of English merchantmen rode in the harbour at Danzig, not a single one passed through the Sound in the year 1497.

A similar story of disruption and setbacks is found in England's centuries-old wine trade with Gascony. In this south-western corner of France, ruled by the kings of England for exactly three hundred years, the economy had been brought to a fine degree of specialisation. Everything was paid for in wine which was so widely and intensively cultivated that even wheat had to be imported from England. There was barely a household without an interest in the trade and the growers ranged from high-born ecclesiastics to artisans.

The wine fleet to England sailed twice a year, in spring and autumn, and might carry the product of as many as two hundred growers. In addition there were free-lance operators, sailing out of Bayonne, who generally beat the main fleet to Southampton and so secured better prices. But the winners of this medieval version of the 'Beaujolais race' were small fry compared with the merchants who ran the 150–200 sail fleets. The admiral was elected from the masters of the ships, some of which had their merchant owners on board, though often the English or Gascon principal traded through an agent. The English agents not only negotiated the wine price at the Bordeaux end, but also disposed of the cargoes of grain shipped from England. The *Gost* of Southampton, Bordeaux-bound in September 1427, took corn on board at Chichester and Shoreham before she sailed, though the bulk of Gascony grain imports came out of Bristol.[6]

Men like John Woodcock of Southampton or Stephen de la Ree of Bordeaux, who travelled with the fleets, could offer a more personal service than Richard Harvey of London, who was the agent for Grimond of Bordeaux, but their operation was generally smaller and a resident agent did have advantages. Walter William of Southampton worked

through Roger Hogge, one of the resident English community at Bordeaux, and Hogge, like other regular factors,
came to enjoy partner status. Such an association generally
began with a contract for a single voyage so that the merchant
could test the efficiency of a new agent. Roger Taunton,
based in Newport, Isle of Wight, engaged John Thorne to
handle his 1423 consignment from Bordeaux to London. The
job involved negotiating the sale of Taunton's export of
cloth, the purchase of the wine and the supervision of its lading on the ships specified by Taunton. This was an important
and involved operation. Even the vast size of the wine fleet
did not guarantee immunity from piracy and to spread the
risk all but the very smallest dealers parcelled their buy out
among different ships.

The operation was involved because each ship operated as
an independent unit with a separate charter party between
each master and the merchants he was carrying for. This
stated the total amount of wine on board; the names of the
merchants; the quantity that each was freighting; the alternative destinations each merchant would accept in event of bad
weather or evasive action; the corresponding scale of charges
for each destination; the porterage fees that would be allowed
as bonus to master and members of the crew; and finally,
not least important, an agreed definition of the terms used –
for example, that a 'ton' of ship's lading actually did signify
two pipes of wine landed. Thorne had to ensure that the
items on the charter party concerning Taunton's business
were accurate. His work finished, he made up a detailed
report.

The terms of the charter party concerned the crew
members as closely as the master. The porterage owing to
each depended on rank, whether 'valett', 'hedgrome' or
garçon, while some of the sailors might be trading on their
own account. One Southampton merchant used the purser
of his own ship as his permanent factor at Bordeaux, but on
many ships each seaman had his own hold space which he

could use for a cargo of his own or a friend. If the cargo had to be jettisoned he could even expect some compensation if the ship made it back to port. In this event a general levy was made on the cargoes that had been spared for the common fund. Any seaman who 'had carried himself at sea like a man' during the storm, was exempted payment on the first tun of his cargo. A man who died on the voyage knew that his basic 'hire', though not the porterage, would go to his heirs, and a mariner who failed to put his best into saving the ship lost his hire.

The physical conditions on shipboard were, in general, pretty harsh. A caravel owned by Sir John Howard had a galley which took six days to build in and needed 800 bricks, 250 housetiles, and 13 paving tiles, and the accommodation for owner and passengers would have been correspondingly luxurious. Howard seems to have run his ships as a branch of the household and his sailors were given mourning clothes, like his retainers, when Lady Howard died in 1465. But his great caravel was an exception even in his fleet, and a luxury liner compared with most merchant shipping. Cabins were rare, though they might be specially erected for important passengers; food was the standard dreary diet of the sea – salt fish, salt beef and ship's biscuit (an innovation of the late fourteenth century).[7] As a result owners, whether on the scale of Canynges of Bristol – whose payroll for eight years in mid-century carries more than 800 names – or single ship masters, had to accept responsibility for surprisingly generous terms of compensation for crews.

Inadequate though it may have been, the food during the voyage was provided by the owner, not out of the crew's hire. In case of wreck, the seamen expected to be paid salvage or given their passage home. If they fell ill on board they had to be kept at the expense of the owner and, if necessary, lodgings ashore found for them. If the master or owner breached his part of the conditions of service, he could expect vigorous counteraction. The master of a Dutch ship, freighted by William White, a merchant of Poole, was unable or refused to pay off the crew when he returned to the Downs after a run to Bourgneuf Bay. The cargo of salt, bought on White's behalf from the proceeds of the cloth and wool he had exported, was sold for £18 to William Brown of Sandwich, who, on orders from the mayor of Sandwich, allowed the English seamen aboard to attach part of the payment in lieu of their wages. We know of the case because White sued Brown for the money in chancery.

Ordinary seamen often had some say in the running of the ship. Group decisions were needed even to decide the time of sailing while, in a storm, if a third of the crew supported the master's decision to jettison cargo, the objections of any merchants who might be on board were over-ruled. And group decision could govern even discipline. The penalty for striking the master was a fine of 5s or loss of the hand, but if the dispute between master and a mariner did not come to blows, the ship's company decided the compensation due. Nevertheless, at sea the master of a vessel could play the tyrant; if he did so the victim could seek redress in the courts. In 1445 the master of a Norfolk ship was presented for inflicting injuries and mayhem on a sailor. The fact that he was acquitted when supported 'by the major part of the mariners who had journeyed in the said ship' may be taken to show that he, or the ship's owner, could afford the going price of justice then obtaining in the county.

His report written and delivered into the hands of the ship's purser or master, Thorne's job was done. Others sailed back with the fleet, keeping a watchful eye on their own cargoes. Back in England the wine was sold either to wholesalers, who dealt with the merchants of inland towns, the taverners or other retail outlets, or possibly in bulk to great houses or religious institutions. On rare occasions the taverner himself might sail with the fleet. John Bradley of Oxford, for example, took a cargo of tallow out on the *Marie* of Hampton and brought back four pipes of wine, bought with the proceeds of the sale, on the *Trinity* of Bursledon. The export-import business seems to have engrossed him since he is described as vintner in later records. But in fact, as the vintners of London often protested, the term did not always signify. Despite their best efforts, they were never able to control the wine trade. Not only did Gascon merchants play a massive role in the import trade, virtually any English merchant trading abroad would bring back wine if he got the chance. Cloth merchants dealing with the Italians took wine as payment. Grocers, ironmongers, tailors, goldsmiths, all did the same. Even the gentry and nobility, who bought in bulk for their household needs, might also have an eye to profit. A Hertfordshire knight, on a visit to London, buys no less than £48 worth of wine from an ironmonger and then stores it until he can sell at a profit.

Wine was the drink of Everyman. Only the very poorest had to limit themselves to ale. For the rest, wine flowed into England, as today, from Gascony, Spain, Italy, the Rhine and Greece. Wine was so generally in demand anybody who had the chance would deal in it; it was always a safe bargain. It could be bartered; used to pay fines; it was almost a form of currency.

The bulk of the trade was with Gascony. Inevitably, the wars with France caused some upheavals. The figures for imports to Southampton demonstrate the point pungently; the 1027 tons of 1448–9 sank to 207 tons in 1449–50; the fact that, according to a Parisian commentator, 1448–9 was an outstanding year, was of marginal importance. The French were pressing towards the gates of Bordeaux in 1450 and the following year the town fell on 12 June. There was no wine fleet that year and only three ships of any size sailed to England. The largest, the *St John*, was freighted by two Bayonne merchants, Arnold Makanam and Ponset de Sala. The only Southampton ship for the year carried a paltry seven tons. Overnight the English, for three hundred years compatriots of the Gascons, had become aliens. As such they were promptly subjected to authorisations and sailing documents.

But the economy of the region was so dependent on the English connection that the trade had to revive. On the day Bordeaux capitulated, Charles VII's chancellery issued a safe conduct to an English ship and the following January twenty-three made their way up the Gironde to Bordeaux – some with safe conducts issued by the admiral of Bordeaux from the fort at the mouth of the estuary, others with papers obtained, by agreement with the French authorities, in England.

The French conquest was not good news to the Gascons. As contemporaries had observed back in the fourteenth century, the distant rule of England was far to be preferred to the tax collectors of Paris. For a twelvemonth, it seemed there was still hope. In October 1452, the English re-entered the town and held on until October the following year. But the realists had already seen the pattern of the future. Baldwin Makanam, probably Arnold's brother, was making arrangements to set up business in London. The Gascons in Southampton, who had been treated as denizens up to the loss of English Gascony, prepared for changes and to welcome friends and relations as they emigrated there from their French homes. In the late 1450s it began to look as though Southampton's share of the wine trade was going to be taken over completely by the immigrants and in London, too, Gascons like Richard Luncastell and Peter de Formey rapidly rose to prominence. It was not difficult. They were merely subjects of Henry VI and II of England and France who had decided, in the light of new political conditions, to move their headquarters from Bordeaux to London. What the year before had been flourishing 'export' Gascon businesses became English 'importers' with the agency now in Bordeaux.

The trade soon began to revive, but Anglo-French relations continued uneasy and in October 1455 Charles VII banned the issue of safe conducts in England. Henceforth skippers could only get their permits at the fort at the mouth of the Gironde. Additional fees had to be paid for the storage and inventorying of any arms on board which were held at the fort and only returned when the ship was outward bound. Even with the formalities duly observed, the English were liable to harassment. In November 1458, the *Anne* of Sandwich and two other ships were stopped and boarded in the estuary by royal officers, on the pretext that the safe conducts they had paid for barely a week before, on their way into Bordeaux, were 'out of order'. Her cargo was plundered and the safe conduct returned only on payment of 300 crowns. It is hardly surprising that English participation in the Gascon wine trade dropped off, and intervention by government made matters still worse.

When Charles VII was succeeded by his son Louis XI many of the London Gascons returned to Bordeaux anticipating a change of policy. In fact the new king was anxious to revive trade there and encouraged Flemish, Dutch, Hanse, and Spanish merchants. Englishmen were banned unless they could produce a certificate of loyalty from Henry VI or Queen Margaret – with such a certificate they might reside in Gascony though since England was governed by the Yorkist Edward IV they could hardly expect to trade with their home country. Edward retaliated with a ban on wine grown in Aquitaine, Bordeaux, Bayonne or Rochelle. It was temporarily suspended in favour of the Earl of Warwick in September 1464, when it had been in force for two years, and after that it seems to have been relaxed on a number of other occasions. Even so the break with England was causing dire trouble in Gascony and an official report to Louis emphasised the stagnation of the Bordeaux economy after the British departure. The wine fleets, it was pointed out, brought almost all the basic commodities as well as bringing in English gold; the author of the report, Messire Regnauld Girard, predicted that Portugal and the Rhineland would displace France as the principal wine exporter to England; finally he pointed out that the closure of Bordeaux left Calais as the only entre-pôt for Anglo-French trade and this was of course in English hands. The economic facts were too strong for the French government to resist. In the late 1460s, by a treaty between Edward IV and Duke Francis of Brittany, Gascon wine came back to the English market through Breton merchants and, by the 1480s, the English and the Gascons were restoring the trade to something like its former dimensions.

9

The Sign of the Red Pale

According to his advertisement, incidentally the earliest printed piece of advertising to have survived, Caxton's workshop was at the sign of the Red Pale in the Almonry of Westminster Abbey. Westminster was the seat of the court and of parliament as well as being the home of scores of highly learned clerks. Caxton's publications were well tailored for such a market. The advertisement itself offered a service order book according to the English Sarum rite as well as books of romances and chivalric etiquette, and numerous homiletic or what the Victorians would have called 'improving' works. Even so, the choice of Westminster is an interesting one for a man whose business success was rooted in the city of London. The fact is that in an age of social climbing William Caxton had arrived in society long before he returned to England. His career is of such interest precisely because, in his journey from London to Westminster via Bruges, he won acclaim and respect among the aristocracy as well as in the city.

He was born in Kent about the year 1421 and died in 1491. It is generally assumed that Caxton senior was a wealthy bourgeois for, when the time came for putting his son to his apprenticeship, he was able to place him with Robert Large, one of the four wardens of the Mercer's Company. Large had become a sheriff of London in 1430, and in 1439, the year after young William Caxton signed his articles, was elected Lord Mayor and Escheator.

London was a bemusing experience for a young man just up from Kent and he needed his wits about him. The author of *London Lickpenny* describes a rustic coming up to the capital to find a lawyer – by the end of the day he has realised that he will never be able to afford the fees, but before he goes back to Kent he has lost his hood at one end of town and found it for sale in the flea market at Cornhill at the other end. Pushing his way through the crowded streets he is accosted by Flemish street traders offering 'fine felt hats or spectacles to read'. At midday, still trying to track down legal advice that will not bankrupt him, the stranger in town heads for the Westminster gate and finds the eating houses beginning to spread the cloths on the pavement tables for lunch – spare ribs is the dish of the day. But he is far too poor and indeed does not seem able to afford even 'hot sheep's feet' from a street vendor.

The year William Caxton came up from Kent was an eventful one. Crop failures had produced such a widespread famine that Stephen Brown, the mayor, and a member of the Grocers' Company, organised a ring to import grain from Prussia. During the summer there was a great six-week joust at Smithfield and it was here that Caxton very probably was first fascinated by the trappings of chivalry. The following year two great Venetian galleys left the docks of London carrying 5000 cloths between them – about a tenth of the total exports for the year. Robert Large's 'riding as Mayor to Westminster', to the court, was presumably the highlight of 1439 for his apprentices. When he came to publish the *Polycronicon* Caxton continued the history of England from 1400 up to 1460. Since the mayoral riding was an annual event, he understandably makes no reference to it, even though he must have been personally involved in the preparations for the 1439 one. It is a pity that he was so objective. For the next year, he does record an event which one would have expected to have been far less interesting to a nineteen-year-old apprentice. This was the death of the Lollard priest Richard Wyche and Caxton's words suggest strongly that he was present at the burning and was deeply impressed by it. 'This year,' he wrote forty years later, 'Sir Richard Wyche, vicar of Harmondsworth, was burnt at Tower Hill as for an heretic on St Botolphus day, who well at his death he died a good Christian man.' We have seen the unrest caused in the city by the execution; one feels that the young Caxton had sympathy with the protesters.

The next year the conventional pattern of his apprenticeship was dramatically broken by the unexpected death of his master which brought Caxton the very sizeable legacy of £13. Since this represented a year's income for a minor squire, it seems obvious that the young man had already made his mark. Large made no provision for the continuation of his apprentice's articles and soon afterwards Caxton went to Bruges. Given the independence of his later career, it is tempting to imagine that the young man used part of his windfall to venture oversea on his own account and finish his articles with another master in the English community. There he prospered so well that he was accepted as surety for a debt of £50 incurred by a John Granton, a fellow merchant. Three years after this, in 1453, Caxton returned to London to be formally inducted as a member of the Mercers' Company. Once again there is the unconventional note. He and three friends, the formalities concluded, left London for Bruges, without staying to attend the inauguration of the mayor, who was that year a mercer. The 'riding of the Mayor to Westminster', to be officially received by the king, was the most solemn event in the city year at which all members of his company, especially new ones, were expected to be present. It was the great occasion for display, to impress the citizenry and outshine the show put on by other companies. The absence of four new members from their mayor's procession was a blow to the worship of the Mercers' Company,

and Caxton and his friends were fined. The following year
the officials of the company must have been still more morti-
fied when the Drapers sent their new mayor to Westminster
by river. It was the first time it had been done and the glittering flotilla of ceremonial barges was generally considered a
brilliant innovation.[1]

No doubt the Drapers embarked upstream of London
Bridge. The older members would have vivid memories of
the merriment on the waterfront some thirty years back at
the expense of the Duke of Norfolk, when his bargemaster
attempted to shoot the hazardous rapids through the narrow
arches of the bridge and 'his barge was rent against the arch
of the said bridge'.[2] That kind of indignity had no part in
the Drapers' image of themselves. But colourful ceremonial,
though the most public activity of the great city companies,
was merely the window-dressing of their commercial
powers. The Grocers, for example, nominated two important public officers – the weigher of the king's beam and the
garbeller of spices. Since every wholesale transaction was
supposed to be weighed at the king's beam, the control of
it gave the company detailed knowledge of their competi-
tors' business. Control of the garbelling or cleaning of spices
was a vital check in the protection of their own interests,
especially, as they claimed, against the unscrupulous dealing
of Italian importers. These bales, it was said, contained so
much dust and chaff that the grocer who resold them in good
faith, sometimes had to face a charge of malpractice.

By the middle of the century, the London grocers were
authorised, by act of parliament, to garble the spices at Sandwich and Southampton. It seems that they did not find this
public service profitable, since later we find complaints that
many spice shipments were being sent to these ports where
the scrutiny was laxer than in London. In fact, it was to their
advantage for the London spice market to be accepted as the
national centre for quality, and in the early decades of the
century they built a monopoly of the trade on this reputation.

The goldsmiths, on the other hand, fully exploited the powers conferred on them outside the capital.

From the early fourteenth century, provincial goldsmiths had been obliged to come to London to have their goods assayed for finesse. In 1404 the Londoners' powers were extended to the right of supervision of gold wares in all the common fairs of the kingdom; in the 1460s, the ordinance was strengthened to give their wardens rights of search and spot check assays of all gold and silver ware on sale. Early in the reign of Henry VIII, a provincial smith fined at the Bristol and Stourbridge fairs was to complain that the 'wardens, when they ride, and search, do nothing but rob men'.[3] Though in fairness it must be said that Londoners were equally liable to exposure. The notorious case of Thomas à Wode shows how thorough the wardens were, and needed to be, in the capital. After numerous minor offences, he was found to have in his shop 'two drinking cups deceivably painted and wrought in deceit...and the silver was right bad'. He was fined, but only months later the wardens 'entered the house of the said Thomas à Wode, finding there diverse men working girdles, chalices, altar and candlesticks, salts and other plate...whereof the wardens made assay there and found [the metal] greatly faulty'. À Wode was ordered to bring all his stock to Goldsmiths' Hall and a second summons was needed to get all the fourteen girdles seen on his premises by the wardens to the assay office. All were faulty.

Like many other crafts, the goldsmiths drew their apprentices from all over the kingdom and also from Wales and even Ireland. The Hugh Bryce who financed Caxton's *Mirror of the World* was a Dublin man by origin and rose to become master of the London mint. Girls as well as boys flocked to find their fortune in the capital. Members of the London Guild of Silkwomen are found with apprentices from Warwickshire, Yorkshire and Lincolnshire,[4] but many of the young hopefuls must have ended on the streets, in the brothels or at best as kitchen drudges to unscrupulous housewives. Two lasses from Northumberland were tough and lucky enough to get their case before the authorities. A certain Dame Alice had induced them to sign articles for a seven-year apprenticeship to her in the craft of embroidery but, as they soon discovered, she was not skilled and her husband was not even a freeman of the city.

The pulling power of the great city was already a large factor in the national life. The story of Dick Whittington comes from the early years of this century and if Whittington, the son of a prosperous Gloucestershire gentleman, had rather more than a cat to launch him in life, he did come up from the country to seek his fortune and he did become mayor. Like Caxton, he began his career as a member of the Mercers' Company. While every apprentice who had served his term and could afford the fee for enfranchisement had to be presented for the freemanship of the city by his master, barely half the apprentices enrolled in fact made this vital step. Some dropped out, some died, many found themselves heavily in debt to their masters when their indenture expired, for although the master engaged to see the boy clothed and fed, there is clear evidence that the parents or guardians were expected to contribute to the cost. If they would not and the apprentice had no other means, debt was the only way out. The pattern varied from master to master and from company to company, but even if he was lucky the apprentice could easily find himself debarred from setting up shop on his own account by further regulations of his company designed to protect the interests of full members. The Mercers, for example, ruled that no one might set up in their trade without capital of at least £100.

This incredible figure reflects the high position that the company held in the city hierarchy. They were one of the few companies to exercise an effective monopoly. It was based on their control of the overseas branch of the Merchant Adventurers which enabled them to dominate the trade in fine fabrics and luxury cloths. In the early fourteenth century the English merchants trading to the Low Countries had been overwhelmingly woolmen. The government control of the trade and the shift of its base to the Staple at Calais left the small number of cloth merchants in the Low Countries to operate independently. When the scale of cloth exports expanded during the fifteenth century the association of traders in it came to embrace all other members of the English community overseas. His position as governor of Merchant Adventurers at Bruges gave Caxton an extremely influential place in English trading policies. It was natural that, when relations between England and Burgundy became strained, he should have been one of the ambassadors appointed by Edward IV to the ducal court. The negotiations were unsuccessful, however, and the Mercers, finding their old privileges at Bruges restricted, moved to Utrecht, where they were enthusiastically welcomed and given the right to hold an annual cloth fair. The honourable welcome given to Caxton as their leader is mentioned in the Utrecht records. During much of the brief exile, however, he was engaged in further negotiations with Burgundy and, in 1468, welcomed the arrival of Margaret of York, the king's sister, at Bruges for her marriage to Charles, Duke of Burgundy. At this time he met Lord Rivers, the head of the entourage which escorted the princess to the Low Countries. It was to prove a fruitful encounter for both merchant and aristocrat.

All over Europe, the fifteenth century was a period of a burgeoning self-confidence for lay culture. The orators of the great Italian city states had introduced a new Latin style to the diplomatic exchanges between them. Modelled on the classical authors of antiquity, it was considered purer and more elegant than the living, changing and, as it came to be seen, debased Latin of the Church. The movement began in the Italian chanceries and was competitively fostered for reasons of political prestige. It spread rapidly – the formal Latin address of the modern ambassador became the vehicle for humanist oratory. The fifteenth-century Renaissance had

its roots in a revolution in scholarship, expressed in the new
Latin; its ideas were percolating north of the Alps, but the
ideas of chivalry remained far more important.

According to Huizinga the renaissance of chivalry was 'a
naive and imperfect prelude to the Renaissance proper'.
Without accepting the implied value judgement, we can
agree the northern Europeans, by and large, did believe that
the revival of chivalry (as they saw it) would bring about
a revival of the virtues of the ancient world. We have seen
how Henry V was thought to have 'maintained the discipline
of chivalry well, as did the Romans formerly'. In his book
Le livre de faicts, Jean Sire de Boucicaut, marshal of France,
wrote 'Two things...sustain the order of divine and human
laws...Chivalry and Learning.' Like Charles of Orleans he
was captured at Agincourt, and like him wrote poems during
his English captivity. Love and chivalry were the chief
themes of such courtly literati. Their remarkable contemporary, Christine de Pisan, possibly the first 'free-lance'
woman writer and feminist, knew her market well when she
translated the Roman military manual by Vegetius under the
title *Le livre de fais d'armes et de chevalerie*, and a little later
wrote a book '...*of the duke of True Lovers*'. The north European imagination was enchanted by Arthur and his knights,
and the high medieval cult of this northern chivalry had such
cultural dynamism that it broke through into the courts of
Italy.

In July 1469 Lorenzo dei Medici went to Milan to stand
as godfather to the son of Duke Galeazzo Maria Sforza. The
event was celebrated in the same way as the marriage of Margaret of York and Charles of Burgundy had been, the previous year. Lorenzo tells us in his memoirs that 'to do as
others had done', he 'held a joust in the Piazza S. Croce at
great expense and with great pomp. I find we spent about
10,000 ducats.' The picture hardly squares with the clichéd
image of Lorenzo as the great Renaissance prince. But then
the Italian princes were by no means all, or all the time,

devoted exclusively to the ideals of humanism and art. Ber-
toldo di Giovanni, the Florentine architect, accepted a
commission under Count Girolamo of Lucca; in a letter to
Lorenzo he described his disillusionment. 'I would to God
I had been trained by Cibacca [a famous cook] instead of by
Donatello, for, seeing how times go, before I had made a
couple of *giacomini* or a few jellies, the count would have
created me Prior of Pisa.'

The court of Burgundy was the capital of European chivalry, its glitter and luxury resting on the commercial wealth
of the Flemish towns. Some of the Italian businessmen who
came as agents for the Medici or other companies, looked
on their period of service as an exile – others 'went native'
in high style. Of these the most expansive was Tommaso Portinari, Lorenzo's factor in Bruges. When, thanks to him, the
business went bankrupt and the books were at last examined
in Florence it was found, as Lorenzo bitterly noted in his sum-
ming up of the disaster, that Portinari 'in order to court the
duke's favour and make himself important, did not care
whether it was at our expense'. During the twelve years he
ran the Bruges branch, from 1465 to its collapse in 1477, Portinari had been one of the city's most brilliant figures. His
lavish loans (of Medici money) won him an honoured place
in the ducal council of state. His Hôtel de Bladelin, built, so
he protested, for the honour of the firm, was in fact run as
his private palace. At the joustings and feastings of the court
he, a mere merchant in northern eyes, outshone many a
nobleman in the brilliant extravagance of his dress. His fall
was dramatic, though, thanks to shrewd contracts, he evaded
responsibility for many of the bad debts he incurred.

Across the Channel, the London branch went the same
way somewhat earlier, thanks to the immense 'loans' it
advanced to Edward IV in return for licences to ship wool
direct to Italy free of tolls at the Staple in Calais. Once again,
however, it was the distant Italian headquarters that suffered.
The manager, Gherardo Canigiani, or Gerard Caniziani as

it was Englished, became an English subject in 1473 and shortly after married a rich heiress, Elizabeth Stockton. The king, in recognition of the more than £6000 of Medici money that Caniziani had advanced him over the years, and in repayment of a loan of £360 of the merchant's own money, granted him the Buckingham manor of Great Lynford. Accepted as a member of the Mercers' Company, Caniziani finished his days as a prominent London citizen.

Though a financial lightweight beside these Italian operators, Caxton fitted naturally into the atmosphere of commerce, chivalry and learning at the court of Philip the Good and Charles the Bold. All that Caxton tells us about his education was that his parents sent him to school. But it is obvious from his translations that he acquired far more than the standard reading and writing skills expected of an apprentice who hoped to rise in his trade. Living on the fringe of Europe's most exciting court he must have early resolved to become part of the action. Perhaps the example of Portinari inspired him; perhaps he had contacts with the Englishmen in the ducal service. Of these the most important were the musicians, like Robert Morton, who served both Philip the Good and his son Charles. It is unlikely that Caxton, with his interest in the arts, would have failed to meet Morton and his compatriots in the ducal service.

Certainly he made the most of all the opportunities to get to know the court. On a visit to Hesdin he did a tour of the castle there and made a special note of the remarkable room of Medea. This enchantress, who helped Jason in the quest for the Golden Fleece, was naturally honoured at a court with the Order of the Golden Fleece as its highest award of chivalry. In his prologue to the *Book of Jason* (1474; English translation 1477) Caxton describes the way the engines concealed in walls and ceiling made snow and rain to order, just like the enchantments of Medea herself. He makes no comment on the numerous other rooms and devices. When the works in the castle were renovated in 1433 the clerk noted the lurid details with delight. Among other things restoration was needed to 'the room where water can be made to spray down just like rain... Also for the paving of this room which was not previously paved, including the place where people go to avoid the rain, whence they are precipitated into a sack full of feathers below.' In another room, 'there are several devices... which, when set off, spray large quantities of water on to the people in it, as well as six figures... which soak people in different ways. In the entrance there are eight conduits for wetting women from below and three conduits which, when people stop in front of them, cover them all over with flour.' And so the catalogue of grisly japes continues.

The court which commissioned its portraits from Rogier van der Weyden, which had financed the genius of van Eyck and patronised the great musicians – Busnois, Binchois, and Ockeghem – paid the painter Melchior Broederlam at the rate of a *valet de chambre* with responsibility among other things for keeping the engines in order and painted decorations fresh and vivid. This side of the aristocratic way of life had little appeal to the somewhat sober-minded Caxton but he did share his noble patrons' love of Chivalry and Learning, those twin pillars of 'divine and human laws'. When he returned he was to publish many more books of chivalry, among them a translation of Christine de Pisan's *Chivalry*.

He was installed at his first shop in Westminster in 1476. It was between the buttresses of the chapter house near the entrance to the south transept of the Abbey – the door which now leads to Poet's Corner. Apparently out of the way, the site was well chosen since, when parliament was sitting, the Commons conducted their business in the chapter house and the lords in the Palace of Westminster. Caxton's shop was on the path that linked the two. In the 1480s need for storage space took him to new rooms, just inside the Abbey precincts at the gate leading to the Almonry. This was, it is presumed, the sign of the Red Pale, though there is no reference in the

Abbey's records or rent books to such a designation. Before Caxton set up shop, few people in England had seen a printed book. Sir John Russell had brought one back from a diplomatic mission to Bruges in the mid-1460s, but this was rare. Since he lacked official sponsorship and any consistent patronage from Church or State, Caxton had to rely on his intuition as a publisher to make his book printing pay. The way he did this tells us as much about the England of his day as about his business judgement. The very idea of bringing printing to England must have struck many of his contemporaries as risky. Although literacy was spreading, the reading habit as such was hardly general. Where William Worcestre, it was said, loved a good book better than Sir John Fastolf, his master, loved a French castle, Sir John himself kept his dozen or so books in the bathroom. The bequests of books in the wills of London citizens are notable by their rarity, and while there were men of considerable culture among the nobility, as a whole the class was not over-enlightened.

Printing came late to England. Johannes Gutenberg of Mainz had brought the art to commercial viability by the year 1450; in 1452 his workshop set up the first lines of type for the great 42-line Bible, and the publication was complete by August 1456. In the next twenty years, presses were set up at Cologne (1464), Basel, Rome (1467), Venice, Paris (1470), Florence, Valencia, Budapest (1473), Cracow, and a dozen other cities. Caxton returned to England in 1476 and his first book did not appear till the following year; technically he was to be one of the less distinguished of the early printers. Yet the fourteen years during which he conducted business at the sign of the Red Pale in the precincts of Westminster Abbey are among the most fascinating episodes in Europe's printing history.

His very first book was a publishing event without precedent, being in English and by a living Englishman. It was fitting that Gutenberg should have initiated the new art of the book with a Bible, but thereafter the arrival of printing in a country was marked by some Latin work. In Italy, Cicero's *De Oratore*; in Switzerland, St Gregory's commentary on the book of Job; in France a collection of Latin prose texts for students. Anthony Lord Rivers, brother-in-law of Edward IV, was the first European layman to see his work in print when, in 1477, William Caxton brought out his *Dictes and Sayings of the Philosophers*. Of the more than ninety books Caxton published, seventy-four were in English and twenty of these were translations by the publisher himself.

At first sight, it is not clear why William Caxton became a printer. Just turned fifty, he could look back on a highly successful career in business and was among the most respected members of the English merchant community in the Low Countries. This new venture meant the learning of a new trade, entering a new apprenticeship in effect; it was the decision of a resilient and vigorous personality but not the behaviour expected of a comfortable, middle-aged burgess. A recent biographer argues that from the spring of 1469, when he embarked on the translation of the *Recueilles d'histoires de Troyes*, Caxton was systematically preparing the ground for the English publishing enterprise he established seven years later. The idea certainly provides the neat, positive motivation one feels should lie behind a major historical development. Caxton's own account is less tidy, but more convincing.

In 1468 the Merchant Adventurers returned to Bruges and Margaret of York married Charles, Duke of Burgundy. The following year Caxton seems to have given up his governorship. At any rate he was finding time heavy on his hands. In March, fearing lest the devil find evil work for idle hands to do, he embarked on the translation of the French romance of Troy. 'And for as much as this book was new and late made and drawn into French, and never had been seen in our English tongue, I thought it should be a good business [i.e. to busy myself with it] to translate it into English to the end that it might be had as well in the realm of England as in other lands.'

After a bold start his confidence began to falter. 'I remembered my simpleness and unperfectness in French and in English for in France been I never and was born and learnt my English in Kent in the Weald where, I doubt not, is spoken broad and rude English as in any place in England.' At about this time he became a feed pensioner of the duchess's household and it was she who persuaded him to finish the work. Her interest soon brought in demands for copies of the book from other members of the English community. By the time he had finished Caxton found that he had 'promised to diverse gentlemen and to my friends to addresse to them as hastily as I might this said book'. What had begun as a retirement hobby had become a business opportunity. Therefore he 'practised and learned at my great expense to ordain this said book in print after the manner and form as you here may here see. And [it] is not written with pen and ink as other books be, to the end that every man may have them at once…all the books of this story thus emprinted.'

Where Italian bishops and French academics summoned printers from Germany, Caxton the merchant went to learn the trade at first hand. In 1470, the year when the enterprise was shaping in his mind, a German printing works was being set up in Utrecht; but although he was known and respected there, Caxton preferred the slightly longer journey to Cologne, which had been a major centre for a generation past. He was there from July 1471 to the winter of 1472 learning everything he could and, with a refreshing disregard for the 'worship' due an ex-governor of the English merchants of Bruges, working on the shop floor. He returned to Bruges well enough qualified for his own purpose and with a press, type, matrixes and arrangements for a supply of the all-important printing ink. It was probably at Cologne that he met Wynkyn de Worde (i.e. Wörth in Alsace), who was to be his assistant for the rest of his life and continue the business after his death. More immediately important was his business partnership with Colard Mansion, a leading Bruges book-seller and scrivener.

Gutenberg's invention had been launched on a rising market. The wealthy could always hire a scribe to copy books for their libraries but by the early 1400s, the demand for books was so large that booksellers were making speculative commissions of even the most elaborate and costly manu-scripts from the illuminators, in the sure knowledge that there would be a buyer by the time the work was done. The Florentine bookseller, Vespasiano da Bisticci, employed up to fifty scribes and further down market, standard legal and theological textbooks were hired out by the piece (*per pecia*) in sections of ten or so pages at a time so that students could make their own copies. At Paris and other large university towns, the copyists formed their own guilds while Bruges itself had long been a major centre of manuscript production. Mansion was the dean of the booksellers' guild of St John the Evangelist and as such was the most useful collaborator Caxton could have had.

The partnership was, if anything, still more valuable for Mansion since from Caxton he learnt the art of printing. With his own contacts in the English community and an out-let to the wider locale assured, Caxton followed up the *Recuyell of the Historyes of Troye* with the *Game and Playe of the Chesse*, a second edition of the *Recuyell*, and two devotional treatises and a romance of Jason and the Golden Fleece all in French. Having brought the art of printing to his adoptive city, and having established his name as a publisher, this busy Englishman prepared to open up the 'home market'. The groundwork was well laid.

As he was to insist in prologues to his later publications, Caxton was primarily interested in the top end of the market. 'This present book,' he advised prospective buyers of his ver-sion of Virgil's *Eneydos*, 'is not for a rude uplandish man to labour therein but only for a clerk and noble gentleman.' The

Order of Chivalry 'is not requisite for every common man to have, but to noble gentlemen that by their virtue intend to enter into the noble order of chivalry'. When he established himself at Westminster in late 1476 or early 1477 he already had his beachhead among the ranks of the 'noble gentlemen' in the person of Anthony Lord Rivers.

In the next decade, Caxton served his noble patrons well and the history of English literature munificently...as publisher and translator. As translator he brought the English their first version of Aesop's fables, a history of the life of Charlemagne, the story of the First Crusade, as well as major works by Cicero. As publisher he produced a comprehensive list of current interest and taste ranging from a popular encyclopaedia to a history of Britain – *The Brut* – and a history of the world – *Polychronicon*. But it is to Caxton that, above all, we owe the *editiones principes* of the masterpieces of Chaucer, Gower and Malory.

In its first year Caxton's press put out Chaucer's mildly ironical *Parliament of Fowls*. This was followed, in 1478, by the first printed edition of the *Canterbury Tales* and the poet's prose translation of Boethius' *Consolations of Philosophy*. Six years later came the second edition of the *Tales*, the *House of Fame* and *Troilus and Criseyde*. In addition he printed works by Lydgate and John Gower's fourteenth-century masterpiece, *Confessio Amantis*. The fact that Caxton did not publish *The Vision of Piers Plowman*, is today something of a blot on his remarkable achievement as the sponsor of vernacular classics, but his contemporaries would not have agreed. The poem is in the old English tradition of alliterative verse, already somewhat passé at the time it was written and distinctly old-fashioned by Caxton's day.

It must be admitted that the decision to publish the *Canterbury Tales* demanded neither special aesthetic insight nor commercial courage. The work had been in constant demand since its appearance; it had been plagiarised and 'continued' and by the 1470s could be had in numerous versions, some good, some very bad indeed. But Caxton's publication of three other poems by the great poet proves that money was not his only thought. Indeed, at his own expense, he made two astonishing gestures of his admiration. The second edition of the *Canterbury Tales* was no mere reprint, which would have met the commercial demand perfectly well, but an entirely new version. In his prologue Caxton explained why it was necessary to bring out the new version 'made according to his making'. 'For I find many of the said books which writers have abridged and many things left out. And in some places have set certain verses that he never set in his book, of which books, so incorrect, was one brought to me six years past which I had supposed been very true and correct. And according to the same I did emprint a certain number of them which anon were sold.' But after publication a young man 'came to him' and pointed out that it was 'not according to the book Geoffrey Chaucer had made'. Admitting that he had 'erred in hurting and defaming' Chaucer's work, Caxton needed a more authentic version. After some diplomatic persuasion the young man arranged the loan of his father's copy 'which he had loved well and kept by him many years'.

Concern for the accuracy of his translations is a recurring theme in Caxton's prologues and it is not surprising that he should have been so anxious for a good text of the English masterpiece. His second tribute to the master is more surprising, for sometime about 1478 he commissioned an elegy on the poet to be hung above his tomb in Westminster Abbey. The author was the Italian humanist Stefano Surigone. After leaving his teaching post at Oxford about the year 1470 he had gone to Cologne, matriculating at the university in 1471. It was probably here that he and Caxton first met; the acquaintance was renewed when Surigone returned to England, practising as a doctor of canon law at Cambridge in 1476 and coming to London soon after. Caxton tells us that the encomium for Chaucer hung on the pillar by the tomb.

Most of all he admired the poet's precision – but he could not match it : '...he comprehended his matters in short, quick and high sentences eschewing prolixity, casting away the chaff of superfluity and showing the picked grain of sentence'. Style was something that did concern him, though after thirty years abroad he was probably more attuned to the rhythms of French than English. One of the reasons he gives for translating *Eneydos*, a French version of Virgil, was the 'great pleasure' he had from the book 'by cause of the fair and honest words in French, which I never saw before the like, nor none so pleasant nor so well ordered'. His own work was often anything but well ordered, thanks to the remarkable speed at which he worked to keep the press supplied. The *Mirror of the World*, which made up two-hundred printed pages, was done in just over two months – 2 January to 8 March 1481. The story of Godfrey of Bouillon and the First Crusade, 280 printed pages, was translated between 8 March and 7 June of the same year, and the tale of Reynart the Fox, translated from Dutch, was also done at the same time, being finished on 6 June. It ran to 180 printed pages.

The dates are from Caxton's own notes, but he says nothing of his mode of working. Given the sheer physical labour of quill pushing on rough paper, the speed of his output indicates the use of a professional scrivener. The style of many of the translations reinforces the suspicion that they were dictated. Often the syntax of the original is slavishly followed and gives awkward effects in English while sometimes, with no English equivalent on the tip of his tongue, Caxton simply uses the French word. Since the educated, upper classes for whom he published generally had a smattering of French, this disturbed them less than some of his English vocabulary.

In the prologues and epilogues to his translations, Caxton comes back time and again to this problem of langauge. Three aspects troubled him. First, the changes in spoken English even during his own lifetime; secondly, demands

from academics for more sophisticated and recherché vocabulary in his versions of the classics; thirdly, the regional
variations of English. Because his solutions to this third point
have, rightly, given Caxton the reputation as the founder of
modern standard English, it is the only one of his three
dilemmas to interest modern commentators. The vivid anec-
dote he used to drive the point home has become a cliché
of social history. A company of merchants becalmed in
Thames mouth, went ashore at Foreland for a meal while
they waited for a wind to take them to Zeeland. One of them,
a mercer called Sheffield and so presumably a northerner,
ordered a dish of 'eggys'. To his considerable irritation the
housewife asked his companions to interpret as 'she could
speak no French'. As good an Englishman as the rest of them,
he retorted that 'he also could speak no French but would
have some eggys'. Eventually one of his friends explained
that the, by now near apopleptic, gentleman merely desired
a plate of 'eyren'. 'What,' concludes Caxton, 'should man
in these days write, "eggys" or "eyren".' He settled for
eggys.

The move to uniformity he inaugurated continued after
his death. For his 1495 edition of Bartholomaeus Anglicus,
Wynkyn de Worde used an English version some fifty years
old, but first he copy-edited the manuscript to conform with
Caxton's usage. *Clepe* became 'call' or 'name'; *wend* became
'go'; *twey*, 'two'; *thridde*, 'third'; and so with all the other
changes, the modern 'standard' was established. Yet when
Caxton had complained 'it is hard to please everyman', he
had had in mind not only the geographical 'diversity' of language but also its 'change' in time.

It is tantalising to speculate on the changes that struck him
on his return to London after thirty years abroad. He does
record that it had been 'much more wealthy and prosperous
than it is today', but somewhat weakens this as a serious
comment on economic developments by the old man's moral
he draws. The 'cause is that there is almost none known that

intendeth to the common weal but only everyman for his singular profit' and, of course, 'that the children born within the said city profit not like their fathers and elders...but ...after they be come to...years of discretion...scarcely two among ten thrive'.[5] His sole other observation on the changes of those thirty years is on language and this does carry authority. He found that 'the language now used varieth far from that which was used and spoken when I was born'. There is a moral here, too, though coloured more, perhaps, by Continental views of perfidious Albion, than advancing years. 'For we Englishmen be born under the domination of the moon which is never steadfast but ever wavering...'

Whether or not a changing language is a symptom of national shiftiness, it certainly gave Caxton problems. The most extreme instance was 'some evidences written in old English' which the Abbot of Westminster once asked him to 'reduce into English now used'; he had to refuse the commission because he 'could not bring it to understanding'. But the matter of vocabulary was endlessly complicated. When he came 'to oversee and correct' the first few pages of the *Eneydos* translation and 'saw the fair strange terms therein' he glumly resigned himself to criticism. No question, but it would 'not please some gentlemen which lately blamed me, saying that in my translations I had over curious terms which could not be understood of common people'. What these traditionalists demanded was 'old and homely terms'. In the weary hope he might please everyman he 'took up an old book and read therein but certainly the English was so rude and broad that I could not well understand it'. Ignoring his old friends' nostalgia for good old English Caxton preferred where possible 'the common terms daily used...in my judgement lighter to understand than ancient English'.

But in a scholarly classic like *Eneydos* such a policy brought the academic fraternity about his ears. The 'fair strange terms' that irritated his merchant colleagues, delighted the clerks who 'have asked me write the most curious terms that I could find'. From their point of view it was bad enough to have this dilettante trader minting money in the groves of academe without having to endure his 'common terms'. Diffidence as to his qualifications had led Caxton to shelve work on his first project, the *Recuyell*; modesty, or perhaps wariness, made him disparage his translations in almost every prologue he wrote. The number of times he refers to the version given him to work on, or protests 'I have but followed my copy in French as nigh as me possible', highlights the greatest occupational hazard of printers at the close of the manuscript era. Variant readings, more or less divergent, were inevitable when books were copied by hand. The case of the Chaucer first edition brought the point home to Caxton. But there were few opportunities for comparison until printing made possible the wide distribution of identical copies. The young man and his Chaucer must have been only one of many dissatisfied clients who came to the sign of the Red Pale to point out discrepancies between the new printed version and some treasured manuscript in the library of a friend or the neighbouring monastery. By reminding critics that he was working from only one manuscript among many, Caxton also hoped to forestall the scholars.

In a case like the *Eneydos* he was especially vulnerable as he well knew. A popular English translation of a French paraphrase of a Latin classic invited attack at a time when, even in England, the new standards of humanist scholarship were coming to acceptance. In an earlier book he had tartly recommended dissatisfied critics to go back to the original if they objected to his version. In the prologue to *Eneydos* he mounts a respectful pre-emptive strike:

> pray hold me excused for the translation of it for I knowledge myself ignorant of cunning to emprise me on so high and noble a work. But I pray Master John Skelton, late create poet laureate in the university of Oxford, to oversee and correct the said book, and to expound whereas shall

be found fault to them that shall require it. For he hath translated the letters of Cicero, the work of Diodorus Sicullus, and diverse other works of Latin into polished English, as he hath read poets and orators to me unknown.

But while modestly deprecating his own efforts as translator, Caxton praised the work of the actual author with all the confident reverence of a modern blurb writer. The edition of Landry de la Tour is described as:

a book by which all gentlewomen, especially, may learn to behave themselves virtuously – which book is come to my hands by request and desire of a noble lady which hath brought forth many noble daughters and required me to translate this book out of the French into our vulgar English. In which I find many virtuous enseignements. Then for as much as this book is necessary to every gentlewoman of what estate she be, I advise every gentleman and woman having such children to get and have this book.

The anonymous gentlewoman, for whose soul the grateful buyer is urged to pray incidentally, provides the personal testimonial so beloved by advertisers; other such personal 'recommends' include the esquire who requested a translation of the *Order of Chivalry* (1484) – 'done in my best wise according to the copy he delivered to me'. The fact that they are unnamed prompts more than a suspicion that they were just a salesman's fiction. Elsewhere Caxton does specify sponsors. William Pratt, a lifelong friend, is named in the prologue for the *Book of Good Manners* while *The Mirror of the World* was done for 'and at the request, desire, cost and dispense of the honourable worshipful man, Hugh Bryce, alderman and citizen of London'.

He was probably a brother of the Thomas Bryce who had been inaugurated into the Mercers at the same time as Pratt and Caxton and so, presumably, a close friend. According to the prologue, he told Caxton that he wanted to present the work to Lord Hastings. It was an odd commission to a printer. Presentation of a unique hand-illuminated manuscript made sense; presentation of some 200 copies of an identical edition makes hardly any sense at all. The apparently 'personalised' nature of the edition becomes more suspect still when it is realised that the manuscript from which Caxton did the translation was 'engrossed in the town of Bruges in the year 1464' and so, presumably, was part of the stock the printer had brought over with him. In any case, even if we accept that by luck the very book that Bryce knew would best please his lordship happened to be in the printer's workshop, it is hard to imagine the nobleman being especially pleased by the dedication of a popular encyclopaedia. It seems reasonable to suppose that Caxton wanted to publish on commercial grounds and persuaded Hastings, a leading courtier, to accept this form of dedication and Bryce, a leading figure in the city, to put up the capital.

The *Mirror* appeared in 1481, to be followed, later in the same year, by the history of *Godfrey of Bouillon* and the First Crusade. Despite its venerable historical theme this is perhaps the first example of instant publishing. From the outset Caxton, like virtually every printer in Europe, had made a steady income from printing indulgences – one, dated 13 December 1476, was filled out in the names of Mr and Mrs Langley, who bought it from the Abbot of Abingdon in Berkshire. In 1480, Caxton found this lucrative side of his business faced with competition when John Lettou (presumably 'the Lithuanian') set up a press in London using smaller type, thus enabling him to produce smaller and so cheaper indulgences. Paper, which had to be imported, was a heavy item in costings. At the same time John Kendall, the English commander of the turcopole soldiers of the island of Rhodes, was in England to raise funds for the Knights of St John against a new attack from the sultan. Caxton, by adopting a smaller type size, was able to get a healthy order for the indulgences Kendall needed. But when, in the next year, John Giglis, a papal collector, also arrived to raise money for the Turkish expedition, Caxton saw he could capitalise on the topical enthusiasm for things crusading and at the same time up-stage the competition. The very day he finished the translation of the *Mirror of the World* he began work on the Godfrey manuscript. The book was on sale by the autumn with the pious aim, according to its prologue, 'that every man be better encouraged to enterprise war for the defence of Christendom'.

The advantageous blend of piety and profit is reminiscent of the motto of the Dantini family of Prato in Italy – 'For God and Profit'. After a lifetime of honourable and distinguished service to his merchant company William Caxton came home to live on his wits and the commissions of his friends. The machine he brought with him and the business he launched, marked one of those turning points in the history of the country which only posterity can place, but which it cannot mistake.

Notes

1: Who were the English?

1. See *The Book of Margery Kempe* edited by S. B. Meech and H. E. Allen (London, 1940).

2. Crotch, W. J. B., editor, *Caxton's Epilogues and Prologues* (EETS, London, 1928).

3. Marcus, C. J., *A Naval History of England*, vol. i (London, 1961), p. 10.

4. Richardson, H. G., 'Business Training in Medieval Oxford', *American Historical Review*, xlvi (New York, 1941), p. 271.

5. Scattergood, V. J., *Politics and Poetry in the Fifteenth Century* (London, 1971), p. 12.

6. Sugget, Helen, 'The Use of French in the Later Middle Ages', in *Essays in Medieval History*, edited by R. W. Southern (London, 1968), p. 222.

7. Knoop, Douglas and G. P. Jones, 'The English Medieval Quarry', *Ec. Hist. Rev.*, ix, 1 (London, 1967), p. 35.

8. Worcestre, William, *The Itineraries*, edited by John H. Harvey (London, 1969).

9. Quoted in R. J. Mitchell, *The Spring Voyage* (London, 1965), p. 17.

10. Ibid., p. 19. *The Spring Voyage* forms the basis of this description of a fifteenth-century pilgrimage.

11. Ruddock, Alwyn A., *Italian Merchants and Shipping in Southampton 1270–1600* (Southampton, 1951), p. 151.

12. Ibid., p. 159.

13. Reddaway, T. F., 'The London Goldsmith's Company c. 1500', *TRHS*, 5th series, 12 (London, 1962), p. 53.

14. Bolton, J. L., *Alien Merchants in England in the Reign of Henry VI, 1422–61* (Unpublished thesis, Oxford, 1971), pp. 7–8.

15. Ibid., p. 11.
16. See R. J. Mitchell, *The Spring Voyage* (London, 1965).
17. Quoted by J. G. Dickinson in *The Congress of Arras* (Oxford, 1955), p. 25 note.

2: *The French Connection*

1. Quoted in J. R. Lander, *Conflict and Stability in Fifteenth-Century England* (London, 1969), p. 67.
2. Allmand, C. T., 'The Lancastrian Land Settlement in Normandy 1417–50', *Ec. Hist. Rev.*, xxi, 3 (London, 1968).
3. Pernoud, Régine, *Joan of Arc*, Eng. trs. (London, 1964), p. 101.
4. Scattergood, V. J., *Politics and Poetry...* (London, 1971), p. 72.
5. Ibid., p. 127.
6. Quoted in H. Cole, *The Wars of the Roses* (London, 1973), p. 30.
7. Vale, M. G. A., 'The Last Years of English Gascony 1451–53', *TRHS*, 5th series, 19 (London, 1969).
8. French original quoted in Charles Ross, *Edward IV* (London, 1974), p. 235.
9. Ibid., p. 423.
10. Scattergood, op. cit., p. 89.

3: *The Governance of England*

1. Storey, R. L., *The End of the House of Lancaster* (London, 1966), p. 34.
2. Scattergood, V. J., *Politics and Poetry...*, p. 38.
3. McFarlane, K. B., *The Nobility of Later Medieval England* (Oxford, 1973), p. 121.
4. Ruddock, Alwyn A., *Italian Merchants and Shipping in Southampton, 1270–1600* (Southampton, 1951), pp. 177–8.
5. Calendar Patent Rolls, Henry VI 29–36, p. 72.
6. This and other details of piracy are to be found in *The Royal Administration and the Keeping of the Seas, 1422–1485* by C. F. Richmond (Unpublished thesis, Oxford, 1962).
7. Jeffs, Robin, *The Later Medieval Sheriff and the Royal Household... 1437–1547* (Unpublished thesis, Oxford, 1960), p. 8.
8. Storey op. cit., pp. 55–7.
9. Jeffs, op. cit., p. 21.
10. Details of Rokewood's contingent are given in Winifred I. Haward's 'Economic Aspects of the Wars of the Roses in East Anglia', *EHR*, 41 (London, 1926).
11. Quoted in Charles Ross, *Edward IV* (London, 1974), p. 305.

12. McKisack, May, 'The Parliamentary Representation of King's Lynn before 1500', *EHR*, 42 (London, 1927).
13. Ibid.

4: *Town and Country*

1. O'Neill, B. H. St-John, *Castles and Cannon* (Oxford, 1960).
2. Furnivall, F. J. and W. G. Stone, editors, *The Tale of Beryn. Prologue of the Merry Adventure of the Pardoner with the Tapster at Canterbury* (EETS, London, 1887).
3. Storey, R. L., *The End of the House of Lancaster* (London, 1966), p. 1.
4. Carus-Wilson, E. M., *Medieval Merchant Venturers*, 2nd edition (London, 1967), p. 225.
5. The account of medieval Castle Combe is based on E. M. Carus Wilson's 'Evidence of Industrial Growth on Some Fifteenth-century Manors', *Ec. Hist. Rev.* (1959–60).
6. The account of the medieval iron industry is based on H. R. Schubert's *A History of the British Iron and Steel Industry* (London, 1957).
7. Quoted in Davies, R. T., editor, *Medieval English Lyrics* (London, 1963).
8. Schubert, op. cit., p. 42.
9. Salzman, L. R., *Building in England to 1540* (Oxford, 1952).
10. Cook, G. H., *Medieval Chantries and Chantry Chapels*, 2nd edition (London, 1963).
11. Quoted from John Lydgate's *Troy Book* in Salzman, op. cit.
12. Salzman, op. cit., p. 20.
13. Dobson, R. B. *The Priory of Durham in the Time of John Wessington, 1414–1446* (Unpublished thesis, Oxford, 1962), p. 347.
14. Richardson, H. G., 'Business Training in Medieval Oxford', *American Historical Review*, xlvi (New York, 1941), p. 259.
15. Tucker, Melvin J., 'The Household Accounts, 1490–1, of John de Vere', *EHR*, 75 (London, 1960).
16. Beresford, M. W., *Lost Villages of England* (London, 1954), p. 103.
17. Ibid, p. 64.
18. Ibid., p. 102.
19. Ibid., p. 105.
20. Owen, Dorothy M., *Church and Society in Medieval Lincolnshire* (Lincoln, 1971), p. 69.
21. Baker, Alan R. H., 'Open Fields and Partible Inheritance on a Kent Manor', *Ec. Hist. Rev.*, xvii, 1 (London, 1964).
22. Storey, op. cit., p. 215.

23. Mitchell, R. J. and M. D. R. Leys, *A History of London Life* (London, 1958), p. 49.

24. This account of the theatre is much indebted to R. Southern's *The Medieval Theatre in the Round* (London, 1957).

25. Mitchell and Leys, op. cit., p. 49.

26. Owst, G. R., *Preaching in Medieval England...1350–1450* (Cambridge, 1926), p. 180.

27. Ibid., p. 183.

28. Clay, R. M., *The Medieval Hospitals of England* (London, 1909), p. 63.

5: Church, Churchmen and Dissent

1. Davies, R. T., editor, *Medieval English Lyrics. A Critical Anthology* (London, 1963), p. 258.

2. Thomas, Keith, *Religion and the Decline of Magic* (London, 1971), p. 42.

3. Scattergood, V. J., *Politics and Poetry in the Fifteenth Century* (London, 1971), p. 121.

4. Thomson, John A. F., *The Later Lollards 1414–1520* (London, 1965), p. 77; the treatment of Lollardy which follows is largely based on this work.

5. Jeffs, Robin, *The Later Medieval Sheriff and the Royal Household...1437–1547* (Unpublished thesis, Oxford, 1960).

6. Thomson, op. cit., p. 73.

7. Owst, G. R., *Preaching in Medieval England...1350–1450* (Cambridge, 1926), p. 71.

8. Scattergood, op. cit., p. 227.

9. Owst, op. cit., p. 182.

10. Ibid., p. 37.

11. Jacobs, E. F., 'Archbishop John Stafford', *TRHS*, 5th series, 12 (London, 1962), p. 1.

12. Heyworth, P. L., editor, *Jack Upland, Friar Daw's Reply, and Upland's Rejoinder* (Oxford, 1968), lines 23–5.

13. Owst, op. cit., p. 167.

14. Quoted ibid., p. 172.

15. Owen, Dorothy M., *Church and Society in Medieval Lincolnshire* (Lincoln, 1971), p. 89.

16. Quoted in Scattergood, op. cit., p. 239.

17. Ibid., pp. 241–2.

18. Owen, op. cit., p. 42.

19. Cook, G. H., *Medieval Chantries and Chantry Chapels*, 2nd edition (London, 1963), p. 48.

20. Clay, op. cit., p. 120.
21. Colvin, H. M., *A History of Deddington, Oxfordshire* (London, 1963), p. 111.
22. Fletcher, J. M., *The Teaching and Study of the Arts at Oxford c. 1400–1520* (Unpublished thesis, Oxford, 1961), pp. 8–10.
23. Ibid., p. 62.
24. Emden, A. B., *A Biographical Dictionary of Oxford University* (Oxford, 1957).
25. Woods, William, *A History of the Devil* (London, 1973), p. 192.

6: The Woman's Place

1. Thomson, John A. F., *The Later Lollards, 1414–1520* (Oxford, 1967), p. 106.
2. Thrupp, Sylvia, *The Merchant Class of Medieval London* (Chicago, 1948), p. 266.
3. Ibid., p. 106.
4. Dale, M. K., 'The London Silkwomen in the Fifteenth Century', *Ec. Hist. Rev.*, iv, 3 (London, 1933).
5. Richmond, C. F., *The Royal Administration and the Keeping of the Seas 1422–85* (Unpublished thesis, Oxford, 1962), p. 66.
6. Carus Wilson, E. M., *Medieval Merchant Venturers* (London, 1954), p. 93.

7: The Life of Privilege

1. Davies, R. T., editor, *Medieval English Lyrics* (London, 1963).
2. Scattergood, V. J., *Politics and Poetry...* (London, 1971), p. 322.
3. Mitchell, R. J. and M. D. R. Leys, *A History of London Life* (London, 1958).
4. Greene, R. L., editor, *The Early English Carols* (Oxford, 1935), number 381.
5. Keen, M. H., *The Laws of War in the Late Middle Ages* (London, 1965), pp. 48–9.
6. Storey, R. L., *The End of the House of Lancaster* (London, 1966), pp. 158–9.
7. Myers, A. R., *The Household of Edward IV* (Manchester, 1959).

8: Merchants, Mercers and Trade

1. Richmond, C. F., *The Royal Administration and the Keeping of the Seas* (Unpublished thesis, Oxford, 1962), p. 40.
2. Scattergood, V. J., *Poetry and Politics...* (London, 1971), p. 180.
3. Marcus, C. J., 'The Mariner's Compass...', *History*, new series, xli (London, 1956).

4. Marcus, C. J., *A Naval History of England*, vol. i (London, 1961), p. 6.
5. For details of England's fifteenth-century 'Iceland Venture' see E. M. Carus Wilson, *Medieval Merchant Venturers* (London, 1954), pp. 98–142.
6. James, M. K., *The Gascon Wine Trade of Southampton*... (Oxford, Unpublished thesis, 1948), pp. 68–9.
7. Burwash, Dorothy, *English Merchant Shipping 1460–1540* (Toronto, 1947).

9: The Sign of the Red Pale

1. Burwash, Dorothy, *English Merchant Shipping 1460–1540* (Toronto, 1947), p. 111.
2. Ibid.
3. Reddaway, T. F., 'The London Goldsmiths *c.* 1500', *TRHS*, 5th series, 12 (London, 1962), p. 51.
4. Dale, M. K., 'The London Silkwomen of the Fifteenth Century' *Ec. Hist. Rev.*, iv, 3 (London, 1933), p. 325.
5. Crotch W. J. B., *Caxton's Epilogues and Prologues* EETS, London, 1928), p. 77.

Addendum

One of the more intriguing mysteries of fifteenth-century history concerns the fate of Edward IV's brother George, Duke of Clarence. There is no doubt that he died in the Tower at his brother's order in 1478, but the mode of his death has been the subject of legend and speculation ever since. At the nub of the problem is the long-standing tradition that he was 'drowned in a butt of malmsey'. Historians have variously discounted this as a colourful metaphor at the expense of the duke's reputation for drinking or accepted it, reluctantly, as the truth. The matter is, perhaps, not worth deep research. However, it now seems that we can confidently propose that Clarence was in fact drowned in his bath.

An early fifteenth-century inventory of the goods of Sir John Dinham gives the clue. It lists 'ij vatis for the lordys bathyng ymad of a bot of malmesyn'. Interestingly enough, Edward, when Earl of March, overnighted at Dinham's house on his flight from Ludlow in 1461 ; whether he had a bath there is not recorded. But there is no reason to suppose that Dinham's house was the only household to use butts for this purpose. And so, as so often, tradition is probably right and the Duke of Clarence probably was drowned in a butt made for malmsey.

Select Bibliography

Allmand, C. T., 'The Lancastrian Land Settlement in Normandy 1417–50', *Economic History Review*, 2nd series, xxi, 3 (London, 1968).

Armstrong, C. A. J., 'The Inauguration Ceremonies of the Yorkist Kings and their Title to the Throne', *Transactions of the Royal Historical Society*, 4th series, xxx (London, 1948)

Ault, W. O., 'Manor Court and Parish Church in Fifteenth-Century England...', *Speculum*, xlii (Cambridge, Mass., 1967)

Baker, Alan R. H., 'Open Fields and Partible Inheritance on a Kent Manor', *Ec. Hist. Rev.*, xvii, 1 (1964)

Beresford, M. W., *Lost Villages of England* (London, 1954)

Blake, N. F., *Caxton and His World* (London, 1969)

Blanchard, Ian, 'Miner and Medieval Agricultural Community', *Agricultural Historical Review*, 20 (Leicester, 1972)

Bolton, J. L., *Alien Merchants in England in the Reign of Henry VI, 1422–61* (Unpublished thesis, Oxford University, 1970)

Boyle, E. and Richard H. Rouse, 'A Fifteenth-century List of the Books of Edmund B. Norton', *Speculum*, l (Cambridge, Mass., 1975)

Bridbury, A. R., *England and the Salt Trade in the Later Middle Ages* (Oxford, 1955)

Bullough, D. A., 'The Games People Played: Drama and Ritual...in Medieval Europe', *TRHS*, 5th series, 24 (London, 1974)

Burwash, Dorothy, *English Merchant Shipping 1460–1540* (Toronto, 1947)

Byles, A. T. P., editor, *The Book of the Fayttes of Armes and Chyvalrye* (EETS, London, 1937)

Cam, Helen M., *Liberties and Communities in Medieval England* (Cambridge, 1944)

Carus-Wilson, E. M., 'An Industrial Revolution of the Thirteenth Century', *Ec. Hist. Rev.* xi, 1 (London, 1941)

—— *Medieval Merchant Venturers*, 2nd edition (London, 1967)
—— 'Evidence of Industrial Growth on Some Fifteenth-Century Manors', *Ec. Hist. Rev.*, 2nd series, xii (London, 1959–60)
Clay, R. M., *The Medieval Hospitals of England* (London, 1909)
Collis, Louise, *The Apprentice Saint* (London, 1964)
Colvin, H. M., *A History of Deddington, Oxfordshire* (London, 1963)
Cook, G. H., *Medieval Chantries and Chantry Chapels*, 2nd edition (London, 1963)
Crotch, W. J. B., editor, *Caxton's Epilogues and Prologues* (London, 1928)
Crowder, C. M. D., *Some Aspects of the 'English Nation' at the Council of Constance*... (Unpublished thesis, Oxford University, 1953)
Dale, M. K., 'The London Silkwomen in the Fifteenth Century', *Ec. Hist. Rev.*, iv, 3 (London, 1933)
Davidson, Thomas, 'Plough Rituals in England and Scotland', *Agric. Hist. Rev.*
Davies, R. T., editor, *Medieval English Lyrics* (London, 1963)
Deacon, Richard, *William Caxton: The First English Editor* (London, 1976)
Dickinson, Joy G., *The Congress of Arras* (Oxford, 1955)
Dillon, Viscount, and W. H. St-John Hope, *Pageant...of Richard Beauchamp Earl of Warwick K. G. 1389–1439* (London, 1914)
Dobson, R. B., *The Priory of Durham in the Time of John Wessington, Prior 1416–46* (Unpublished thesis, Oxford University, 1962)
Du Boulay, F. R. H., *An Age of Ambition* (London, 1970)
—— 'A Rentier Economy in the Later Middle Ages: The Archbishopric of Canterbury', *Ec. Hist. Rev.*, 2nd series, xvi (London, 1963–4)
Edwards, Goronwy, 'The Emergence of Majority Rule in English Parliamentary Elections', *TRHS*, 5th series, xiv (London, 1964)
Emden, A. B., *A Biographical Dictionary of Oxford University* (Oxford, 1957)
Fletcher, J. M., *The Teaching and Study of Arts at Oxford, c. 1400–1520* (Unpublished thesis, Oxford University, 1961)
Furnivall, F. J. and W. G. Stone, editors, *The Tale of Beryn. A Prologue of the Merry Adventures of the Pardoner with the Tapster at Canterbury* (EETS, London, 1887)
Harriss, G. L., 'The Struggle for Calais', *English Historical Review*, 75 (London, 1960)
Hart, Cyril E., *The Free Miners* (Gloucester, 1953)
—— *The Industrial History of Dean* (Newton Abbot, 1971)
Hatcher, John, 'A Diversified Economy: Later Medieval Cornwall', *Ec. Hist. Rev.*, 2nd series, xxii (London, 1969)

Haward, Winifred I., 'Economic Aspects of the Wars of the Roses in East Anglia', *EHR*, 41 (London, 1926)

Heyworth, P. L., editor, *Jack Upland, Friar Daw's Reply, and Upland's Rejoinder* (Oxford, 1968)

Hilton, R. H., *The English Peasantry in the Later Middle Ages* (Oxford, 1975)

Holmes, G. A., 'Florentine Merchants in England 1346–1436', *Ec. Hist. Rev.*, 2nd series, xiii, 2 (London, 1958)

Hoskins, W. G., *The Making of the English Landscape* (London, 1955)

Houghton, K. N., 'Theory and Practice in Borough Elections to Parliament during the late Fifteenth Century,' *Bulletin of the Institute of Historical Research*, xxxix (London, 1966)

Jacobs, E. F. 'Archbishop John Stafford', *TRHS*, 5th series, 12 (London, 1962)

James, M. K., *The Gascon Wine Trade of Southampton during the Reigns of Henry VI and Edward IV* (Unpublished thesis, Oxford University, 1948)

Jeffs, Robin, *The Later Medieval Sheriff and the Royal Household 1437–1547* (Unpublished thesis, Oxford University, 1960)

Johnston, Alexandra F., 'The Play of the Religious Guilds of York...', *Speculum*, l, (Cambridge, Mass., 1975)

Jones, Michael, translator and editor, *Phillippe de Commynes. Memoirs* (Harmondsworth, 1972)

Kahrl, Stanley J., *Traditions of Medieval English Drama* (London, 1974)

Keen, M. H., 'Treason Trials under the Law of Arms', *TRHS*, 5th series, 12 (London, 1962)

—— *The Laws of War in the Late Middle Ages* (London, 1965)

Kendall, Paul Murray, *Warwick the Kingmaker* (London, 1957)

Kinghorn, A. M., *Medieval Drama* (London, 1968)

Kingsford, C. L., *English Historical Literature in the Fifteenth Century* (Oxford, 1913)

Knoop, Douglas and G. P. Jones, 'The English Medieval Quarry', *Ec. Hist. Rev.*, ix (London, 1938–39)

—— 'Masons in Medieval England', *Ec. Hist. Rev.*, ii, 2 (London, 1931)

Labarge, Margaret Wade, *A Baronial Household of the Thirteenth Century* (London, 1965)

Lander, J. R., 'Attainder and Forfeiture, 1453–1509', *Historical Journal*, iv, 2 (London, 1961)

—— *Conflict and Stability in Fifteenth-Century England* (London, 1969)

Lasken, H. W., *At the Sign of the Red Pale* (Maidstone, 1961)

McCann, Helen, *Liberties and Communities in Medieval England* (Cambridge, 1944)

McFarlane, K. B., *The Nobility of Later Medieval England* (Oxford, 1973)
—— *Parliament and Bastard Feudalism*, *TRHS*, 4th series, 26 (London, 1944)
McGuffie, T. H., 'The Longbow as a Decisive Weapon', *History Today*, 5 (1955)
McKenna, J. W., 'The Coronation Oil of the Yorkist Kings', *EHR*, 82 (London, 1967)
McKisack, May, *The Parliamentary Representation of King's Lynn before 1500* (London, 1966)
Mallett, M. E., 'Anglo-Florentine Commercial Relations, 1465–91', *Ec. Hist. Rev.*, 2nd series, xv, 2 (London, 1962)
Malory, Sir Thomas, *Morte D'Arthur*, editor Janet Cowen (Harmondsworth, 1969)
Marcus, C. J., 'The Mariners Compass; Its Influence upon Navigation in the Later Middle Ages', *History*, new series, xli (London, 1956)
—— *A Naval History of England*, vol. i (London, 1961)
Miner, J. N., 'Schools and Literature in Later Medieval England', *British Journal of Educational Studies*, xi (London, 1963)
Mitchell, R. J., *The Spring Voyage* (London, 1965; RU edition)
—— *John Tiptoft* (London, 1938)
—— 'English Law Students at Bologna in the Fifteenth Century', *EHR*, 51 (London, 1936)
—— and M. D. R. Leys, *A History of London Life* (London, 1958)
Morgan, D. A. L., 'The King's Affinity in the Policy of Yorkist England', *TRHS*, 5th series, 23 (London, 1973)
Myers, A. R., *The Household of Edward IV* (Manchester, 1959)
—— *England in the Later Middle Ages* (Harmondsworth, 1971)
Nelson, Alan H., *The English Medieval Stage* (London, 1974)
O'Neill, B. H. St-John, *Castles and Cannon* (Oxford, 1960)
Owen, Dorothy M., *Church and Society in Medieval Lincolnshire* (Lincoln, 1971)
Owst, G. R., *Preaching in Medieval England* (Cambridge, 1926)
Pernoud, Régine, *Joan of Arc* (Paris, 1962; translated Edward Hyams, London, 1964)
Power, Eileen and M. M. Postan, *Studies in English Trade in the Fifteenth Century* (London, 1933)
Reddaway, T. F., 'The London Goldsmiths *c.* 1500', *TRHS*, 5th series, 12 (London, 1962)
Richardson, H. G., 'An Oxford Teacher of the Fifteenth Century', *Bulletin of the John Rylands Library*, xxiii (Manchester, 1939)
—— 'Business Training in Medieval Oxford', *American Historical Review*, xlvi (New York, 1941)

Richmond, C. F., 'Fauconberg's Kentish Rising of May 1471', *EHR*, 85 (London, 1970)

Roskell, J. S., *The Commons and their Speakers in English Parliament 1376–1523* (Manchester, 1965)

Ross, Charles, *Edward IV* (London, 1975)

Ruddock, Alwyn A., *Italian Merchants and Shipping in Southampton 1270–1600* (Southampton, 1951)

Sabine, Ernest L., 'Latrines and Cesspools of Medieval London', *Speculum*, ix (Cambridge, Mass., 1934)

—— 'City Cleaning in Medieval London', *Speculum*, xii (Cambridge, Mass., 1937)

Salzman, L. R., *Building in England to 1540* (Oxford, 1952)

Scamell, G. V., 'Shipowning in England c. 1450–1550', *TRHS*, 5th series, 12 (London, 1962)

Scattergood, V. J., *Politics and Poetry in the Fifteenth Century* (London, 1971)

Schubert, H. R., *A History of the British Iron and Steel Industry to A.D. 1775* (London, 1957)

Scofield, Cora L., 'An Engagement of Service to Warwick the Kingmaker, 1462', *EHR*, 29 (London, 1914)

Shrewsbury, J. F. D., *A History of the Bubonic Plague* (Cambridge, 1971)

Southern, R., *The Medieval Theatre in the Round* (London, 1957)

—— *The Staging of Plays Before Shakespeare* (London, 1973)

Storey, R. L., *The End of the House of Lancaster* (London, 1966)

Suggett, Helen, 'The Use of French in England in the Later Middle Ages', in *Essays in Medieval History*, editor R. W. Southern (London, 1968)

Thomas, Keith, *Religion and the Decline of Magic* (London, 1971)

Thomson, John A. F., *The Later Lollards, 1414–1520* (2nd edition, Oxford, 1967)

Thrupp, Sylvia L., *The Merchant Class of Medieval London* (Chicago, 1948)

Tucker, Melvin J., 'The Household Accounts, 1490–1491, of John de Vere', *EHR*, 75 (1960)

Vale, M. G. A., 'The Last Years of English Gascony, 1451–1453', *TRHS*, 5th series, 19 (London, 1969)

Weinbaum, Martin, editor, *British Borough Charters, 1307–1660* (Cambridge, 1943)

Wickham, Glynne, *Medieval English Stages* (London, 1959–72)

Wolffe, B. P., *The Royal Demesne in English History* (London, 1971)

Woods, William, *A History of the Devil* (London, 1973)

Worcestre, William, *Itineraries*, edited by John H. Harvey (London, 1969)

Index